TWENTY-THREE WEEKS

TWENTY-THREE
WEEKS

The Story of a Micro-preemie Baby and Her Mother

KAREN FRASER-MORRIS

Epigraph Books
Rhinebeck, New York

Disclaimer: This is a work of nonfiction. No events have been fictionalized. All people and places are actual, but names have been changed.

Paperback ISBN 978-1-960090-28-7

Library of Congress Control Number: 2023914105

Book design by Colin Rolfe

Epigraph Books
22 East Market Street, Suite 304
Rhinebeck, New York 12572
(845) 876-4861
epigraphps.com

Dedicated to Cosette Adeline

My baby was born yesterday at 12:30 a.m. That is the estimated time. No one really knows the exact minute. When my baby grows up and asks me what time she was born I will either have to lie and say 12:30 a.m. or tell her we're not sure, but it was around 12:30. My baby will grow up.

Her birthday is September 29, 2019. It's four months before her due date. One hundred and thirteen days early. That's 113 days she will not spend growing inside of me, safe and warm. That's 113 days that I am left to hope she will spend in the Neonatal Intensive Care Unit at the University of Virginia Hospital. This is the wish because the alternative is living no days and dying.

The nurse told us right away that our baby would stay in the hospital at least until her due date. In my haze of shock I thought she could come home sooner if she got big enough. People deliver a month early and take their babies home. But she will not be a normal baby at eight months. She is very sick. Babies are not supposed to be born at 23 weeks. She is missing big things like what makes lungs open and close to breathe. She will spend the first months of her life in a small, plastic box. She will live there instead of inside of me. She will live. I will go to see her every day. I will sit outside of her box next to all of the other boxes with babies in them and help her grow. I can still be her mother even though I only brought her halfway.

We named her Cosette. Cosette Adeline. Cosette means little one and victorious. That is what she will be. When they asked for a name I thought for a second that I didn't want to use Cosette. That I wanted to save it for a future baby who lives. I did not want to bury Cosette. But then I realized it would be too sad to give her name to someone else, that I would always feel sad when I said that name. I will be sad for a very, very long time. Maybe forever.

I was pregnant and now I am not. There is just skin covering an empty womb. She was so close and now she's not.

* * * *

FOUR MONTHS EARLIER

Sunday, May 12, 2019

Hi, journal. It's been a while. Sorry for the gap in writing. I have some time so I thought I'd revisit you. I know, this is what always happens, I come back for a little burst and then disappear again. I will try to do better. I woke up feeling a shift this morning in myself, so maybe that will translate to more time for introspection. We had a group of friends over last night to warm our new house, which we moved into in April. A friend even called to say he couldn't make the two hour drive from D.C., but then there was a late knock on the door. I love surprises like that.

Although a new house is a big deal, today, journal, I've shown up to place this thought on paper – I'm ready to have a baby. Is it only because today is Mother's Day? I don't think so. But check with me tomorrow. Perhaps I've finally grown up enough and been to enough meditation retreats to make me ready for something half the population does. If they can do it, I can do it, right? And time is kind of running out. I turned 36 two months ago.

I have been married for five months. You and I both know that I imagined being married for a few years before trying to have a baby. In that pre-baby time, my husband and I would travel across Europe and later move into a quaint apartment in a city like Chicago or Seattle. We would have a favorite bar on our neighborhood street full of other childless couples who were our best friends. Late nights full of carefree laughter were the main characteristic of this fictional age.

My relationship with Ben has shared none of that vision. It took almost four months for us to meet in person after we met virtually. In an age when people connect on an app and meet a few hours later, four months is a very long courting-over-the-phone time. Ben's situation was difficult to love. When we met, he had recently separated from his wife after seven years of marriage. He got married very young, fresh out of a time of crisis in his early twenties. I was old enough and had dated enough that I felt like I was getting a chance to be with someone who was recycling back into the dating world as a better version of himself. A tasty fish tossed in who would flounder on his own without a partner to help him live and parent his toddler. Ben has Henry, his three year-old son, who was one and a half when we met. But I didn't meet Henry until he was two. You'll probably remember that I swore not to date a divorced man, this was a tenet I held close to my heart. And let alone a divorcee with a child. But there was something about our chats that made me continue. Maybe it was the fact that I felt there was no risk in talking to him because I would never date a man with a child, a child who was practically still a baby. Maybe it was our shared anguish over Donald Trump's election. Yes, that really happened. Romance in a time of tragedy. I was sympathetic to Ben's situation and believed he deserved a chance, especially if he adored me as much as he seemed to. As my towering pile of previous journals prove, I am not used to being adored. It felt great.

I spoke to a psychic who told me that Ben was a meringue pie that had not set; he was unbaked, not ready for the likes of me who was very ready. Though she said if I waited a year, the patient support might pay off. Sitting in my car on the phone with her during a break at work, watching my seventh grade class in the distance play basketball at recess, a year did not sound that long. I was still working at the same school, nine years at that point. My life was excruciatingly steady. I had no idea what was coming in that year with Ben, but when you're in love, every song and movie about earning love and standing by your man are written for you. I planted myself next to him and 18 months later we got engaged.

It was different than how it was with James. With James, I had spent five of our five-and-a-half years together planning our future married life. I woke up on Saturday mornings and fawned over wedding venues in that precious, quiet hour when he was still asleep and I could safely pretend that he was going to propose soon. The previous pages of this journal are full of my musings on just that topic. Then there was that August day he came home from work looking pale and distraught. I asked a question I had confronted him with many times on different occasions. "What's wrong?" He stood in the doorway with tears on his face and moved out the next morning. Journal, you know all about this, of course. I started seeing someone new a month later. I was aware I would stop if James came back. And then a year and a half later – Ben.

After I got home from our first meeting in a coffee shop, Ben texted me: "I think it goes without saying, I had a really great time tonight." He was direct with his feelings and not scared to tell me he was interested. This was very attractive after months of playing coy games with aloof men. He asked me if I wanted to go to dinner three nights later. He would find a babysitter for Henry. His arrangement with his ex included keeping his son for weekend nights in addition to many days of the week. I was supposed to meet Ben at his house and he would drive us to the restaurant from there. I assumed I might see his son that first night, which later seemed extremely naïve. Ben was driving his friend's car while she was overseas. Ben and his ex-wife still shared a car. That's how entwined he was, but he assured me he was getting his own car soon. We went to the restaurant and there was a long wait, so we walked to a nearby bar. He told me stories about his friends and asked about my writing. He had a great laugh and smile. I liked him, a lot. He flirted with his eyes almost as much as I do. After dinner we walked to another place for dessert. It was my favorite post-dinner spot in the chilly basement of a rustic restaurant. C&O, named after the railroad. There were only a few tables and a bar that faced a wall of weathered books and mirrors. On the walk there, I held Ben's arm and linked him to me. He leaned in like it was the best thing that ever happened to him.

I was smitten after the first date, and I began to hope James would not show up at my door because I could not return to him.

Ben and I stopped being careful about not having a baby two weeks ago. I don't feel anything, no changes, and do not expect it to work the first month. I am wondering if the bad concussion I got in February could prevent me from conceiving right away, like my body is not totally back to normal yet and ready to house a new life. We didn't even aim for the day my app indicated ovulation, just around it. I have strong negative feelings about my baby being a Capricorn, which would be possible if I conceived in April. I thought about waiting for May for that reason but figure we have no idea how long it will take.

The fifth grade field trip is next week and then I'll be preparing for graduation and writing student reports. It will all get done, it always does, but May is the busiest month of the year. I'm volunteering on Memorial Day at Moon Tribe, too. I should think about fertility while I'm there. I'll be back soon, journal, I promise.

Thursday, May 16

My breasts are sore and my period is four days late. That never happens.

Saturday, May 18

I am almost definitely pregnant! I took a test. Ben waited outside the open door. I always thought it took a few minutes to show a result, but the plus sign appeared immediately. There was no time to hope one way or another. By today I really wanted it to be positive.

Thursday, May 23

I had a difficult two days on the fifth grade field trip. It was exhausting work, and the kids would not go to sleep, which meant I didn't get much sleep. This morning my old concussion symptoms hit me badly. I felt dizzy and had the worst pain in my forehead. The head of school was on the trip with us and I told her my baby news last night in a burst of joy. I wanted someone there to know my secret. I gushed to her outside the Lincoln Memorial, a place that holds so much promise.

We were walking down the long series of stone steps after having read the moving words of the Gettysburg Address that are etched into the interior wall of the monument. She asked, "How are things going in married life and being a stepmom?"

"I'm pregnant," I gushed.

So this morning when I was a wreck, she and I sat in the hotel breakfast room and I cried desperate tears. Emotional, yes. In pain, yes. I told her I was scared that a night of no sleep and returned concussion symptoms meant a risk of miscarriage. She offered to drive me home. A two and a half hour drive. I opted to go back to sleep for an hour and join up with the kids later in the morning. It felt dramatic, though, and I hate being the cause of drama. People usually wait until twelve weeks until they tell anyone but their parents. If I tell more people they'll wonder about what that means for my job next year, maternity leave, and the following year. Will I leave the school? Maybe. I don't know. Probably.

Mom and Dad are coming home for the summer after spending the fall and winter with my sister in Austin. We will definitely tell them before twelve weeks. It feels weird that I told my boss before Mom, but that's how it happened. My friends who had miscarriages after telling many people said they would want to talk about the miscarriage anyway. I am enjoying having this secret but am also very fearful of being too confident.

I bought a pretty journal in a gift shop in a museum on the trip. I'm going to use it as a pregnancy journal, separate from this one. I'll write entries directly to the baby. I think it will be meaningful for her to have something like that when she's older. I am reading a book about conversations in the womb. I tried some of the centering and speaking to baby activities. I was surprised by how strong a presence the baby already has when I stop to listen for a voice.

Everything has happened quickly. I need to start eating the right foods, no caffeine, read the books, know all the stuff to do and not do. I made my first doctor's appointments. One is next week and the other is at the end of the first trimester, July 10. It seems like doctors don't want to get too involved until it's definitely happening. I am trying to be positive and not approach this with fear. Whatever happens happens. I feel good. I can do this.

BABY JOURNAL | May 23 | *5 weeks*

Today when I grounded and held my belly, I immediately sensed that you are a girl. A warm flush took over my face and I smiled. Then you let me know that your name is Hannah. I like that name. It's not one I considered before, but I like the sound of it. It means "grace" in Hebrew. You told me that you're okay, forming well, and that I should eat more fish and peanut butter. Lots of protein. And I should stop all coffee and caffeine. I will. Thank you for being so quick to speak to me. It made me feel excited and happy.

Saturday, May 25

We told Mom and Dad today when they came over. Mom inhaled a high pitched squeal, then jumped up to hug me. "Oh, that's wonderful news. What a great surprise! My baby is having a baby!" Tears came quickly to her eyes.

Dad shook Ben's hand and then hugged me. He looked happy, too. Dad doesn't always have large emotional reactions to things, but he cares a lot about family.

I offered them both beers, leftovers from our housewarming party. "It's time to celebrate," my dad said.

"Yes, but it's early." I did not want anyone getting more confident than me. I did not want to manage anyone else's disappointment if the baby did not make it past the first trimester.

"That's no reason not to celebrate, though," Mom said. "You're healthy and we have no history of miscarriage in our family. It's best to stay positive."

I nodded. I know this, but I also know it is safest to stay alert. You can't be caught by surprise if you're half expecting something. I used to imagine all of the worst case scenarios when I was scared about something going wrong. Truly terrible things usually happen when you're not expecting it. But that all got ruined when I was in a SUV driven by someone else, we skidded on black ice, went over the edge of the road, and rolled down a hill. I crawled out with only a cut, but I do this less now, think about worst case scenarios, because it's not a reliable prevention. I still try to see things from both sides, so it will not hurt as much.

Monday, May 27

I took food to the end of Moon Tribe today and participated in the closing ceremony. It's been four years since I did the whole weekend myself. Moon Tribe is intended for women who want to have a rite of passage, something they missed when they were younger. It was that rite for me – mental and physical challenges, an intense experience in a sweat lodge, followed by an overnight alone in the woods without a tent. I was so nervous about that part, and the chance of bears, but it was fine. So I go back each year to celebrate the other women who go through it. The program alternates between pre-teens and women. This year it was for the teens, and mothers show up at the end as a surprise to support them and acknowledge the rite of passage that happened. I cried a little at how touching it all was, how deep and rich the feelings were that they shared, and the naked display of bravery I got to witness. I held my belly and hoped the baby is a girl. I really want a daughter.

BABY JOURNAL | May 28 | *6 weeks*

I don't feel discomfort as much now in my uterus and breasts so it's easier to forget sometimes that this is happening, that you're happening. Yesterday I went to Moon Tribe for teenagers. The girls told their moms things like they want to spend more time with them. The moms said sweet things like how excited they were to have them before they were born.

BABY JOURNAL | May 30

I had my first appointment at the doctor's office today. It was a little disappointing. Just a nurse and urine and blood tests and medical questions. I need to find a better way to acknowledge you and celebrate your start. Maybe energy healing or something like that. I want to be excited and to feel like I'm joyfully bringing you into this world.

Sunday, June 2

I had my first OB appointment on Thursday. It was a tremendous letdown. I cried on the way home.

I went to the appointment alone because Ben was with Henry. I went straight from work and had been looking forward to it all day, all week. The baby would be officially documented.

I was taken to a tiny, windowless office by a nurse who was much younger than me. Without trying, she made me feel old and unusual for having my first child at 36. She asked me a long series of scary questions about my health, Ben's health, and our parents' health. There was nothing celebratory or fun about it. Then I was sent to the lab in the basement to get blood drawn. I told the technician that I get woozy when I have blood taken, and she was very sweet and gentle with me. I did appreciate that. Then I drove home and cried because it felt like what my anthropology professor described all those years ago about gynecology being a sterile, ruinous business was very true.

I must find a more personable side to pregnancy and childbirth. I will give birth in a hospital; I am not a home birth person, nor would Mom ever condone the idea as a retired nurse. But maybe I could find a mentor or look into having a doula. I didn't think I wanted that, but maybe I do. Maybe I want to be surrounded by everyone possible who will make me feel safe and good. I know how important it is for the birth to go well. I've sat through so many child studies at the Waldorf school where everyone discusses the birth in relation to the child's life. Difficult births or cesarean section births were brought up when the preschool child was having trouble adjusting to transitions or settling into the rhythm of the day. It felt so ominous to know you could be setting up your child for hard times even in the first moments of their exit from the womb.

We have one more week of school until summer. I think the song we're singing about the fifth grade graduates will go well. We've spent a lot of time on it. I need to keep up my energy for these last days. An end to the routine of the work day will be great. This summer I need to go easy on myself and not create too many lists and projects. Just be.

Wednesday, June 5

Tomorrow is the last full day of school. I am so ready for summer. I'm in the midst of week seven and still feeling pretty normal. I just watched videos from our wedding. It feels so long ago already. Nothing is permanent, no matter how much time and money is spent on it. I have some memories, however, not as many as I wish. It was a night, a special one, but a night. I'd like to hold onto the wedding tighter, but I can't. The concussion two months later didn't help. This is the way of life. It'll be fun to go to Ben's niece's wedding later this month. Tomorrow, graduation, will be its own special moment to remember. I have clear, beautiful memories of my three other graduations at Waldorf.

I have felt so busy and constrained and tired, but tonight with Ben out with friends, for the first time in a long while, I feel alone. It's okay but different. I'm glad I am doing a meditation retreat; there will be a lot of alone time there. Do I still know how to enjoy being alone? I think so. But it is certainly nice to have consistent company. I am lucky to have Ben. It's still hard to believe I got pregnant so easily and quickly. We're almost two months in. Life changed so fast after being the same for so many years.

BABY JOURNAL | June 5 | *Week 7*

It's been a busy week, the last week of school. Tomorrow you'll be with me as I sing a song in front of a lot of people. It's neat that you're with me for things. Tonight I watched videos from your dad's and my wedding. That was almost six months ago now. Our wedding was very fun and special.

Tonight I held my belly where you're working at being formed. I was very tired last weekend, but the last few days I've felt better. I worry sometimes that you won't be okay. But usually I trust that you will be. We really want you. That wedding was a big step toward you. I'm a little scared of all the changes coming but I believe we're ready. I'm 36, I better be ready! You let me know I should take it easy. I will. Summer is so close. I'll slow down and sit and go on easy morning and evening walks. I'll be careful not to push too hard. I want to be responsible right from the start. I'm glad you're becoming a soul. Someday you'll wonder how time existed before you had thoughts. This is it. This is your pre-life.

Monday, June 10

G raduation went well. The kids gave speeches, David and I sang our song,
people appreciated it, and the parents said kind things to me. One dad told
me he thought I was the main reason his son made it happily through the year,
that his son said about me, "She gets me." That was the best moment of the
night. It was very hot during the ceremony and we had to sing looking into the
sun. Ben and Mom came to watch and we sat together with our plates on our
laps full of delicious potluck food. I looked around at the family units all sitting
together and imagined us one day being like that. Over the past many years, I
always felt sad leaving school events as a teacher instead of a parent. I gave ten
years to other kids and always went home to an empty house. Well, except for
Teddy. He's always been there for me in his cat way. But I can stop being sad
about that now because I'm married and pregnant and am having a baby.

After our inservice day today, colleagues met at a restaurant to celebrate
the end of the school year. Everyone ordered fancy drinks and I had water-
melon water. When no one else was around I whispered to a friend, "I'm not
drinking because I'm pregnant!"

Her face brightened and spread into an ecstatic grin. "I knew it, I knew it!"
she squealed. "I knew this was going to happen soon! I hoped it would."

Joy and more joy.

Tuesday, June 11

I went to the dentist today and when they asked if there were any medical
changes to note on my chart I said, "Well, I'm pregnant." The woman at the
desk said, "Okay, I'll make note of that."

No one pressured me to get x-rays. The dental hygienist asked when I was
due. "January," I said.

"Ah, so not a Christmas baby," she replied.

"No," I said. Did people hope for Christmas babies? Ben's is January 30 so
our baby will be in his company.

"We can schedule your next appointment for when you're eight months
pregnant, get it done before the baby arrives."

At the end of the cleaning, she told me December 13 was my next appointment. It was very strange to think about being so huge and coming to the dentist and lying in that chair. That will be me, though.

BABY JOURNAL | June 11 | *Week 8*

School is almost over, one more day of meetings. I've been tired but mostly okay. I went for a run early this morning before work. I feel slower, but it's okay. We are telling more people about you. I'm thinking about how things will unfold at my job. When I held my belly tonight, I felt that you are going to be shy and sweet. That sounds lovely. I am excited to meet you.

Saturday, June 15

Tonight we told our friends, two couples, that I'm pregnant. It was actually more difficult than I thought it'd be to find the right pause in conversation. When there was finally a space I said, "We're glad you're all here because we want to tell you that we're pregnant."

It was the first time I used that phrasing of we instead of I. It felt a little weird. I think I said it because the friends knew Ben before they knew me so it was like I was sharing his news more than mine. One of the couples is moving away in the summer, and they expressed regret that they won't be here in January when the baby is born. I feel like it's normal where we live, a college town, for people to come and go. I've adjusted to it, and although it makes it difficult to form deep friendships, there are always new people entering, which is comforting. I will have new mother friends next year. Maybe people from prenatal yoga or the infant class at the Waldorf school or baby swimming lessons at the YMCA.

Tuesday, June 18

Today I had an appointment with an herbalist I see from time to time. We talked about taking the right vitamins, eating the healthiest foods, what to cut out of my diet, and she put together a special tea for me to drink. I expressed my concern about miscarriage and she told me to reach out to her right away if I have any bleeding because she could give me something that might turn it around. It was scary to confront the idea of that happening, like imagining the moment when I feel something go wrong and then see blood in my underwear. She told me to take digestive enzymes to help with indigestion, which is my only discomfort of pregnancy right now.

BABY JOURNAL | June 18 | *Week 9*

I am very tired this week. Days when I can stay home are best. I meditated and almost fell asleep.

You're growing and it takes a lot out of me. You are the size of an olive. Three more weeks until the end of the first trimester. It is going quickly. I will be glad to have energy back and a normal appetite. We're going to a family wedding next week. They're all excited about you. We'll see three of my friends, too. Lots of girl time.

Wednesday, June 19

I am in the dregs of the first trimester. I look and feel tired. I'm okay, though. No throwing up. Sleep is strange and I don't want to be touched. Poor Ben. I miss alcohol. All of this will pass. I have three weeks until the end of the trimester. My energy should return then, so they say. That will be in time for Shrine Mont, and my meditation retreat, and our Montreal trip. We're going on a babymoon trip to Montreal at the beginning of August. We planned it after our honeymoon in January to have something to look forward to, but now it works out to be a babymoon, too. It's a funny word that I like.

I'm grateful for this pretty house. I could easily stay home for most of the summer and be content. It's peaceful and feels safe and spacious. This is certainly a big life experience, being pregnant. I'm doing a good job at it so far, I think.

I made an appointment at the local birth center to talk to someone about being pregnant. I said in my email that I want to give birth in a hospital, but that I'm looking for assistance up until that point. I asked if it is possible to pay for sessions individually instead of a package that includes the birth at home or at the center. She said yes so I am going to check it out. The appointment is the day after my first ultrasound.

BABY JOURNAL | June 24 | *Week 10*

We are moving closer to the end of the first trimester. The placenta will be fully formed soon. I went to energy healing today. I wanted to get things cleared out for you. She got two images of you: flowers and sail boats. That second one surprised me, which I like. She said I've made space for you and you are going to ground me. That feels true. She said now is a time when it's going to feel important to have my mom, your Mom Mom, around me. I felt some shifts over the weekend, wanting to be closer to your dad again. Maybe the slightly nauseous, drained feelings are behind me.

Tuesday, June 25

Afew days ago Mom noticed a lump on Teddy's front paw. I had seen something last week, but I hadn't noticed the change in size. Animals get little lumps under the skin. He has them on his back, too, under his thick, orange fur. But last night he was licking and acting like it was bothering him. I called the vet this morning and they had a spot for him to come in right then. The doctor said he had to sedate Teddy to take an X-ray to really know what it was. I went home and waited for him to call. Around one o'clock he called. I was expecting it to be something related to a claw. That is not what he said.

"I have never seen something so large grow on a cat's foot." He went on, "It could be a cyst. He might have broken a bone in his paw and this is scar tissue that has grown over the fracture. The break would've happened months ago for the tissue to look like this. Do you remember a fall? Did he get out of the house and something happened then? Do you remember him limping?"

No, no, no. I thought about the ledge above the kitchen cabinets in our new house and how hard his landing sounds when he comes down. Could he have broken something and not shown pain?

"The other possibility is a tumor. Tumors in cats are very rare but they can happen. Performing a biopsy on the area would be very painful and expensive. I don't recommend doing that."

My voice trembled. This could not be happening. Teddy with cancer? It was supposed to be about his claw, an ingrown nail. "What about amputation?" I asked.

"Amputation is very difficult on a cat. And most likely if he has a tumor of this size then the cancer has spread to other parts of his body. I can tell you from his x-ray that it has not spread to his lungs, which would be the first place I would expect to see it."

I was crying by this point. I told the doctor it was a lot to hear and that I was pregnant and emotional. He said he understood. "What is there to do?" I asked.

"I think you should wait and see what happens. He does not appear to be in pain so just go on as normal. When he starts to decline, we can give him medication to help with the pain. And then at a certain point you will make a decision about his quality of life."

Lose Teddy? My best friend of nine years? Teddy is supposed to meet the baby and be a part of her life.

We're leaving for Oregon tomorrow. It's horrible timing. I may not have much more time with him.

When we got Teddy home, it was like everything was normal. He was relieved to not be at the vet and moved around the house as usual. I don't want to spend the next months being sad every time I look at him. Maybe it's a cyst, it'll always be there, and he'll be fine. This feels like the wisest thing to believe right now for the sake of my own stress and the baby, as well as the fact that he could be perfectly fine and it would be a shame to spend so much time feeling sad.

Sunday, June 29

The flight to Portland on Wednesday afternoon was uneventful. I was concerned about getting too anxious about the baby while flying, but that didn't happen. On Thursday morning, we had breakfast with Ben's parents, then drove with them to Eugene. We stopped at a coffee shop, and I treated myself to the richest hot chocolate I've ever tasted. We told his parents about the baby over the phone many weeks ago, but it's nice to share the glee of our news in person with them.

During lunch I asked Ben's mom about family names. Henry is named after Ben's dad. She told us a few names and said she had recently been looking at family tree work done by her brother. A great-great-grandmother was named Cosette. The name stood out to her as a pretty one. I really love that name.

She told us later that night she was mistaken and the name was actually Cozart and a last name. But, she added, Mary Cassatt is in the family line, too. Cozart blended with Cassatt sounds like Cosette. Victor Hugo apparently made up the name Cosette from the word *chosette* meaning *little one* in french. It has also been assigned the meaning *victorious*.

Our niece got married on Friday evening. It was a fun wedding, but I felt puffy and pregnant. They all know we're expecting, which was nice; it didn't have to be a secret. I am not really showing much yet, but I can tell the difference.

Yesterday we took a bus to Portland. I fell asleep for most of the ride. I texted Mom to tell her about the name Cosette. She said it reminded her of Les Miserables. I didn't ask if that was a good or bad thing because I do not want anything to shadow the name.

Today, Ben flew home because he is starting a summer job tomorrow. I'm on my own in an Air BnB for two nights and will see friends. I'm a little nervous about walking the streets on my own, mostly because I'm pregnant and have a hyper awareness about being safe, and I don't look pregnant so no one will treat me more gently. I feel eager for those days.

Wednesday, July 3

Today I fly home. I'm ready to be done with this trip. It was a good time, but I want to be home. I'm in Charlotte, NC waiting for my connection to Charlottesville. On the first flight, I asked a man to put my suitcase in the carry-on area above my seat. I said, "I'm sorry, but can you lift this for me? I'm pregnant." He did it right away and then sat back down next to his wife. I imagined the woman was judging me for not being able to lift it or being too cautious. She also could have been thinking she felt that way once in the past, but that's not where my head goes first. I want to be strong, but I also want help when it feels warranted.

I stayed with Ashley, a friend from college, for two nights in Portland and we had some good talks. Her daughter is turning one soon. I have never been someone who runs to hold the baby in a room. I don't feel any differently about that while pregnant. I think when the baby is my own I will want to be around her all of the time. I don't feel that way about other people's kids.

Yesterday my sister-in-law and niece came from Eugene to spend the day with me. We went for a hike. The conversation was lively and we talked a lot about pregnancy. I got very hungry and had to pee a bunch of times. After the hike we went to a restaurant. I ate a big burger, and we shared a giant piece of chocolate cake. Before leaving downtown, we went into a stationary store. I looked at baby shower invitations and everything baby related. I found a baby book I want to buy. I had forgotten there are things like that I should be starting now. I'm making some lists, not too many though, just a few.

BABY JOURNAL | July 5 | *Week 11*

I'm almost to twelve weeks! You're feeling more real. I started picking out things for a registry today and am thinking about a baby shower. We went to Portland, Oregon for your cousin's wedding. Everyone was excited about you. I bought a baby book to fill in memories of the first year. Your dad and I have thought of some new names, all french sounding. We thought one was a family name but it's not. Cosette. I really like it. Juliette and Colette are others. I know I felt Hannah but now I'm not sure. Instead it could be a message that you're full of grace because that's what Hannah means in Hebrew.

Wednesday, July 10

Today I had my second pregnancy appointment, the first one with a doctor that happens at twelve weeks. It was scheduled at one o'clock so that Ben could come during his lunch break.

Someone from the office called at 10 a.m. "The doctor has an emergency and needs to leave by 1:15. Can you come at 12:30 instead?"

"My husband is joining me there but can't come until 1."

"It might still be happening at 1. He could join you for the end. Or we could reschedule for another day next week."

I did not want to wait another week. I figured the doctor would probably talk to me for the first part and do the ultrasound at the end. Ben could be there by then.

I sat on the edge of the uncomfortable reclined table, which leaves two options: lay back or sit hunched over. I looked at the poster of the woman with the growing baby inside of her that I had seen so many times while I waited for the doctor to come in for my annual pelvic exams. Many of those years the questions were about if I had a partner. I would answer no in a shaky voice. The doctor didn't need to ask if I wanted to talk about birth control those times. One year I told her I thought I might be married by the next year and thinking about children. But by the following visit, James and I had broken up. Even that year she mentioned geriatric pregnancy. I was just over 30 then. Now here I was at 36 and finally pregnant. It has happened and it feels important and good, but Ben wasn't there, so I was still alone, still not getting it quite right. I cried but made sure to stop before the doctor came in.

She stalled a little after hearing I was waiting for Ben, but not enough. She had hurt her hand and needed to see a doctor herself. That's why my appointment had been changed. "Do you have any questions?" she asked.

What was I supposed to be asking? Maybe that should have been my question. Was the doctor's job to provide some education on what was going on in my body, things I should be doing or not doing?

"I guess not," I said quietly.

She put the jelly on my abdomen and used the wand to look for the baby. She saw the fetus. She turned the screen to show me. A blob moving to a beat. She printed pictures. There was no sound, no heartbeat tracking. Just the noise of a printer. "All looks good," she said. "We'll see you next month."

I put my clothes back on, and as I walked to the elevator Ben texted: "I'm here."

BABY JOURNAL | July 10 | *Week 12*

I had an ultrasound today and got to see you. You're already very cute. Your hand was raised with tiny fingers waving. I have been very tired this week, but I feel happy that you're okay. More ultrasound on Monday.

Thursday, July 11

Today was a very difficult day. I went to the birth center feeling wary but open-minded. It's located in a small house behind the vet hospital where I used to take Teddy. The grounds were uncared for, which unsettled me. I felt similarly in the small waiting room, devoid of people. It was dusty and cramped with furniture. I sat on the edge of an overly soft chair, expecting someone to pop out to acknowledge I had entered. A large shelf of books lined one wall. The books were on a wide range of topics, of course including natural births, but also work with infants and toddlers. From the adjacent room, I could hear two parents talking about their child who was playing on the floor. They were telling a person who I assumed was a therapist about the child. After about ten minutes, the parents and child came into the waiting room looking cheerful and talking loudly. I smiled at them and their child who was much older looking than I had imagined from the voice and play sounds. The woman who had been with them turned to me.

"You're Karen?"

"Yes," I nodded.

"Come on in." She gestured to follow her into the room from which she had just come. "Please sit there." She pointed to a couch on one side of the room. She sat in a chair facing me. "The others will be here soon," she said.

Others? Two other women entered the room and took seats forming a triangle around me. This was the whole team of midwives. I wasn't having an appointment with one person but three.

"If you decide to work with us, you'll be seeing all three of us at your appointments and we never know who will be there at the birth, so it's good for you to get to know all of us." The person speaking was probably in her late 50s with dark gray hair and a solid build. She had clear, stern eyes and a strong voice. Her colleague to my left had long, blonde hair and a jovial affect, probably similar in age. To my right was a much younger woman, maybe thirty, with short hair. She seemed newer to the group and less at ease.

"It's very nice for you all to make the time," I said. I suddenly felt bad for wasting their time because I didn't think this was going to work out.

"You were the one who wanted only pre-birth work but not the birth, right?" She waited for me to nod. "Well, we can't really do that. It wouldn't be fair to you. I do things a certain way here and it's all the opposite of how it's done out there," she pointed toward the window, "and you can't mix what's in here with what's out there. They contradict each other. You'd have a doctor telling you one thing and me telling you another. They're going to try to fill your head with nonsense and I can't work against that."

"Oh," I whispered. I wanted to leave. The couch I was seated on was red with a yellow swirl running through it. How many pregnant women had sat on this couch confident they wanted to give birth down the hall in this small house?

She cleared her throat. "So tell us why you want to give birth in a hospital. Why not a home birth? Tell us."

"Well," I stammered, "Honestly, I think about cleanliness as a factor."

The two older women guffawed. "Cleanliness! We are so much cleaner here than a hospital! Your home is so much cleaner. Have you seen the floor of a hospital? All of the sick people who are walking in and out of the hospital? When are you due? January? Flu season. You'd be better off far away from a hospital with your newborn baby."

"Oh, goodness, yes," agreed the blonde woman, chuckling and nodding her head vigorously.

I felt a small lump form in my throat. I tried again. "My mom is a nurse and I don't think she'd ever let me give birth at home. She'd be scared for me and make me nervous about it. It's just not what people do in my family. And I'm worried about what would happen if there was a problem during the birth."

The owner edged her chair closer to me. "Let's get one thing straight. This is your baby, not your mom's. It's fine to respect your mom but you tell your mom your decisions about your baby, not the other way around. Don't have a baby in a hospital because you don't want to disappoint your mother. It's too big of a decision. Right?" She waited for me to react. I looked at her, unmoving. "And if there's a problem, we go to the hospital. We love c-sections if that's what has to happen. Don't we?" She looked at her partner.

"Love them," she concurred.

"We never wait if we know that's what's needed and we always know. There have been very few cases when there was an issue getting to the hospital on time. We don't like to send our clients there too early though because the hospital insists on pumping in a bunch of unnecessary drugs that will hurt the baby. That's what hospitals like, they like drugs from the drug companies that pay their bills. And they scare you into thinking childbirth hurts a lot so you go there and spend a lot of money staying overnight in their fancy hospital. It's a racket."

"I've had ear aches that hurt more than giving birth," the blonde woman said with a chuckle.

"I had an ovarian cyst a year ago that hurt so much," I said with a question in my voice.

"Oh yea, that could be much worse than childbirth."

That was nice to hear, although the ache in my throat was getting less easy to manage.

"Why did you come here? What led you to us?" The main woman speaking crossed her hands tightly on her lap as if she was actively restraining herself from interrupting me with more information until I got a chance to speak. I looked to the young, silent woman sitting to my right. She was watching, an eager student.

I began, "I've had a few disappointing appointments with my OB at UVa. It feels like it should be more special than how they treated me. Yesterday they changed the time of my appointment and my husband missed the first ultrasound. It bothered me a lot."

All three of them nodded in agreement and with sympathy. "Many of our clients are OBs or nurses who work the maternity floor. They see how bad it is and they want something better."

They went on to tell me horrifying things about the place I was planning to have my baby. They talked and talked with vivid descriptions and veiled threats until I cried.

"I know, it's hard to hear, isn't it? We're not trying to scare you, we just want you to be informed."

"Can I use the restroom?" I excused myself and cried hard. I knew the hormones weren't helping me, but still, this was rough, right? I stared at myself in the mirror and thought about giving the women a chance to explain themselves. I would look around the birth center and consider it. Nothing had to be decided right now. I went back in and sat down, unsure if I would start crying again.

"It's shocking stuff, isn't it? If you choose to give birth in a hospital you should at least have a doula.

You need someone there to protect you and speak up for you. The nurses and doctors will bypass your wishes. You may want to give birth naturally and they'll insist a c-section is necessary even if it isn't. Or they'll cut that umbilical cord so fast after birth, letting none of that important blood pass through to the baby. Your husband can't be trusted in those moments because he'll listen to your pain. And not your mother either, even if she is a nurse."

It went on like that for over an hour. By the end I was exhausted and knew I was late for lunch with a friend. I asked to be shown the birthing rooms. They looked like ordinary bedrooms. I tried not to picture all of the pain and fluids the rooms had seen. Birth felt like such an extraordinary thing, yet these rooms made it seem like it could be done anywhere. Like one moment there was a pregnant woman in the bed, and the next there was a baby in the room and she was no longer pregnant.

Before I left, the meeting leader asked me if I wanted a sonogram so I could hear the heartbeat. I laid back on the table that was in the same room as our talk, and she put her bare hands on my stomach. No doctor had done that yet. She felt around and talked about the position of the baby and made a comment about how many weeks pregnant I was. Then she applied gel and the wand. I heard the heartbeat. It was a really nice moment and I felt cared for.

As I left the small house, I was massively confused. They tricked me into coming there, pushed me to tears, gave me all of this valuable, terrifying information, made me feel seen and heard and cared for, and then left alone to sort through huge contradictions. I have a lot to think about. More than I want to have to think about. Before today I wanted something more sentimental and resembling Moon Tribe in my pregnancy. Now I'm scared of being forced into a bad birth experience by a faceless, heartless doctor in a fluorescent room full of germs. Is it better to be aware and make a knowledgeable choice or is the anxiety bad for the baby?

I'm lying on my bed cradling my belly with one hand and writing with another. I'm going to yoga soon. That will help. Although sometimes I feel frustrated because I can't do many of the positions and there are no prenatal classes at the studio. They're talking about starting one in the fall, though. I could go for a few months before the baby arrives. We leave tomorrow for a weekend church retreat.

Sunday, July 14

The church retreat was a nice weekend away together. The food is not healthy, which did not feel good for the baby, but otherwise the pace was fine. I spent some time reading a baby book. Our friends know that I'm pregnant, which makes things easier. A parent of one of my previous students was there and we sat together for lunch on the first day.

"What's new?" she asked in her chill, California way.

"Well," I said, drawing out the word.

She jerked her head to look at me directly.

"I'm pregnant," I said.

She squealed loudly in delight causing people to turn and look at us. She started to cry. "I knew it when you started talking. And I know how much you want this." Her reaction made me so happy. Yes, this is what I want, validation that this is huge for me and my life story.

Tomorrow is the genetic testing and ultrasound that I am supposed to have because I'm over 35 years-old. I won't get results immediately, but I'm still a little nervous. The test may tell us the gender, too, which means my hope for a girl will be answered soon.

Tuesday, July 16

Mom went with me for the ultrasound. The questions were intense and the different diseases they check for are all scary to think about. They took a vial of my blood and did an ultrasound to take measurements of the head. Before the appointment, they told me to have a full bladder. I was in so much pain from needing to pee I could hardly concentrate on the pictures. I overdid it. I was trying to do everything so right that I could have inadvertently hurt my bladder. The radiologist came in after and said the proportions look fine. I went home and slept deeply. I held my belly and hoped the sound of the ultrasound wand and energy had not hurt the baby's ears. I read in a book how that can happen.

In the afternoon I had a call with a doula who used to send her kids to Waldorf. She was always very kind and I wanted to talk to her about the birth center because the website indicated she worked there. In talking to her, I found out she left over a year ago. The website has not been updated. She said she had been a doula for many hospital births that had gone well. She only witnessed a few where the doctors were pushy. The nurses are known to be excellent at Martha Jefferson Hospital and noted the pace at that hospital was slower than at the university hospital. So now I'm thinking maybe I should switch to Martha Jefferson as a compromise between UVa and the birth center. And maybe even have a doula. The one big drawback of MJ is that they do not have a NICU. They have some capabilities during an emergency, and she has never seen a birth where a baby needed more help than what MJ can offer. I feel like it's best to not face this birth letting fear make decisions. I should assume complications at birth are rare and therefore will most likely not happen to me. I don't want to pick UVa just because I want to be less nervous in case something goes wrong. I have a strong feeling that the baby will be born a few days before the due date and naturally, not a c-section. I very much want to give birth without surgery and without drugs.

BABY JOURNAL | July 16 | *Week 13*

Hi, baby. Here we are at Week 13. I'm having a lot of headaches and am feeling tired with interrupted sleep, but I'm okay. I saw you yesterday on an ultrasound. You're in there flipping and moving around. The doctor called it a "pretty pregnancy." We will find out your gender next week!

BABY JOURNAL | July 18

I'm going to a meditation retreat today. I hope it's a nice time and that I'm able to sleep well. It's for five days. It will be good to be reminded of how important mindfulness is, especially as we start this journey together.

Later the same day: I made it! It's better than I anticipated. I have my own room with a roommate in an attached room, but the bathroom is in my room which is good for all the peeing I do! The meditation hall is very pretty and peaceful. I am glad I came and am doing this. Me and my tiny passenger are on a little trip just the two of us.

BABY JOURNAL | July 19

It is mid-July already. It's good I'm here. I needed time to slow down. No phone, email, things to do. In that way, it is blissful. The food is good. I did not sleep well but I feel okay. It is very hot outside so I can't be out much past the morning. I find myself planning during meditations, but it is just the first day. I need time to unwind and cleanse. They are all pleasant thoughts. I am lucky for that. I wonder what we should do for the baby shower for types of food and activities. I plan to invite a lot of people. It's fun to celebrate and it will be helpful to get gifts for you. These are names I'm thinking about: Juliet, Cosette, Eliza, Claudia, Colette. Once we find out your gender, we should get a name book. I want you to have a meaningful middle name, too. My belly is getting bigger and moving up. I'm starting to look more pregnant.

BABY JOURNAL | July 20

Day two may be harder than one. Sleeping was difficult again. The woman staying next to me got up to use the bathroom five times and woke me each time. This is an experience. It's funny that I pay to do things like this.

I just turned my phone on for the time because my IPOD is dying, and there was a message from UVa. The genetic tests came back all normal. I felt like they would, I mean I feel like everything is fine with you, but it's good to have confirmation. They will have the gender for us Monday if we want it. I want it! I'm tempted to do a gender reveal cake for me and your dad. Some people wait to find out at birth. I've been so set on you being a girl, but of course I'll adjust if you're a boy. It will be good to know soon so I can start shifting if you are a boy.

I will do my best to stay in the present today. It's going to be 98 degrees, lots of indoor time.

BABY JOURNAL | July 21

Last day. I'm leaving tonight instead of tomorrow morning. It was a hard decision to make, but I let go and did it. It feels good to do something for me and what I want instead of what I think I should do. Maybe it's a lesson for what's to come with me quitting work to be home with you. In the end, all of these tiny decisions don't mean much. It might feel giant in the moment -- I found a tick on me this morning and that felt hugely dramatic -- but it's all passing. Some things are big like the arrival of you or stopping work or marrying your dad.

It is so hot here today and it will be so cold when you arrive. Tomorrow is week 14. And then the following week your dad and I go to Montreal for our babymoon! I have a lot to be happy about.

BABY JOURNAL | July 22 | *Week 14*

It is very nice to be home. We are finding out tomorrow if you're a girl or a boy. We're getting a cake made. They'll put vanilla custard inside if you're a girl and chocolate if you're a boy. I am full of anticipation!

Tuesday, July 23

I'm writing this in the morning. Tonight I will know the gender of our baby. It is very strange that I will be able to look back tomorrow at my unknowing voice. In such a short amount of time, my life will be greatly altered. Of course nothing will physically change because the baby has always been a boy or girl inside of me, but my perspective on the rest of my life in terms of raising a daughter or a son will be affected. If we are having a boy, it will be fine, although I know I will be a little disappointed. I will get over it, though. A lot of my favorite students have been boys. Boys often have great senses of humor as middle and high school kids. I think I would like to have two children so if this baby is a boy, then there's still a chance to have a girl in a few years. I do still think she is a girl, though. Ben's mom told me that men on Ben's side only have boys, which was hard to swallow when I'm so set on a girl. But there's no way anyone can know, except the genetic tester person.

BABY JOURNAL | July 24

You're a girl! We found out last night. We're so excited. The glee I felt was so full and real. Your dad and I are thrilled. When we cut the cake and there was vanilla custard, we were so happy. Yay for you and knowing you a little better now. You told me right away. What do you think of Cosette Hannah Fraser-Morris? I'd like to honor your voice and when you told me the name Hannah.

Thursday, July 25

We are having a girl! The surge in my heart when I saw that vanilla custard in the cake was like nothing I have felt before. It was an indescribable glee. I jumped up and down and hugged Ben in a way I haven't since I found out I was pregnant. He is very happy, too. I was also very relieved that I don't need to change all my thoughts on who this baby is and now I can call her "she" without a doubt.

Friday, July 26

We toured the maternity floor of UVa and Martha Jefferson hospitals last night. Being in the main lobby at UVa felt gross. The bathroom smelled worse than anything I can describe. It wasn't a normal, bad bathroom smell but instead like it had not been cleaned in weeks and when it was cleaned it was done with yeast and old black beans. If the bathroom was like that, what does that say about the cleanliness of the rest of the hospital?

The person showing us around was very kind and informative. She teaches the birthing classes at the hospital. I have signed up for that series starting in November, but if we switch to Martha Jefferson then we will do their class instead. The rooms at UVa were barren and full of steel. It was frightening to imagine giving birth in one of them. The nurses' station outside of the rooms looked like a call center, dimly lit by only computer screens.

There were so many people on the tour at MJ versus at UVa. One had just ended at MJ before ours, too. It's like a baby factory in there, but a nice one. The halls were wide, the rooms were more like hotel rooms. There was hotel type art on the wall across from the bed where the delivery could happen, unless you wanted to sit or be in the tub. The tub was giant and the tour guide told us to make sure to tell the person on the phone when we call saying we are coming that we wanted the tub to be filled upon arrival. She made it all sound relaxed and like it could be a nice experience outside of the pain. You get moved to a second room after the delivery with a comfier bed and more privacy.

The tour guide said we might hear a woman yelling who was in the early stages of birth. I tried to listen but didn't hear anything. I was the least pregnant person there. Some of the women could have been ready to give birth next week. It was strange to imagine looking like those women in a few months. I was feeling glad I would be super pregnant in cold months.

There's a cute coffee shop and a sweet looking gift shop outside the doors of the maternity wing. Between those doors and the actual maternity ward is the waiting room. It's spacious and has a wall of windows. I imagined Mom and Dad sitting there waiting to hear about the birth. I have decided I don't want Mom to be at the birth, but instead Ben and a doula. You're only allowed two people. I think I will probably yell and be grumpy at times and I don't want that to be a part of the experience for Mom. Just cute, pudgy granddaughter being held for a first picture, gazing into each other's eyes.

BABY JOURNAL | July 28

We are going to Montreal this week, all three of us. This will be your last-flight in my belly. I bought you a few clothes this week -- a dress with dinosaurs on it, two one-piece outfits, a winter hat, and a bathing suit. It's fun to shop for you. Your dad and I visited two hospitals. I think we're going to decide on Martha Jefferson. I hope it's a fun week away.

Monday, July 29

Our BnB in Montreal is adorable and exactly what I would hope for in a Canadian getaway. It's in the quaint, old part of the city. The streets are crowded because this is a popular time of year to visit, but I don't mind. It's all pedestrian traffic, not cars. The shops are mainly touristy but the buildings are familiar to Europe and remind me of my study abroad days in Florence. I've enjoyed looking up restaurants for each night and small activities for the days. I get tired easily and don't need a packed agenda. It's vacation!

BABY JOURNAL | August 5 | *Week 16*

For Week 15, we were in Montreal. It was a nice trip. Your dad and I enjoyed the time away. We went to a museum, a few churches, and lots of good restaurants. We talked about a name for you. Our favorites are Cosette and Lydia. I think they're both very pretty sounding. I bought you socks from Quebec. It was fun to shop for you. My belly is getting much bigger. They say this week you can hear my voice and I might start feeling you move soon.

Wednesday, August 7

I saw a resident for my appointment today at UVa. She looked much younger than me. We heard the heartbeat, but she didn't touch my belly. She asked if I had any questions.

"I am still exercising almost every day and run a few days a week. I bought a running belt but is that enough?"

She nodded aggressively. Her perfectly trimmed hair brushed against her shoulders. "Yes, that should be fine. Exercise is very good for the baby and staying in shape for labor."

"I feel dehydrated all of the time. I need to wake up in the night to drink water. Is that normal?"

"It's important to drink a lot of water while pregnant and it has been very hot. Anything else?"

My face burned. "I don't think so."

"Well, everything looks great here. You can schedule your twenty week ultrasound at the desk before you leave."

"Oh, actually, I'm planning to change to Martha Jefferson. We toured the maternity floor and I think I want to deliver there so I need to switch soon."

"Good for you," she said genuinely. "We get along well with MJ and support their practice. You have no risks related to your pregnancy so there's no reason for you not to change. Is there anything else I can do for you?"

Maybe educate me on being pregnant? I decided to still make the ultrasound appointment because I wasn't sure if I'd get behind in changing doctors. I want to make sure it happens at twenty weeks, not later. It is set for September 6. I'll be back to work by then. Twenty weeks is a big milestone.

Teddy has been very cute and cuddly since we've been home from our trip. Sometimes I think about the possibility of him being sick, but mostly I don't.

BABY JOURNAL | August 8

I had a doctor's appointment yesterday and heard your heart beat. Everything is fine with you. Your cousins are visiting this week. They're excited for your arrival. We all are.

BABY JOURNAL | August 14 | *Week 17*

All is well. I am looking a lot bigger. You're definitely in there! I haven't felt you move yet, but it's coming. There are only a few more days of summer. I'm soaking them up. I was at school yesterday and it felt okay. I think pregnancy makes me even more mellow and easy-going. I have gotten a lot done this summer and had some fun times. I feel like I'm in a good place. A good place to bring you into the world!

Thursday, August 15

I've been feeling a little glum today. I guess from being at home a lot and doing mundane tasks.

Soon I will be busy and wishing for days like this. I think I'm sad that Ben is leaving for a week, too. I will miss him. It was so quiet here today even with the pets.

I'll be in meetings at school for the week and a work picnic on Sunday. I feel okay about school and like I'll have enough time to get things done next week. I like teaching and it will be a good place to be for the next four months. Time is going by quickly, as always. This week has reminded me of all of my years of being single and living alone. It could get very lonely.

Saturday, August 17

Ben left for England this morning. It was hard to say goodbye to him, in all I can think to call 'my fragile state.' I definitely feel more vulnerable, and I want someone else around in case something happens. I also think about a plane crash or an accident in England that would leave my baby never meeting her father. I imagine these types of fears occur to a lot of women when they're pregnant. Mom is coming over to help address baby shower invitations with me. I'm also looking forward to some time alone and plan to watch a good amount of television. This is the last week of summer and soon being lazy will be only a memory.

Tuesday, August 20

Today was the first day of meetings at work. I sent an email to my colleagues last month when I was telling the parents of my students about being pregnant so everyone already knows, but it felt important and fun to mention it on my turn during summer recap. I drank a lot of water, ate my snacks, and held onto my belly a little as pregnant people do. Sitting in a meeting on emergency protocol for an armed predator on campus was very uncomfortable. I was even pointed out as not being able to move very fast in a few months. It's a horrible thing to think about and it made me feel relieved to know I may not be teaching for a while or ever again. Schools are dangerous places now, more than most other workplaces. And yet, I would send our child to this school in the future. It feels safer than most, although has no barriers from someone walking onto campus. Something I learned today is that women like telling you about their own pregnancies and births when you're pregnant. Some are nice to hear, others are not. It's worrisome anytime someone feels the need to follow up their story by saying "I'm sure it will be easier for you."

After the day of meetings, I went to Martha Jefferson to meet with a nurse for an initial appointment. She was very kind and significantly older than me, which I appreciated. She gave me a lot of information, some of which I already had from UVa, but mostly she just made me feel happy and supported.

I left knowing we made the right decision in switching doctors.

BABY JOURNAL | August 21 | *Week 18*

I just got home from my meditation group. I have a nice community there. Meditating at home is important and I hope it's something you know me as doing. Your dad is away this week in England. He's at a conference at Oxford. I think he's enjoying it. I miss him, but it's been a busy week. Lots of school. I had my first appointment at a new doctor's office yesterday and that went well. Wow, 18 weeks. I'm talking out loud to you these days because you can hear me. I want your dad to play guitar and for us to sing to you. I call you Cosette when I talk to you.

Saturday, August 24

This morning I went to my first prenatal yoga class at Bend studio. It's a studio strictly for pregnant women and women with their babies. It's exciting to think about taking my baby girl there next spring after the flu season is over. This prenatal class that I'll continue to go to each week is at 9 a.m. The teacher is the owner. She said 9 a.m. is a good time on a Saturday for pregnant women because they don't go out on Friday nights. I'm always in bed by 9:30, sometimes 9. The class itself was relaxing and felt good, but the 15 minutes before the practice began was a little anxiety producing. Each woman says what week they are in their pregnancy, how they've been feeling, and if there's any sore body part they would like to work on in class. It was hard to hear all of the complaints from women much further along than me. You have to be 12 weeks pregnant to go to the class. Some women there were 39 and 40 weeks and even a little overdue. They were huge. It's hard for me to imagine getting that big. I'm on my way though, there's no turning back now. I sometimes worry about how my body will recover, but women do it all the time so I know I can too. As long as I don't gain too much weight while pregnant, it shouldn't be that hard to return to my original form. Breastfeeding is supposed to help lose weight, too.

I did enjoy being a part of a special group of people who all have a commonality that is quite intense and important. Today I said I have been feeling fine, no sickness, and no soreness. I mean, I've been running and working out daily. I didn't say that out loud, though. I hope every week I go I am still able to say I'm feeling good, no soreness. Some women had things to complain about that I had never heard of like pain on the pubic bone due to the heaviness of the baby. Pregnancy is a very strange thing. Ben is supposed to be home tonight. I'm ready for him to be back.

Sunday, August 25

I received many congratulations today at the Back to School picnic. Parents seem to be genuinely happy for me. No one is upset that I'll be leaving for maternity leave. I don't know why I think like that. Well, actually I do. When I first started teaching I didn't feel prepared for the job and some parents of my students agreed with that and gave me a hard time. I cared so much about the kids, though, so it really hurt to be considered not good enough. I worked very,

very hard and was definitely good enough. So now when I am doing something out of the normal expectation, causing an inconvenience, it feels like someone is going to tell me I am not enough. That I don't deserve the job. Instead, people here seem very excited about a new baby being around. No teacher has had a baby and gone on leave and returned within the same year in a long time. It was nice to see the kids today, too, especially the returning fifth graders who I taught last year as fourth graders. And David, my co-teacher, is always fun and refreshing to be around. He gets very excited about things that don't phase me as much anymore, and although sometimes last year that made me worry about being unprepared, this year I know what it's all about. I just feel much more secure this year.

BABY JOURNAL | August 26 | *Week 19*

Week 19, Day 1. Feeling good! We just did a long barre workout. The first day of school with kids is tomorrow. I hope we're ready. I think we're ready.

Sunday, September 1

It's September. I've been pregnant for four months. I had a tiny scare of blood this morning after running. It was terrifying to think about anything going wrong now.

I have a doctor's appointment on Tuesday and ultrasound on Friday. I'm eager to hear that everything is okay. I'm a lot bigger, looking pregnant. I'm sleeping better. School started and it's been pretty good. Kids are nice. Once the rhythm is set, it'll be less tiring. I took a nap each day when I got home this week. I put my things down, change into comfier clothes, and collapse onto the couch in the living room. Then everything goes black. I fall asleep so quickly and deeply. It is not like any other sleep I have experienced.

BABY JOURNAL | September 1

It's a new month. I have been pregnant for four. We went to see Mom Mom today. Tomorrow is 20 weeks. We'll get to see pictures of you. I'm looking forward to hearing that you're okay. I am getting a lot bigger, as are you!

Tuesday, September 3

Today Ben and I went to see one of the doctors in the new office. She was very kind and friendly. She knows some of the moms from school. She even delivered some of my students. We listened to the baby's heartbeat, Ben's first time hearing it, and she said everything looks and sounds good. It was a very pleasant appointment, and we left feeling more secure in our decision to switch practices. I told her that I have to wake up at night to drink water because I'm so dehydrated. She said that seemed normal and that my sleep may be interrupted for the entire pregnancy. The need to pee a few times a night stalled after the first trimester as promised. I do still have to go every hour during the day, though, especially with all the water I'm drinking, so I need to leave my classroom during transitions. It's necessary and the kids will need to hold it together while I'm gone. I think they will.

I saw a wise, older friend yesterday and she asked if she could be the baby's fairy godmother. I really like that idea. She has played that role in my life. There is something unnerving about her at times because she's spontaneous and strong-willed and reads me too well, but she cares deeply and is compassionate and interested in me in a way that is not typical of my other relationships. She seems genuinely concerned for my well-being and also admires how I have conducted my life. Her son went to a Waldorf school that she helped found, so we've connected in that way. And we are both Aries.

Yesterday she remarked upon how I created, or summoned, my relationship with Ben that led to marriage, home, and baby. *I'm in awe of you*, she said. All I can do in those moments is feel grateful but also think about how hard it all was, how much I went through with James, and also Ben, to get where I am now, which is a good place, but not void of problems. It is important to keep perspective like this.

BABY JOURNAL | September 3 | *20 weeks*

Twenty weeks yay! We saw a new doctor today and she was great. Your heartbeat sounds healthy.

Friday, September 6

It was a long first full week of school, but I was looking forward to the ultrasound we had today. Ben met me there and I made sure not to overdrink this time. The tech took a ton of pictures of the baby. The whole time she was cooing over the baby's perfect dimensions.

"Look at that position! That's a perfect picture of her head. Oh, that's just gorgeous." At one point she confessed that usually it's difficult to get such detailed pictures because it's hard to get so close if a woman is overweight at all. I feel proud to give my baby a healthy body to grow inside.

She called in the doctor to read the images. The tech said to the doctor, "I have a crush on their baby. She's just so perfect. Look at these images."

At first the doctor just smiled and nodded but then as he started to scroll through he became more alert. "These are fantastic. They're like what they use in teaching manuals."

Ben and I smiled and went along with their vibe but there was not much more to say besides thank you. They wished us luck and said they saw no reason why we would need another ultrasound. The tech showed us toward a different door than the way we came in and said it would get us to the parking lot more quickly. In the empty stairwell, Ben said to me, "We're kind of rocking this pregnancy thing. No morning sickness, perfect ultrasound, people jealous of our baby."

I felt happy too, but the fearful part of me kicked in. "Yea," I said, "but let's not get too far ahead of ourselves. We're halfway there."

"Are you worried about jinxing ourselves or something?

"I guess so." I didn't want to admit it because at this point thinking about something going wrong makes me immediately nauseous, but I also couldn't go along with agreeing we were lucky and rocking pregnancy. Who really believes in luck? It's a word we use often, but it is only a sentiment, a wish, and nothing more.

BABY JOURNAL | September 7

You were perfect in the ultrasound. Everything is forming right. You were wiggly and the tech said she had a crush on you. Your measurements line you up exactly to your due date. We're very fortunate to have such a great baby already. You've been moving around in there a lot the last two days!

Monday, September 9

Mom mailed the baby shower invitations today. That is very exciting to me, that they're all out there announcing our baby is coming. I looked at a lot of invitations, but I picked one with cute baby animals on it that could easily be for a girl or boy even though we know she's a girl. It seems tasteful to have something adorable but muted. I want a big party to celebrate that she's coming, but I don't want it to be too much about me, just who is growing inside of me.

On Saturday at yoga while doing a child's pose, seated cross legged and leaning my chest near the ground, the baby kicked me so hard. Or maybe it was punches. Three really fast punches or kicks in a row. The ultrasound tech said the baby is positioned so her feet are probably hitting the uterine wall where I would feel it. Yes, that's definitely true. The kicks were so hard I actually exclaimed and sat up straight. The instructor saw me looking up and I whispered, "She's kicking so hard right now!" She smiled at me. I think the baby was saying, "Hey, you're squishing me in here!" This was very different from the aches and pains I felt in the first trimester while trying to do some simple yoga poses. Oddly enough, I can do those again without pain. Now it is up to the baby to decide what she likes as well.

BABY JOURNAL | September 11 | *21 weeks*

I feel you move often now. It's a thrill. I wonder what you'll look like and who you will be. I really like this experience of being pregnant. I'm enjoying the unfolding and the mystery of it all.

Saturday, September 14

My week ended too dramatically. Thursday was Back to School Night and because there wasn't enough time to go home and return to school, I made a plan to do something with Mom near school. She picked me up and we went to a huge second-hand sale of baby things that was happening at a church. Thursday was the day for first time moms. There was something about that specialness which made me not want to miss it. So we went and it was overwhelming and I was already tired from the day. It was very hot outside. As we were leaving, I got dizzy and had to grab onto Mom's arm to steady myself.

She took me to get something to eat, but then it was time to go back to work. I made it through the presentations where we talked about the year to twenty-three sets of parents, and I mentioned my maternity leave and how I might not return after winter break because I would be 38 weeks pregnant then. It was fun to think about all of that.

I went home, went to sleep, and the next morning woke up feeling weird and dizzy. Ben drove me to school but when I got there, I felt very strange. I called Mom and she said I should get my blood pressure checked. Preeclampsia is all about having the wrong blood pressure. Ben came back to get me and we drove to CVS, which did not have a checker, so then we went to Kroger which did. It read as normal. I decided to call the doctor's office, though, and they said I should come in to be checked out. So we went back to school, I left a sub plan, a friend offered to teach my classes for me, and I got back in the car with Ben. Mom met us at the doctor's office so that she could drive me home after because Ben needed to do work. All three of us went into the little room and waited for the nurse practitioner to come in.

"You brought your fan club I see," she said in a warm tone. I chuckled, not really in the mood for being funny. She went on quickly, "Your urine shows that you're dehydrated. Tell me what you eat on a regular day."

I listed out what seemed to me a well-balanced array of foods.

She responded, "That's not nearly enough. You need to be eating more protein. Your baby is getting much bigger at this stage and she needs more nutrients, more calories. You need lots of protein all day. Snack every hour. Eat a protein bar if you have to."

My mind went to the disgusting chewy slabs of protein that I used to choke down before cross country meets in high school. That chalky fake chocolate flavor. And there was a peanut butter one, too.

"So get her to eat more, you hear?" She said this to Ben and my mom. They nodded.

"About the dehydration," Ben said. "She drinks more water than anyone I've ever known. And constantly. How could she be drinking more?"

"She might not be able to. It's been very hot and that'll take a lot out of you. It'll be calming down soon as we get further into the fall and that will help. You just keep doing what you're doing and eat more protein. Sound good?" That was to me. Yes, I can do that, I will do that.

That was yesterday. Today we met our doula. We talked about her method of helping during the birth, which is to coach Ben to help me as much as he can.

I also know she will be good at the moment, and I want to hire her. I like the idea of having someone there who has seen a lot of births and has my personal interest in mind, like I'm a big deal to her, versus a nurse who delivers many babies each day.

After the meeting, we went to the Waldorf school for an autumn festival. Even after being gone for just one year, there are many unfamiliar faces. We sat with former colleagues of mine and a previous student and her family. Everyone is very happy for me. It felt nicely validating to be around people I have known for years who are truly joyful for an upcoming event of mine. Being pregnant, bringing a child into the world, is a huge life marker. Sitting at a picnic table in a spot I had walked over countless times over the last decade and having this experience of talking about my future baby... it was good.

Then we went to Ben's friend's birthday party. Last year there was a surprise party for her but no one had bought a cake so Ben and I left during the party to go to the store and buy one. I was tipsy and felt very fun making that decision, being in the store with Ben, and bringing it back through the door with candles lit. The party tonight was different. There were people smoking outside, which was very off putting to me. Ben's friend asked me if it felt weird to be pregnant. I knew exactly where that question came from, I'd wanted to ask it often of others. And now here I was receiving it.

"Yes," I told her. "It is weird. It's like nothing's there and then suddenly there is. I don't really feel that different yet, though."

We didn't stay long. It was an exhausting day, especially on the heels of my Thursday and Friday.

BABY JOURNAL | September 16 | *22 weeks*

Twenty-two weeks here we are! I'm struggling with some dehydration issues. I'm looking forward to it being cooler outside soon. It should be tomorrow. Our baby shower invitations went out in the mail. I hope many people can come. We will be getting a lot of tiny things for you soon.

Friday, September 20

On Monday, I came home to find Teddy licking his paw obsessively. He had licked the fur off around the growth and made a huge welt on his skin. I called the vet and they gave me an appointment for today after school. They cut his nail that is behind the tumor. It was growing into his skin because it's so puffed out. It looks very painful. They told me I will most likely need to bring him in once a month to get the nail cut to keep it from getting infected. So far he has not acted sick. I guess I'm still waiting for that to happen, but for now it's just lots of licking. I know he licks to try to make it feel better, though, so I think he is hurting. I am not sure what else to do for him.

Saturday, September 21

Today was a nice day. I went to yoga and got to say "I'm 22 weeks and feeling really good." Once in the 20s you hear women complain of body pain. But I'm still doing fine. There was a woman there who is also 22 weeks and she's having triplets. Her belly was much bigger than mine. I can't imagine.

After class, I met Mom at the movie theater to see Downton Abbey. We both had vanilla milkshakes.

It was one of the most delicious things I've ever tasted. When we first arrived, our seats that I had picked for us did not have recliners, which is one of the highlights of this theater. I had picked the wrong row. I was so uncomfortable and so adamant to put up my feet, I went out to the lobby and got our seats changed. I told the woman at the counter, "I'm pregnant and I really want to recline and put my feet up." She didn't seem to care, but I wanted her to know I had a good reason.

Sunday, September 22

I'm always ready for the annual church picnic in the fall because it feels so quaint and familiar. I like going to church because of how safe it feels. The routine and how much people care for one another is comforting. It's a peaceful time to reflect, listen to music, and digest the week. Before I met Ben, I was not going to a church and I definitely only started attending because of him, but I really do like it. The first time I went, I sat with two of Ben's friends because the childcare was closed, and so Ben had to stand in an adjacent room with Henry who was only 1.5 years-old. I felt so nostalgic during the ceremonial aspects of the service. I even teared up during the recitation of the Nicene Creed, remembering how intent I was on being the first person to memorize it in my sixth grade class. I was such a good Catholic at my Catholic all-girls school. The church we go to now is Episcopalian, which again, I only picked because that's where Ben was going, but it works for me.

I always make deviled eggs for the picnic. Well, always means for the last three years. It was hot outside but we found shade under a tree and I pulled a chair from a nearby table so I didn't have to sit on the ground. The food was delicious and I ate a lot. Friends asked how I was feeling. "Great," I said. "Work is tiring, but I'm doing fine. I think November and December during the third trimester will be more difficult at work."

One of our friends had plans to go to a winery for a polo match in the afternoon. Lots of drinking happens at those. It made me slightly envious, wanting to have a glass of red wine outside on a beautiful Sunday. But I only felt that way for a minute. My afternoon ahead was fairly empty and that felt okay too.

Ben and I drove in separate cars because he needed to use time up in town before taking Henry to his mom in the afternoon. I drove home and landed on my bed to write. I am feeling the baby kick so much now, especially at night after dinner. She's commenting on my food choices. When I go to sleep, too, she sometimes gets more active. It's like she is busy sleeping all day while I am rocking her by being so active, and then when I'm still, she wakes up. She lets me know when we need more food in the morning, too.

BABY JOURNAL | September 22 | *Week 23*

All is well. You wake me up early some mornings asking for food. Little kicks and punches. I'm getting more and more excited to see who you will be!

Monday, September 23

Today was an upsetting day. There has been some confusion about my maternity leave. It's 3 a.m. and I am writing emails. At one point, I laid back on the couch and sobbed. I'm not sure if I am reacting differently because I'm pregnant, like the hormones are making me more emotional, but if so, that's the case because I am indeed pregnant.

Wednesday, September 25

After school today, I drove to church so Ben and I could talk with the rector about our baby's baptism in the future. It's far ahead to be planning but I know things will get more difficult to do once winter hits. He was happy to talk to us about it, and it brought back pleasant memories of our premarital conferences with him. Our pastor is very easy to talk to and has a great sense of humor. He is approachable, which was not my experience with priests in the Catholic church. We are hoping to have the baby's baptism in April. Maybe Ben's family can visit to meet her for the first time and attend the baptism. It will be past flu season which is most important.

Friday, September 27

Today started out like a normal day but took a bad turn once I got to school. I felt slightly nauseous when I got there, went into the bathroom and there was some bright red blood on the toilet paper. I know that bright red is cause for alarm. I called Mom and she told me to call the doctor's office. I had to wait until 8 a.m. when they opened. Kids would be coming in at 8:15. A nurse answered.

"How many weeks are you?"

"Twenty three."

"Any other symptoms? Cramping?"

"No. Just a little nauseous feeling but that could be from nerves since I saw the blood."

"It's probably nothing, but we'd like to check you out. When can you come?"

I thought about the Friday a few weeks ago when I came to school and left. I did not want to do that again. "Is there anything in the afternoon?"

"A doctor can see you at 2:30. Will that work?"

I agreed and hung up and texted Mom to tell her. I asked what they would check and she said they might do a pelvic exam. I knew that would hurt more while pregnant. I called Ben, told him what was going on and said he needed to meet me at the office at 2:15. I could hear kids in the hallway arriving. I poked my head out and signaled to David to come into my room.

"Being pregnant is the worst," I said. "It will be such a relief when it's over and every little thing doesn't feel like a huge threat. Not to be too graphic but

I'm bleeding a little, which is something that can't be ignored so I'm leaving a little early to go to the doctor."

He commiserated and asked if I wanted to leave right then. No, I didn't, I was fine, and we just needed to be sure.

I sat on a stool at the All School Morning Meeting while everyone else sat on the floor. I am the special pregnant lady. Our kids went to music and Spanish classes and I headed to my classroom to prep. There was a fire alarm scheduled to go off at 10 a.m. I had one hour to calm my worries, which I did somewhat successfully. I did not Google what bleeding during week 23 could mean. Our very kind office manager came in to tell me something and I informed her I was leaving a little early and why. She had a flash of concern on her face, but said she was sure it was nothing.

I taught language arts to both grades, we had lunch, recess followed. We all met in one room for current events class. I had trouble concentrating. I started to feel nauseous again. I gripped my water bottle and tried to persuade myself that I did not feel dizzy. I needed to hang on for twenty more minutes.

Class ended and the kids went to PE. I grabbed my stuff and walked to the outdoor classroom to say goodbye. Most of the kids were engaged already, discussing what they would be playing. But two girls turned around to wave at me.

"Have a nice weekend," I said to them.

"See you soon," said one.

It was a sweet, simple thing to say but the nausea had heightened my emotions and worry, so it hit me deeply. It felt like something to remember but I don't know why.

At the doctor's office, Ben and I sat in the waiting room for a long time, almost thirty minutes. It felt incredibly long because I was very scared about what the doctor might say to me and also for the exam. We weren't there for a normal checkup. When we were taken into the exam room, the nurse told me to prepare for a pelvic exam. The doctor came in and said my urine sample showed everything was normal. She listened to the heartbeat, also normal. She told me the exam might be more painful than usual.

It was excruciating. I cried. I gripped Ben's hand so tightly. My back writhed up in the air. The doctor said it seemed like more pain than she would expect and wanted to send my urine out for further testing to see if I had a urinary tract infection. I had no symptoms of an infection, but it was good to check. She said if anything changes over the weekend we should not hesitate to call the on-call number. We will not be needing that. I'll be fine except that now I am in a lot of pain from the exam.

A friend from work texted me a little while ago before coming up to bed. *Worried friend sitting here wondering how your appointment went today.*

I replied, *Thanks for checking. Baby is fine. They couldn't find anything wrong.*

Phew! That is terrific news.

It was terrific news. Baby is fine. I pat her. I know she's fine, she's never given me any reason to think otherwise. Just a little blood. Unfortunately it hasn't stopped and the exam seems to have made the volume increase.

Saturday, September 28

Today the baby shower replies are due. Mom hasn't heard back from many people. Not giving an RSVP is one of my biggest pet peeves. We are sending an email out this weekend to everyone who did not reply asking if they will tell us. I think some people assume silence equals a no but that seems rude. How difficult is it to write the email saying no, I can't attend? It makes me doubt my friends, which I don't like. In the past, occasionally, it has felt like maybe not having a party is better because then I don't need to face the level of disinterest. But there have been some very good parties, too. And many people have said they are coming, which is nice. Fewer than I thought, but still a good group.

I went swimming this morning. I am still in so much pain from the pelvic exam, but I wanted to exercise and I thought the pool might help. It still hurt, I was crampy, but I was able to swim gently. I felt very slow and fragile, though. I talked to the baby in my head while I swam. I told her she was okay even though I was hurting. And I said I hoped it felt good inside the placenta swimming and also swimming in a pool. Double lightness.

After we got back from the pool, Ben had to leave for a workshop for the day. I went to meet a former student at a coffee house in the afternoon. She told me about preparing to be a senior in high school and all of the things she is looking forward to. She has grown up a lot since she graduated eighth grade with me as her teacher, and yet many of her personality traits are consistent, which is comforting to see. I was still feeling bad during the meeting. I had a blueberry muffin but that made me feel worse. I got flushed and felt a little nauseous so I told her I needed to go. I came home and tried to nap, but a loud storm woke me up after twenty minutes. I went downstairs and laid on the couch. It didn't feel like I could handle doing much more than that. It was even starting to feel difficult to walk. That exam really hurt yesterday, but I had no idea it could have this effect on me. I regret doing it. Ben came home and ordered us take-out food. I didn't have much of an appetite. We tried to watch a little television, but I was so uncomfortable I decided to go to bed early. And here I am, 8:30 p.m., in bed hoping sleep will restore me.

Monday, September 30

My baby was born yesterday at 12:30 a.m. That is the estimated time. No one really knows the exact minute. When my baby grows up and asks me what time she was born I will either have to lie and say 12:30 a.m. or tell her we're not sure, but it was around 12:30. My baby will grow up.

Her birthday is September 29, 2019. It's four months before her due date. One hundred and thirteen days early. That's 113 days she will not spend growing inside of me, safe and warm. That's 113 days that I am left to hope she will spend in the Neonatal Intensive Care Unit at the University of Virginia Hospital. This is the wish because the alternative is living no days and dying.

The nurse told us right away that our baby would stay in the hospital at least until her due date. In my haze of shock I thought she could come home sooner if she got big enough. People deliver a month early and take their babies home. But she will not be a normal baby at eight months. She is very sick. Babies are not supposed to be born at 23 weeks. She is missing big things like what makes lungs open and close to breathe. She will spend the first months of her life in a small, plastic box. She will live there instead of inside of me. She will live. I will go to see her every day. I will sit outside of her box next to all of the other boxes with babies in them and help her grow. I can still be her mother even though I only brought her halfway.

We named her Cosette. Cosette Adeline. Cosette means little one and victorious. That is what she will be. When they asked for a name I thought for a second that I didn't want to use Cosette. That I wanted to save it for a future baby who lives. I did not want to bury Cosette. But then I realized it would be too sad to give her name to someone else, that I would always feel sad when I said that name. I will be sad for a very, very long time. Maybe forever. I was pregnant and now I am not. There is just skin covering an empty womb. She was so close and now she's not.

When we arrived at the hospital on Sunday afternoon, still technically her birthday, we had to check in at the front desk like we were guests. Guests to see my baby who was a part of me hours before. I feel like I'm the patient but I am not. I am not pregnant, I am not having a baby, I am done. Ben asked for a wheelchair because most women stay in the hospital for two nights after giving birth and I stayed fourteen hours. No one tried to make me stay longer, there was no reason to. A man brought the chair and led us to the elevator that took us up to the NICU. It's the floor below the maternity unit where we went for the tour. By the main door, there is a giant poster of a baby with a breathing tube in his nose looking happy. There is a buzzer on the wall to get in. The unit itself is contained and looks very private. Not just anyone can go in there. The door swung open and Ben pushed me into a hallway. There is a window along the wall and a woman asked for our names. She put green plastic bracelets on our wrists that say Care Partner. My hand shook as she wrapped it around my thin wrist.

"That's too long for you," she said and cut off the remainder. "Only parents get these. If you have other guests, they'll need to sign in at the main desk in the front lobby as well as here. As Care Partners you don't need to go to the main desk each time you come."

Every day for months and months, I thought. This is my new life. We washed our hands and a door at the end of the hall opened. Someone appeared who would lead us to Cosette.

Ben wheeled me through the dimly lit room full of screens and small incubators. Some babies were large, full-term, and in small, open bassinets. The baby next to ours looked very, very sick. His stomach was inflated and he had many machines around him. I tried not to stare.

And then we were with Cosette. She is hooked up to many wires and she has a large tube down her throat, but she looked better than she did a few hours after the birth. But she does not look like a baby. She's tiny, just 1.5 pounds with thin limbs and a small head. Her skin is burgundy, the color of beets. She is not cute, but I love her. I love her already so much which is petrifying because there is a very large chance she will not live past this week. The kind nurse named Susan who was caring for Cosette said that the first seven days are the most important regarding survival. If she does live, she could have major physical or developmental problems. We could have a lifetime of difficult care ahead of us.

My baby, my baby. I shake.

Tuesday, October 1

I soak the sheets every night. A mixture of sweat and tears. The only thing that makes me wake up is knowing I need to get there and see her. I am pumping milk and I take that to her in small tubes. I pump milk all day in the hospital, too. I am supposed to do it eight times a day and right now each session is 30-45 minutes. I really want to make milk for her. I am up during the night anyway to cry so I pump then. Ben sleeps unless I sob so hard that I move the bed. Then he wakes and holds me until I push him away. I have failed Cosette and him. I could not bring his daughter into the world in the right way. I wonder if he regrets meeting me and marrying me because I am deficient. I will pump milk as well as I can. This is something I can do for her.

The separate rooms in the NICU are called pods. There is a tiny room connected to her pod, B-pod, and there are two pumps inside of that room. I spend a lot of time there working to make milk for Cosette. She is not drinking it yet, but they said she will be able to have some soon. In that way she is already alive and in the world because she will drink milk rather than just live in the placenta. In many other ways they try to act like she is still in the womb. But it is impossible to fake. Her isolette, which is her little box home, stays warm and moist because her skin is so fragile. And a blanket remains over the isolette to keep it dark. But she has an IV in her arm and sometimes they move it to her foot. Stickers on her rubbery skin keep cords connected to her that track her heart rate and oxidation levels. These numbers appear on a screen in bright blue and green behind her isolette. When the numbers go below or above a certain range, they flash red and make a loud noise. This happens constantly. The nurses tell us not to stare at the flashing numbers, but it is like telling a driver to not watch the howling ambulance as it whizzes by. The stickers that pull at her skin leaving tiny drops of blood and the needles are bad, but the worst is the tube that goes down her throat.

That was the first thing I saw when I looked at her on the night she was born, when they wheeled me to see her in the nursery before they took her to UVa. She was in a box raised up on a cart and she was wearing the tiniest pink hat that was still too big for her. Her face was narrow and sallow with a large tube going down her throat that was throwing her neck back in an awkward position. Her chest was translucent, showing tiny ribs, and they had blankets on her to keep her warm. The UVa transport team was there. In the room were three people from UVa, the nurse assigned to me named Ruby, and Ben and

Mom. It felt like a lot of people. Everyone was somber. That room was supposed to be a happy one but it was not that night. No one was trying to be happy. They knew I would cry when I saw her and I did. Even though I was still in shock I was able to cry a little. Someone said congratulations. I did not respond. One of them told Mom to take a picture. Maybe they said that because if she died we would have a picture of her alive. I felt Ben's hand on my shoulder. I looked back at him. His hand was over his mouth.

Today there was a breakfast set up in one of the lounges. A woman standing by the food told us she is the coordinator of meals and activities for families. She talked like we are in some sort of club now, that we are people who need to be cared for in a special way. I don't understand why she thinks that. It's my baby who needs care. I have no time for bagels on Mondays and pizza on Thursdays. When I am at the hospital, I'm with Cosette. And we are going to get through this and then take her home. I do not want to talk to other parents about their babies or sit at a table and share how hard it is. I drive to the hospital. I park in the garage. I validate my parking pass. I take the elevator to the seventh floor. I push the button for them to let me in. I sign my name on the Fraser-Morris guest sheet. I promise I do not have flu symptoms. They give me a sticker to wear on my shirt that signals I do not have flu symptoms. By the double sink, I put down my bag or try to hold it between my legs and roll up my sleeves. I wash my hands for twenty seconds with harsh soap while I read the sign that says how well one must wash their hands. It says take off rings. Will the stone of my wedding ring kill Cosette by carrying germs inside? I pick up my things from the floor. I wait for the person at the window to push another button to let me inside. I look at the welcome screen that shows Now and Then pictures of babies who were there sometime in the past. Cosette will be one of the success stories. Maybe they will ask to put pictures of her on the screen.

I turn left passing through C-pod to enter B-pod. I walk by three other bed-spots and the nurses' station, and then I arrive at B-17 which is in the corner by the blood gas machine. B-17 is where I sit and cry and talk by Cosette for six hours unless a doctor or nurse or social worker or chaplain is talking to me. It has only been three days, but it feels like weeks. I am so tired. More tired than a person should ever feel. But sleep brings holding my empty belly and feeling that she is so far away. It is a type of longing I have never experienced. I'm in purgatory. There is nowhere that I feel okay. They said seven days is an important milestone but so is three. I carry the phone around with me at night praying that it does not ring.

Wednesday, October 2

Last night we created a page about Cosette on a health journey website. I know parents who made a Caring Bridge page for their daughter and that was how everyone could learn how she was and send messages without bombarding her parents. That's what I want, to hear from people but not answer emails and texts or risk having people say the wrong thing to me. I also know how that girl's page ended, with reporting her death, and the idea of that as Cosette's conclusion makes me disintegrate inside. But the doctors talk hopefully enough about her that I think it's okay to make the page. She has lived for three days and that is a good sign. It feels much longer than that. I will want comfort if things go badly, too. Like my friends who have had miscarriages. But I will not think like that. While driving, pumping, and not sleeping, I have gone over in my head what to write in the synopsis of events on her webpage. I remind myself that I am a writer and writing helps me process and connect. I am neither looking for attention nor pity, well, maybe some pity, but mostly it feels like if others know and can tell me things, then I will not dissolve into a million tiny pieces. I need my experience reflected back at me to understand that it is real and that my world might actually be okay again someday in the future.

I am learning more about the human body and how it functions than I ever wanted to know. I taught the respiratory and circulatory systems to my three different seventh grades so I understand some things already, but I am absorbing much more. Cosette is alive because she has a breathing tube down her throat that puts air into her lungs. On the night she was born, the doctors at UVa injected her with surfactant, which is a chemical that makes the lungs open and close. Babies are born with surfactant if they are born on time. Premature babies like Cosette, called micro-preemies, do not have surfactant. I hate the word preemie. I despise it. It sounds tight and overly cute. Micro-preemie makes me think of a small toy race car. If Cosette had been born a decade ago, she would have had a much lower chance of survival because then they did not know how to give surfactant. If I had been in preterm labor in a hospital, they would have given doses of surfactant as an injection through my belly in expectation of the birth. But if I had been in the hospital, they may have given me magnesium to delay the birth, which could have made her groggy and less able to survive in those first hours. The doctor who was there after Cosette's birth told me that, maybe to make me feel better. It worked a little; I have clung tightly onto the idea. She said the pain and fear I experienced in going through rapid labor without help could have saved Cosette's life.

The breathing tube is connected to a ventilator that pushes air into her lungs. It's taped to her mouth and chin so that she cannot pull it out or move it. She is protected from outside air in her isolette, so the tube has to go through one of the portals on the side, and there are towels packed up around it to prevent gaps. The tube is stiff and it's a balancing project to have it leave the ventilator, go through the portal, and fix to her mouth accurately. A respiratory specialist comes to move it every so often, and they are constantly sticking another tube into the tube to clear it of liquid and accumulated mucus. The persistent flowing air into her body creates mucus that builds up and cannot be coughed out. Her oxygen levels go down when there is too much mucus, the alarms go off, and eventually someone comes. But the nurses and respiratory therapists are very used to hearing the alarms so they aren't actually alarmed by them. When they go off, I feel like I need to look around and make sure someone understands what's happening. And then there is the question of what is going on when I am not there. They gave us a card when we first arrived that has the phone number for the NICU printed on it, and we are allowed to call any hour of the day. We have not called at night yet, but I imagine we will start at some point.

Today Cosette had on mini sunglasses. Ultraviolet lights are directed at her to help with skin pigmentation. Her bilirubin level is very high. A week or so under the lights should help. It's hard not to see her face. It makes it feel like she is more alone.

Cosette moves much more than I would expect, but she did move a lot in the womb. Watching her though, outside of me, the movements are jerky and seem like responses to danger. A creature on alert in a foreign environment. A creature, dark and limber with a body that moves like a puppet in stiff and sudden ways. They say she is not in pain, but I don't know how they can know that. However, I do trust the doctors and nurses. I would be in an even worse place if I didn't. They seem very sure of what they are doing and talk about how many times they have treated babies as small and as young as Cosette. I had no idea babies could be born this early and live. It is a whole world I did not know. They say "twenty-three weeker" in a familiar way. She is another one of those to them. No one talks about her not making it. Their confidence is uplifting. Multiple medical professionals have told us that we are lucky Cosette is a girl.

Apparently babies born at her gestational age are more likely to survive if they are female. They fight harder, is what they say.

One thing I have heard many times already is what a rollercoaster this experience will be for us. I say us not me because Ben is going through this as well. I don't have the energy to write about him. It's just me and Cosette in these pages for now. When they say that to me, about the rollercoaster, I nod because I know they are trying to be kind and cautious, not to mislead me with false hope. These nurses and doctors hold my daughter's life in their hands. I must be likable to them. They insinuate that overall she will survive but the journey to get there will be hell because one day she'll be fine and the next not. Beware seems to be the real word versus rollercoaster. Beware, do not get too comfortable. Okay, I nod. What else am I supposed to say? Thanks for letting me know that it will be bad? I am already aware of that. Let me live it instead of trying to tell me not to feel confident. But I do not say any of that because I believe they each think they have come up with an original analogy. Yes, thank you, a rollercoaster, I will watch and be prepared for the dips. My least favorite part of a rollercoaster is the slow way up. So basically it's all going to be terribly painful.

BABY JOURNAL | October 2 | *24 Weeks*

My dearest Cosette, you were born on Sunday, September 29 at 12:30 a.m. You have been in the NICU at UVa for four days now. You are doing really well for weighing only 1.5 lbs at your birth. I am so proud of you for being strong. It's hard to see you look so uncomfortable when I know you were happy and safe in my belly. I miss you being there so, so much. I miss your flutters and kicks in the morning. I feel empty without you and wish I had gotten four more months with you growing and me feeding you. As much as I may wish for those things, that's not how it is. I am working hard to pump milk for you. You will be getting that soon. You're alive in the world and for that I am grateful. I didn't think there was much of a chance of that when I realized you were coming out. I thought my contractions were false labor because how could they not be? Everything had been perfect and the doctor said on Friday that you were fine. I was in so much pain but I didn't want to go to the hospital. The doctor said not to come. I took it as long as I could and then we went. I labored in the backseat while your dad drove. I started to feel you come out when we were close to the hospital. Your dad ran to get help and you were born in the backseat. They took us inside attached and worked on you and me. They took you away and they wheeled me into a room to remove the placenta. They came and told us your heart was beating. A while later we got to see you before they moved you to UVa. You will be there at least until your due date in January. I will visit you every day. The time will go by and you'll get bigger and we will get to hold you and change your diapers. We can touch your arms and legs for now with a single finger. It is hard to leave you and go home at night, but your nurses are great and they are taking excellent care of you. Your dad and I are very sad that your start had to be so hard and that you're experiencing the world before you are ready. But we're trusting you will be okay and that our family will be whole and fun and so full of gratitude always with you by our side. I love you, Cosette. I hope you like your name. It means little one and victorious.

Thursday, October 3

I went to see Dr. H today. I had never met her before the night of Cosette's birth, but now I think she needs to be my regular gynecologist. She knows the story. It is time for me to record that story here before it moves too far into the past. It feels like I will remember every excruciating moment forever, but that may not be true. I am not writing it because I will want to reminisce about it in the future, but it is haunting me, so writing it down may release parts of it.

On that Saturday night, I had gone to bed early with a lot of pain, pelvic pain but also all over my body. It felt hard to move off the couch, but I was being brave and getting through it. About thirty minutes after I had fallen asleep, I was awoken by a release of liquid. A gushing sensation. There had been more discharge that week, that was a part of the whole reason I went to the doctor, but this was more than usual. I got up and went into the bathroom. There was nothing distinct or obvious about what had come out of me. It wasn't blood, just clear and watery. As I was coming to full consciousness, I thought, "A gush of water? Is this my water breaking?" It couldn't be. I got back in bed but felt too worried about that idea to close my eyes. I went to the top of the steps and yelled down to Ben. "Ben, Ben!" I called. He was working on a presentation he was supposed to give the next morning at church.

"Yea?" he called back.

"Can you come up here, please, and bring my phone?" I always left my phone downstairs on airplane mode when I went to bed.

He appeared quickly and we sat in bed as I described what happened. I called Mom. She was doubtful it could be my water breaking and asked how much it felt like, just a little or a lot? I didn't know. Kind of a lot. But with each word of acknowledgement that something could be wrong I wanted to take it back and say, "I'm sure it's nothing." She told me to call the doctor's office. Ben called the number, a woman asked for my details and said a doctor would call us back within twenty minutes. If no one called in twenty minutes we were supposed to call again.

Then the level of pain increased. It stabbed me from inside. Something was tearing my stomach lining in half over and over. It made me cringe and double over and then release. This, of course, was a contraction. But I did not think about that in the moment because I could not be having a baby. I was only 23 weeks pregnant and we had a perfect pregnancy.

I kept asking Ben how long it had been since we called. He told me the minutes as I writhed in the bed trying to find a position that felt better. After eighteen minutes, the doctor called. She was not someone I had seen at the office yet. I trusted her voice immediately. She sounded concerned and wise. She asked for my symptoms, the history of the past few days, and my weeks number. "It's probably Braxton-Hicks contractions," she said. "They're very common around this time in a pregnancy and they may be made worse by the pelvic exam. Try to relax. Take a warm shower. The more you can relax your body, the more likely they'll go away. Call me back if anything changes."

I got in the shower. But I couldn't stand in the shower. It hurt too much. I lay on the floor of the tub wishing it was cleaner. I knew this wasn't right. This hurt too much. I was having trouble breathing. I got out of the shower. Ben was waiting for me in the bed looking worried. I tried to lay down but couldn't. I kept moving back to my hands and knees on the bed. That was the only way to get through the internal ripping. We moved downstairs. I do not remember why we made that decision but when I tried to sit on the couch I couldn't. I was on all fours on the carpeted floor.

Ben said, "I am starting to time these. They seem like contractions and they're happening more closely together." I told Ben to call the doctor again. The woman who answered took the information and said we would hear from someone within twenty minutes.

The pain during the contractions was so intense by this point that I felt like I was going to throw up. I moved to the bathroom and held my head over the toilet. I gagged but nothing else happened. Ben had a timer counting down from twenty minutes. I stared at the carpet, off white with tiny squares. I stared and stared and then I said, "We need to go to the hospital. This is too much. There's no shame in going to the hospital." Twenty minutes had passed with no call.

Ben agreed and put on his shoes and got his car keys while calling the office again. I was in my nightgown and did not put on anything else, just sandals. I didn't even take my wallet. I waited for a contraction to end, then crawled from the carpeted room to the door. Another contraction.

Then I got outside and moved to the steps that lead up to the cars.

It was after 11 p.m. The air was thick with summer heat. The cicadas were singing their nightly song. The neighborhood was still and calm. People were in their beds after a Saturday night out. I crawled up the steps on my hands and knees, knowing another contraction was coming. Ben opened the passenger door. I told him I couldn't sit. I needed to lie across the back seat. But I couldn't do that, I could only be on my hands and knees.

He drove and I wailed. After about five minutes, the doctor called. She heard me screaming.

"It sounds like it's gotten much worse."

Yes, yes. "We're coming," I called into the speaker phone.

"We'll see you when you arrive," she said.

I was clawing at the fabric of the seat and slapping it. I looked to the side and saw the back of Ben's head. I don't know if we talked on the ride. I was trying to breathe. I screamed and wailed. Sweat covered my body. He had the air conditioner on but I rolled down the window, too. I needed air. I looked again to the side, to the road ahead of us. It seemed like he was speeding, but we were not getting there fast enough. There were a few ways to the hospital. It was a thirty minute drive no matter what. The hospital was on the far other side of town. UVa was closer but that wasn't where we were headed. We should have just gone there, then we would have been at the NICU, but I didn't understand that I was having a baby. It is also possible if we'd gone there they would have given me something that could have hurt the baby.

We were still a few minutes from the hospital when the sensations changed. "I don't think I can do this anymore," I said. Ben told me that we were almost there. "No," I said, "something's happening. Something's happening." My voice was full of hysterical worry. There was suddenly so much pressure. I felt like I was going to have a bowel movement but then I understood. Her head was coming out. I put my index and middle fingers between my legs and touched the top of her head. That had to be her head. I slightly pushed against her, wanting her to stay in. She felt soft and spongy. I would later worry this pressing gave her a brain bleed. I did not process that I was giving labor or los-ing my child. All I could think was: pain, pain, pain.

Ben parked in the ambulance area and left me to get help. I breathed and screamed and gently held the top of her head with my fingers. The outside air was hot. My body was slick with sweat. Puddles of moisture had collected under my arms and ran down my back. I heard peepers and bugs fulfilling their nightly routine. There was a street lamp above us, spilling a mustard yellow glow on the backseat. Ben opened the door. He had a wheelchair.

"No! I can't sit. I can't get in that. Get help."

He turned and left again. The door stayed open. I could see the asphalt. I had no sense of where we were. The pain was excruciating. She was pushing to come out more. She wasn't able to wait any longer. "Help me!" I screamed. "Help me!" I thought of the story where all of the people ignore a woman calling for help because no one wants to get involved. I thought: *This is going to scar me forever.*

"Help me!" I screamed again.

A gruff male voice called from a far distance, "What can we do?"

"Help me!" I screamed. It's all I could say.

Two male voices talked to each other. Then to me: "They're coming. They're coming to you now."

Ben would tell me later that when he went in the first time and told the ER workers that his wife was in labor they pointed to a wheelchair. He took it, doing what they instructed. When he went back with the empty wheelchair, he couldn't get anyone's attention. Then an ambulance driver who heard my screams went in and said they needed to get out there.

A female doctor appeared in front of me, then went to the other door, opened it and sat beside me. She looked at me and told me to get on my back.

"She's crowning, the head is already mostly out," I heard her say. There were a few people holding me and talking to me. "Give one good push now." I did that with a deep groan. There was a rush of movement and liquid between my legs. And the pain stopped. They had a gurney and told me to get out of the car.

"I can't stand up," I said.

"We know. We're going to lift you onto it. The baby is still connected, we're going to hold her in these towels above you while we wheel you inside. We need to get inside."

I saw the night sky briefly. I saw glass doors closing and then white ceiling panels with tiny holes. Someone pulled my nightgown down over me to go through the lobby. We were in an area of the ER. Curtains were pulled on either side of us. Ben was on my right. A female doctor or nurse on my left. She held my hand. "It's going to be okay," she said.

Ben moved away so that someone could start an IV in my right arm. I looked back to the nurse on my left. "Is she alive?" I asked. She looked at me but did not answer.

Ben returned. He was looking down to where I couldn't see. He was crying. Hard, shaking sobs. I didn't see what he saw. His face came back to mine. I stared blankly at him. He held my hand and wiped sweat from my forehead.

Then there was a face at the end of the bed telling me she was Dr. H who I had spoken to on the phone. She was younger than I had imagined. Her eyes looked kind and glassy.

"It hurt so much," I said. "The pain."

She nodded. "I know," she said. "You're alright now. It's over."

My real pain was just starting though.

The cord was cut. They took the baby away and wheeled me to an elevator. My body was relieved that the pain was over. That's all I could think about. They took me to a room, like one we had seen on the tour. A laboring room. Dr. H delivered the placenta by pushing on my belly. It hurt a lot. She would come back and do that a few times in the next hours.

"What is happening with the baby?" I asked or Ben asked.

"They're working on her," she said the first time. I didn't know what that meant. Later I would find out they were trying to get a heartbeat. They were able to intubate her quickly, then proceeded with chest compressions.

Time went by. About 30 minutes. I just laid there waiting. Dr. H came in again and she said, "They got a heartbeat. She's stable enough to be transferred to the NICU at UVa. They're getting her ready for that, and we'll take you into the nursery to see her before they leave."

I had no idea she could live through what we just experienced. She was so little, so early.

I drank a lot of water. The nurse assigned to me, Ruby, helped me get up to use the bathroom. I saw the fancy tub I was supposed to use before labor. I told Ben to call Mom. He left the room to do that. He also went to move my car because it was still in the ambulance bay. A woman came in and asked for my health insurance card. I didn't have my wallet. She was very irritated. I told her we would figure it out. I felt like I was in trouble and something bad was going to happen. Would they make us leave?

Ruby sat by me while Ben was gone. She tried to ask me normalizing questions like about my job and how long we had lived in the area. I answered them politely.

When Mom arrived I thought she knew what had happened, but she didn't. She came into the room looking worried and tired. It was after 1 am. "Are you okay?" she asked.

I nodded. "It hurt a lot," I said. "We don't know yet about the baby."

"Have they examined you?" she asked.

I didn't understand. "She's not here." I put my hand on my stomach.

"You had the baby?" she asked. I nodded. "Oh," she said and her face turned to a cry, "Oh," she repeated and held my hand.

"I thought Ben told you."

"No, he just said to come."

Ben shook his head. "I'm sorry, I thought I said it but maybe not clearly. It's all been so much."

"It's okay," Mom said. "I'm here now."

"Should we say a prayer?" I asked Ben. "We should ask to see the chaplain." Ben was at the start of a three month chaplaincy program at an assisted living center. He was working toward ordination, for a second time, and it was required. He was supposed to be getting the long, unpaid part done before the baby arrived. We said the Our Father. I had expected Ben to make up something to say. A prayer we all knew was okay too. He held my hands.

Shortly after that they came to take us to see Cosette in the nursery. It was very close to my room. They must have put me there knowing the baby would be in the nursery. She was the only one there, in her large transport box. We said goodbye to her as she was transported to UVa. At that point, I didn't know if it was the last time I would see her alive. The rest of the night was nurses talking to me, mostly about breastfeeding. One nurse asked me if I planned to breastfeed. Yes.

"We'll bring a pump to you," she said. "You need to start soon if you want to do it. But it's okay if you don't want to. You've been through a lot. It's totally up to you."

I looked at Mom. "What happens if, you know, she doesn't make it?"

"They can give you something to stop the milk," Mom said.

It felt like a circumstance to say no because I had given no thought to pumping milk for my newborn. That was going to be for when I went back to work twelve weeks after her birth. I turned to the nurse. "Yes, I want to."

The doctor came to tell me she was getting some sleep but would be available if needed. She would be there tomorrow, too. I drank a lot of water and went to the bathroom frequently. And then my body started to acknowledge what had happened.

It got quiet and dark, and I cried. I cried hard and for a long time. Mom held my hand. Ben had fallen asleep on the couch intended for dads. He was always able to sleep at times when I couldn't. I wasn't mad at him for finding enough peace to sleep. I was too terrified to feel anything but shock and grief.

I remember saying to Mom that I couldn't go back to work on Monday. "No," she said. "You'll take maternity leave. You just had a baby."

I just had a baby. Did I? How did that happen? I was pregnant on a Saturday and on Sunday I was empty and my baby was ten minutes away in a hospital getting worked on. They were trying to keep her alive for me and for Ben. She was not breathing when she was born. They could have let her die, but they didn't. It would not have made any difference in their individual lives, but they did it for us. They saved our baby Cosette at least for those hours and then they sent her to others to care for her.

Ruby gave me the number for the NICU at UVa and told me to call but to give them a few hours because they would be busy. She also said Ben could go right then if he wanted. I looked at him sleeping. No, he should stay with me. We would go tomorrow. And then Monday I would not go to work. How strange. Maybe I wouldn't go for weeks. Would I be visiting the baby in the hospital or would I be grieving her death?

At around 4 am the NICU called Ben's phone, but there was no service in the room so it went straight to voicemail. He called back when he saw the missed call, but the receptionist said the NICU nurse was busy with Cosette. That was comforting, to know someone was by her side. My phone was close to losing all charge. Ruby found me a charger.

I fell asleep for a few minutes and was awoken by the phone close to daybreak. It was the NICU calling again to get my information. The baby's nurse could not talk to me yet, but they told me to try calling in thirty minutes.

"Do you have a name for her?" the voice asked me. I had her on speaker phone.

I looked at Ben. He nodded.

"Cosette," I said. I spelled it for her.

"That's a pretty name," she said. "And a middle name?"

Again I looked to him. "Adeline?" I asked. He nodded again.

"Adeline," I said. Mom's head dropped to the side and she looked both happy and sad. Adeline was my grandmother's name, her mother's.

Cosette Adeline. Our baby.

Ruby came to hand me off to the dayshift nurse. I almost cried saying bye to Ruby. She had been kind and understanding and I knew I would never see her again. She was a big part of the worst night of my life, yet also my daughter's birthday.

We were moving to the recovery room, the after labor room. Mom went to get coffee for her and Ben in the lobby. I could drink coffee now if I wanted because I was no longer pregnant, but I chose to keep pretending I shouldn't. Mom asked if I wanted anything to eat. A smoothie. All I wanted was more liquid. The dayshift nurse was tasked with taking us to the new room in a different area of the unit, and I would be assigned another nurse there. As she wheeled me past nurses in the hallway talking in normal voices about ordinary things, I wondered if they knew who I was and what had happened. I did not look like a woman who just had a baby. My belly was nowhere near the right size.

The new room was brighter, too bright. It would have been a cheery view in a normal situation. Ben closed some of the curtains. I got in the bed and the nurse told me a lactation specialist would be in soon to help me with the breast pump. There had been a lot of urgency last night about getting started quickly but no one had come with a pump. I hadn't even opened the pump sitting at home in Cosette's future room. The pump had come free from my insurance company. They wouldn't even let you order it until you were four months pregnant.

Once we were left alone in the room I turned to Ben and started to cry again. He reached out and held my hand. I opened my mouth to speak. My throat was dry. My head hurt from all of the crying.

"We're going to be okay," I said. I swallowed. "I mean if she dies. We're not going to be those people whose relationship falls apart because they lose a child." These words seemed to be coming from somewhere besides my own head and thoughts. They just came out of me. Was I thinking of a book? A movie where this happened? If I was losing my baby, I could not also be losing my husband with the same event. The words were a desperate proclamation of love and shame. Ben nodded and held my hand harder, then reached to hug me in the bed. I sobbed into his shirt.

"Let's try calling the hospital again," he said.

The nurse who had been with Cosette overnight had left, but the dayshift nurse who had just come on, Susan, told us that Cosette was stable for the moment. "She's very tiny but we see a lot of babies her size come in here and make their way. It's just going to be a very long, hard journey. A roller coaster. I know it's already been a hard entrance for her. She was born in the parking lot, is that right?"

We told Susan we would see her as soon as I got discharged. She sounded very nice and capable. Comforting. Ben left to go home and take care of Teddy and his dog, Lyle. He also needed to get my wallet for my insurance card and some clothes for me to wear. I couldn't wear my nightgown to the NICU and even if I had wanted to, it had been thrown away last night. It was covered in blood.

Mom stayed with me. I asked her to call David and tell him what had happened. They needed to start making a substitute plan for me. A long term one. She called in the hallway and told me she left a voicemail. I imagined him listening to it and his whole body sinking. Later that night, I texted him and told him more details of what happened. I explained it was in a parking lot. I said, "Don't tell the kids that. But it's okay if adults know." I wanted them to understand I'd had a horrible experience and wouldn't be available to talk for a while.

Pumping felt awkward, but it did not hurt. The lactation specialist instructed me to "Do this for 15-20 minutes every two or three hours. Don't expect milk to come right away but after a few times it should." She knew our baby was in the NICU. She wished me luck and left. I tried to sleep. Ben returned.

Then the chaplain came in. She gave me a wide, knitted scarf. It was autumn colors – green, brown, and red. She placed it on my legs and said a prayer over me. I cried telling her what had happened. Ben cried too. I don't remember much of what she said, but her demeanor was warm and genuine. A few hours later, around noon, the rector from our church came. Ben had delivered the message earlier in the morning that he couldn't come to do the adult education hour at church, the presentation he had been working on when my water broke, and so people at church knew what had happened.

I was in the bathroom when he arrived. I could hear him talking to Ben but I couldn't make out their words. I opened the door, still with my IV, and crawled back into the bed. I started to cry immediately. We had just seen him at our baptism meeting earlier in the week. We told the whole story of the night again. It felt strange to know he had just come from the 10 a.m. service, doing normal, routine things, seeing all the people we see every Sunday morning. After he left, I tried pumping again. No milk yet. Then we just waited to leave. I had to be discharged.

Dr. H came in to see us. She told me that there was nothing I could have done to help Cosette. I did everything right. "Waiting to come to the hospital must have been terrifying and so painful, but if you had come here when you first called, we would have given you magnesium to try to stop labor. It wouldn't have helped. She was coming out no matter what. But magnesium can make the baby drowsy and it could have been more difficult to get her intubated and breathing. You may have saved her life by waiting."

I realized in that moment if we had waited any longer at home, the baby would have come out in our downstairs bathroom. She would have died in my hands, connected to my body.

Dr. H said, "The placenta had a funny smell to it so there may have been an infection. I've sent it for testing to find out. It will be a week or longer until we get results. Sometimes these things just happen though and there are no reasons for us to uncover."

"I went swimming on Saturday morning. Could it have been brought on by that? It felt a little painful to do. Maybe I pushed too much? Or from the pelvic exam on Friday?"

She shook her head. "Swimming did not cause this. The exam didn't either. Those things could not cause early labor. I know you won't believe me right now, but you need to hear me say this was not your fault. There is nothing you could have done. Now you move forward and try to care for your baby as best you can."

After talking to her I really wanted to leave and get to the NICU. We waited and waited. Finally at 2 p.m. the nurse took out my IV and brought a wheelchair for me.

"Take anything you want in the room," she said. "You paid for all of it."

I took the pack of giant pads and mesh underwear and the slipper socks with little nubs on the bottom. Ben packed up the snacks.

I was wheeled through the maternity floor. No baby to hold. No congratulations balloon tied to the handle. No flowers. Just me with a plastic bag on my lap.

That Sunday night after coming home from the NICU, Mom was already at the house. She had gotten food for us. We told her how promising the doctors and nurses sounded when talking about Cosette. But as soon as there was a quiet moment, I began to cry. I held my head over my plate, fork slipping from my fingers, and watched salt water splatter my food. It was Cosette's birthday. I sobbed for her and for me.

* * *

As soon as Dr. H walked into the room for my followup appointment, I began to cry.

Friday, October 4

Today I went back to Martha Jefferson hospital to register Cosette for her birth certificate. I thought it might be something I could do at the reception desk by the lobby for the maternity wing, but it was not. I was sent to the very back of the unit, which meant walking past all of the rooms that looked like the ones I had been in a few days ago. The smell, the colors of the walls, it was familiar in a bad way. I handed the form I had filled out to the woman at the desk. She told me to sit on a stool and wait for her to put in all of the information in case she had any questions. She seemed a little irritated that I had given her a task to do. I sat and looked around and tried not to cry. I listened to the nurses talk. I heard a baby cry.

After about five minutes, the woman turned to me and said, "Is she doing okay?" She must have gotten to the line that said 1.5 lb for birth weight.

My face tightened into tears. "As good as she can be," I replied.

The woman nodded. She entered the remaining information and then told me I should get a birth certificate in the mail in the next three to four weeks. My immediate thought was I hope Cosette is still alive then.

"Good luck," she said as she handed me back my form. Her demeanor was warm and entirely different than when I had entered.

People have been very, very kind. Flowers and a card were left on our porch by my supervisor at work along with the leave of absence forms I need to fill out. And there have been other gifts too. A friend created a food signup, which is helpful because otherwise I may not eat anything. I get home from the hospital so late. I take some of the donated food to eat there for lunch. Yesterday I emailed the teacher at the yoga studio and told her what had happened. She replied right away and offered to help in any way she could. She said she knows other mothers who have had their babies in the NICU at UVa and they raved about the level of care. She said if I want to connect with any of those mothers she can help me do that. I feel so talked out, I don't think I want that right now, but it was kind of her to offer. I am going to miss those classes so much. Maybe one day me and Cosette can go to the baby and me class together. I said that in my reply email said she will hope for that too and we can go to as many classes as we want for free. The generosity is touching, and it confirms how wrenching a situation I am in. This level of giving is reserved for tragic events.

Mary, a friend from college who lives nearby but with whom I've mostly lost touch has reached out to help. She brought groceries to the house. She's always been a steady friend who understands me, and I find her so interesting and well spoken. She is someone I've always enjoyed being around. But she has three kids and is a doctor, so she is busy. We do not see each other often even though we ended up both living in Charlottesville after college. But now Mary is texting me every day to check on me. She and Ashley, both pediatricians, are the friends I want to talk to because they know what things mean. I feel supported by so many, I do. But is it enough? Enough for what? What is the goal? My baby is in the hospital, the goal cannot be happiness or peace. The aim is to get by, not shrivel up due to dehydration from too many tears. The aim is to be okay enough to make decisions for the baby and be a good mother to her if she makes it.

My sister is flying in tonight to visit. She is staying with Mom and will come to the hospital tomorrow. I am surprised that she is coming so quickly, yet also realize it's the kind of situation that warrants it. I know that it will be sad to see her. We had some nice talks this summer about babies and naming the baby. I remember that when she was pregnant she worried about different things that could go wrong. I did not worry that much and something bad happened to me.

In the elevator this morning, a mom had a stroller with a baby in it. We were going to the same floor. She said to me, "Do you have a baby in the NICU?"

"Yes," I said. Pause. "Do you?"

"Yea, they're twins. This one came home two days ago and hopefully the other will come out in a few more."

"How long has it been?" I asked.

"A week. The longest week of my life."

I nodded. I did not speak again, and she didn't ask me anything. One week. Try seventeen. I wanted her to ask me so I could say I've got four months ahead of me. But she didn't ask so I just wished her well when the doors opened.

CARING BRIDGE POST | October 4

Yesterday Cosette received a small amount (1.8 oz) of my milk through a feeding tube. Since then she has received a few more feedings. She seems to be responding well to it. She enjoys stretching her legs and arms and responds well to touch. We have been told by the doctors that her stability could fluctuate, but for now she is doing well. We have felt supported and safe in the hands of her care team, and we are taking things day by day. We love our little Cosette.

Saturday, October 5

A week ago today I was swimming in the morning. I was feeling the baby in my belly and hoping she liked the light feeling of being in the pool. I imagined taking her for swim lessons some day. This morning I drove to the hospital like I have every morning this week. It's October now and it feels like autumn outside. The sky is a glorious blue, the air is fresh, and on a typical weekend, it would feel full of promise. Cool weather after a hot summer always makes me feel like things are possible that maybe did not feel possible in the middle of July. Relationships simmer, organizing is accomplished, life can be less messy and more enjoyable.

Cosette is at the university hospital, which means college football games, crowds, and traffic. I would never drive through town near campus on a weekend unless forced to. Once I am awake in the morning, every minute that I'm not at the hospital with Cosette feels like a moment I should be. The traffic is a hindrance to getting there quickly, but it also irritates me to see people doing ordinary things and having fun. If I could take a highway directly to the parking garage that would be much better. Instead I sit at red lights while giant groups of kids buzzed from day drinking walk across the street. They take a long time to cross because the cars mean nothing to them, they're on top of the world, and also because they are talking to people behind them, walking backwards, not missing a second of whatever clever, flirtatious conversation they're having. And me, I sit frowning, knowing they have no idea how much hardship may lie ahead of them. I used to be one of those kids meandering across those same streets, feeling like crosswalks were a weird reminder of an outside world of adults going to jobs and having families. But I was a first year in college eighteen years ago. That was so long ago. That's the age of a freshman in college. I have doubled that life. I've been in a car accident since then that I was lucky to survive, I've helped a loved one through a drug relapse, I've bought a house and sold a house and bought another house, I've adopted a cat, I've lost grandparents and students to cancer. I know there have been many good things, but when I imagine myself frolicking to fraternity houses to dance and consume free PBR, I think of all that I didn't know. I certainly did not know that one fall in the future I would spend an endless number of days in a hospital neonatal intensive care unit standing guard by my preterm baby. How would life be different if I knew some of these things?

Cosette's nurses this week have been warm, nurturing women with senses of humor. After the first two days with Susan, I wanted her to be there every day and felt frightened to have a new nurse. But then came Rachel who is equally amazing, sweet and informative. She thinks Cosette is so adorable and says hopeful things to us. Beth was there yesterday and she was also very nice and comforting. She said my milk supply was great, which is one of the few compliments that hits home right now. I do not need to meet too many more nurses. The ideal is just a handful that rotate through caring for Cosette.

There are a number of nurse practitioners in charge of Cosette. We have seen the same attending doctor all week though. She stays mostly quiet during rounds while the NP and others speak about Cosette. But she is there for the final word and to answer any questions. She said there will be a new attending next week and he will be with us for two weeks and then they switch again. UVa is a teaching hospital so this is how it works. The care seems exceptional, though. I have no concerns about that.

For a few days, a social worker talked to us about Medicaid and how Cosette's care will automatically be covered by Medicaid if she's in the hospital for more than thirty days, which she definitely will be. I don't know what happens if she dies before thirty days, but I am not asking anyone about that. With almost one week of life behind her, a sudden death feels less like a possibility. We would never be able to afford this level of care for four months without something like Medicaid. I looked up how much on average the NICU costs for a day and the amount is $3000. If she stays for four months, around 120 days, that's $360,000. That's the cost of a house much bigger than ours. It is definitely a relief to not have to think about money while going through this.

My sister came to see me and Cosette today. I went out to the lobby to meet her and Mom. When she saw me she reached out her arms to hug me.

"I'm sorry," she said while nodding her head like she was trying to acknowledge the pain and also feeling a lot of pain herself.

"Thanks for coming," I said. And I began to cry. Her teary face and seeing how nervous she looked to be there brought it all into reality. I am deep in it now, after just seven days. To bring someone else into that space, and not care about acting a certain way because you have no energy for something like that, feels strange. Although I was crying, I quickly stopped and wanted to feel more positive. I turned around to see Mom also crying. I'm glad my sister is here to give Mom company for a few days. This is very hard on her too, but I am not the person to take care of her right now. I led them to the check-in desk, suddenly feeling how locked down and serious the place appears. When the woman at the desk asked my sister if she could respond to the flu questions, she carefully read each one and then said no. We all washed our hands and the door swung open.

I walked between the isolettes to Cosette and lifted the cover. It was dark and I knew my sister could barely see her, but she said, "She's beautiful."

I wanted to say, "I don't know about that." But I didn't. I stood silently for a few seconds. I think she had given some thought to this moment before arriving. What do you say to your sister about her baby when she is connected to wires and looks like a spindly, half-cooked creature? I had no expectations for what she would say or do or how she would act. It was all fine. I really have no energy for anyone else's experience of this, not even Ben's really, not yet anyway. I do not expect anyone to understand how bad it is, but I do expect for them to tell me it sounds awful and it isn't fair and that they are thinking of me. I now realize how cowardly it is not to contact someone if they are going through a hard time. It is not a gesture of being respectful by giving them space; it's ignoring their pain. It is possible to contact someone without forcing them to talk if that's not what they want. It could be hard to keep friends who do not acknowledge this is happening in my life.

BABY JOURNAL | October 6

Happy one week of life, Cosette. You are doing very well for your tiny size. I got to hold you today. You were so small and clung to me. Your little hands were flat against the skin of my chest. Your tubes were all in place and I felt your breath go in and out. I was so content. It was scary to pick you up but I did it and it all went fine. You were on me for almost two hours. I will look forward to doing that again. The doctor said your intubation tube may come out soon. That will be so great. Your belly line came out today so your belly button can form soon. It's just a stump now. You are starting to open your left eye. You're going to look at us soon! A healing circle prayed for us today. I hope you felt that. I feel lighter than I have in a week. I know we have a long journey, but I'm so proud of how well you're doing. It's okay to feel happy about that. And you had your first big poop today. Good job! It was a big day. Your head looks good, too. It's very hard to leave you at the end of the night but you are in good hands. This time is so hard but you will be home with me soon, my dear one. You loved my heartbeat while I held you and I love yours.

CARING BRIDGE POST | October 6

Today was a big day for us. It is Cosette's seventh day of life. Because Cosette is doing well enough, the doctors encouraged skin-to-skin contact between me and Cosette. This was the first time I got to hold her. The nurses helped with Cosette's wires and breathing tube and then left me to enjoy two hours with Cosette cuddling against my chest. I don't have the words to describe how good this felt.

Other news today: her seven-day head ultrasound came back with good results, her arterial line was removed from her belly, her milk dosage was increased because she's accepting it well, her GI tract is waking up (she pooped!), and near the time of skin-to-skin her left eye began to open slightly.

The doctors remind us every day that although Cosette is doing well for her age, the typical pattern in the NICU is two steps forward, one step back. Seeing her do well is so encouraging, yet it is getting harder and harder to leave her at the end of each day. Your messages have been so nourishing. I read them while I am pumping in the tiny pump room of the NICU and it helps me feel supported.

Monday, October 7

I got to hold Cosette yesterday. She felt so light and fluttery. Her breathing apparatus makes her tremble. I could feel air moving in and out of her.

The tiny weight of her on my chest was such an amazing sensation. My little creature, my little girl who was inside my belly who I talked to, now laying on my skin. Her numbers stayed steady while she was on me and the nurse said Cosette seemed to relax. Her eyes are not open yet so it's not like she was looking all around and then got calm and sleepy, but I could feel it too, a melting into me. Like *Oh, Mom is here now.* It was very difficult to give her up at the end, although it was also stressful to hold her because I was afraid something bad would happen. I just stayed frozen and one leg and one hand fell asleep. I held her for two hours, which felt long because I was staring straight ahead of me the whole time, but it's not like I would rather do anything else. They say the typical hold time is three hours, especially when they are so little because they lose calories coming out of the isolette due to the temperature change and being moved. I know I kept her warm, but she was exposed more than usual. I will not be greedy about holding her. I'll do whatever is best for her. They do say holding helps regulate her nervous system and is overall good for her. She smells me, knows me. I will start to know her too.

I wrote on Caring Bridge about holding Cosette and some other positive updates. The responses from people are so kind but they also irritate me a little. They are too happy and optimistic. Like I'm going through this fun, exuberant experience that warrants exclamation points. I know people are just being supportive but it feels like comments should start with: "This is all awful but at least. . ." or "It's so unfair this has happened, but you sound balanced and strong."

Our pastor asked if I wanted a eucharistic minister to come to the hospital yesterday to see me. Ben was at his job for a service he had to lead. I said yes because I want every power of prayer working for Cosette and for me. But it was hard. Two women came. One I knew from church, and she was kind and quiet. The other I had never seen before and she asked me a lot of questions about the birth and Cosette. I was polite but it took more energy than I had to give. My patience level for formalities is so low right now.

I am writing this on Monday morning before I leave for the hospital. Tomorrow I will see a therapist. I arranged that right away at the beginning of last week. The birth was traumatic and all of this is so much. I am trying to do the right thing by taking care of myself so that I can be okay when Cosette comes home.

There's a nurse practitioner who sees Cosette and she is pregnant. I think she is just a little further along than I was, maybe two weeks more than me. She's sweet, smiley, and she wears very fashionable outfits complete with a lot of makeup and big earrings. Often she wears tight spandex dresses that reveal her baby bump. I had a dress like hers. I remember one day two weeks ago when I wore it to work and my friend said, "You are just the cutest pregnant lady. I love this dress." I beamed.

Now I grimace and hold back tears when I see this NP. It's not like she shouldn't be allowed to work in the NICU because she's pregnant. I imagine it is scary for any woman who works here to be pregnant. They probably hold their breath between week 23 and 30, just hoping they get past 30. Then relief. They know so much that most of us do not know. I certainly didn't know. This NP calls Cosette's area Cosette's Cozy Corner. She likes her name a lot.

I find myself bowing down to the NPs and attendings. They hold my daughter's life in their hands. When they arrive at her isolette for rounds, it's like God is talking to me. I hang on every word. I ask questions. I am trying to be a knowledgeable advocate for her. Ben is working during the day, but he comes in the evenings and sometimes for lunch breaks.

We were supposed to have Henry last week but that did not happen. His mom is keeping him for two extra weeks. I cannot even begin to think about what it will be like to have him in the house next week. He will see I look different, he'll ask questions, he'll ask where the baby is. Ben's mother is coming the day before Henry returns to help take care of him. It will be a week, and then he'll go, he'll come back again, and Cosette will still be in the hospital. And I will still be deeply sad.

CARING BRIDGE POST | October 8

Yesterday was a difficult day. Jubilant from Sunday's progress, I entered the NICU in the morning to find Cosette receiving a blood transfusion through a new IV in her leg due to low electrolytes, something that could indicate she is getting an infection. I found out this morning from a phone call that the transfusion helped level her electrolytes and will learn more when I get to the hospital today. Every day at least three people tell me that days, weeks, months in the NICU are a roller coaster. I think I am being told this as a warning and because it's an effort to make it sound okay, that this is what is expected. But hearing the words and feeling the feelings are two very different things.

Well into week two now, I have begun to accept that this happened. I will not take birthing classes, I will not have a typical baby shower, I will not have a two night stay in a hospital and nurse my baby immediately after birth. I have no use for any of the birthing books I read, I will never have a food craving related to being pregnant, I will never feel her push and wiggle inside of me again.

My neighbors look at me curiously, the woman who was running and walking looking pregnant, and now with a belly that is rapidly shrinking. These things I can accept but what is harder to accept is the inability to help my baby who has entered this world too early, susceptible to infection, forced to hear the beeping of machines all day and night, and have a tube down her throat that looks so painful. I can pray that these things will change and she will be okay, but for now, it is hard. My supply of tears is limitless.

Tuesday, October 8

Some people say the right things. I think Mary knows how hard it is because I text her so much and because she's a doctor and has spent time in the NICU. She wrote on Caring Bridge, "Thank you for your honesty. The pain of this experience is unimaginable for most of us and no amount of well wishes or kind words can take it away, though we wish it could. Know that the love you have for Cosette is limitless, as is the love we have for you."

A former colleague wrote, "Dear Karen, Even though there are no words powerful enough to change what is, I write just so that you see in black and white that I am sharing your pain. Even though my sharing your pain doesn't lessen your pain, I write to let you know that I am sending my love. Even though the words only symbolize the surface of love and the deep and churning feelings of a mother in pain, know that your experiences, however unlike what you anticipated, are the experiences of a mother, and the love I send is the love of another mother whose heart weeps with yours. We love you, and that word represents the portion we hold of the universal Love that words cannot describe."

She thought deeply about what to say and expressed a sympathy that feels true and gut wrenching.

It was a nauseating day. I go to sleep crying tonight.

BABY JOURNAL | October 9 | *25 Weeks*

I'm going to hold you again today. It's good for both of us. Monday was a harder day because I saw you getting blood and they were worried you may be sick. But now you are stable. Asleep right now, you look so cozy. Everyone here thinks you're the cutest. You are very cute. You like putting your hands up by your face. Your nurse yesterday placed a weighted pillow on your legs so you can't flail your legs as much.

I have a lot of hopes for you, wanting you to thrive and be healthy. There are many unknowns right now about how you will be, but I have faith that you are going to be okay. I will love you and take care of you no matter what challenges come. So many people are praying for you and thinking of you. Over 200 people have looked at the website we made to write updates about you. One day at a time. For now, as you are 25 weeks in my eyes, you are doing well. Our little miracle. I love you.

Wednesday, October 9

I have gotten braver about doing Cosette's cares each day. I make sure I am there for at least one set but ideally two. Ben often does her evening ones. The nurses say she knows the difference between me and Ben touching her and a new nurse touching her, so the more shifts we cover the better. Care time involves changing her diaper, cleaning her mouth, offering her some of my milk on a swab, and changing her position in the bed. The nurse and respiratory therapist change her position because it involves adjusting her breathing tube. I like changing her diaper because I can see her reacting to my touch. We are not supposed to stimulate her in any way, so I am very careful and gentle. We use a small wipe to clean her bottom, then put on a tiny new diaper. I like giving her the milk, but I prefer for the nurses to suction her mouth. I have to move the suction around her tube and I'm afraid I will go too far back or be too gentle and not clean properly. Some nurses are very precise in the way they go through these rituals and others are less so.

Each day when I arrive, I tell Ben and Mom who the nurse is for the day. There have been many. It makes a big difference on how the day will go and feel for me. The ones who are very attentive make me less nervous. Sometimes I feel like I need to ask the nurse to switch Cosette's positioning or how she is wrapped because she is swinging her limbs too much or her neck looks arched.

Those are the harder days. I don't understand why they cannot assign the same nurses to her for more than a day or two. I had hoped in the beginning it would be like that, but it definitely has not been.

This afternoon I went to see a cranial sacral therapist who is somewhat famous in Charlottesville. I have known quite a few people who trained with her and recommended her to me. She and three students worked on me on the table. They held my kidneys, my head, my arms and legs. I was able to relax slightly. She told me that Cosette and I are still attached and that Cosette can feel me reassuring her even when I am not in the hospital. She said the cord is not cut and I can continue with my pregnancy as if she is still inside me. I should talk to her in the car and at home like I used to. I should pat my belly and soothe her. It felt good to hear and it certainly was not something that I considered before. I am grieving the pregnancy, that is certain, so to have someone tell me it doesn't need to be over felt like a small gift. She also asked me to speak what Cosette would say to me right now if she could talk.

"What is she saying to you?" she whispered. "If there is one thing she wants to tell you, what is it?"

I immediately heard the words play across my mind but took my time to respond. "That she's okay. That it's going to be okay. We will get through this together." I cried hard. I wasn't making that up. It's really what I heard her saying to me from her little isolette.

I went back to see her after the appointment even though it was past 3 pm. I could not wait until the next morning to see her again.

The therapist I saw yesterday was not as rejuvenating as the cranial sacral visit. Maybe a talk therapist is not what I need right now. I am going to acupuncture tomorrow because the night sweats have continued. Sometimes I change the sheets twice a night. Maybe I should go through every alternative therapy, all types of body work, and forget about thinking for a while.

Thursday, October 10

On the way to the hospital from the acupuncture appointment Mom texted me. *They're changing her ventilator,* she wrote. *Everything is fine but they think she needs this one for a while.*

I was a few blocks from the hospital when I got the text. I started to sweat and tear up. I wasn't there for Cosette during this decision and change. Instead I had been lying in a dark room with needles stuck in me, telling the man who has cured me of allergies and other maladies about my premature labor. I nearly fell asleep on the table. He said the treatment should help with balancing my hormones and stop the night sweats.

When I walked into B-pod, Mom was sitting calmly by Cosette's isolette.

"The nurse practitioner said she would come talk to you once you arrived. You know they can't tell me anything when you're not here. But it's what they warned us about, how she may do fine on the one ventilator but after a few weeks she could get too tired and need more support."

I nodded, letting warm tears fall down my cheeks as I looked at Cosette. This ventilator was more intense, which I didn't know was possible. Her entire body was vibrating. Her chest rattled up and down like a hummingbird had found a home inside of her. She was trying to move her head from side to side and her legs flew up occasionally. She looked like a baby in pain.

"I don't think she likes it," I said out loud. "She doesn't look comfortable."

"It's new. She'll get used to it. It may look bad but it is doing more of the work of breathing for her. She needs the support."

I looked at the white board on the cabinet by Cosette's bed. The respiratory therapist assigned to her for the day was my favorite because he always had time to explain things to me. He had a nice smile, too. When he came to check on her, I asked him how long Cosette might be on this respirator.

"It could be many weeks," he said. "They took an x-ray this morning and her lungs are hazy. There was too much moisture in them. She wasn't able to breathe well enough on the other system. A lot of premature babies go on the oscillator at some point in their NICU stay. The team will probably decide to give her some Lasix to clean out that wetness."

This would be her second dose of Lasix, a diuretic. The bad side effect of it for Cosette is that it also depletes her of important minerals that she must have. They fortify my milk with minerals she needs but it is hard to imagine actually stripping her body of good stuff while doing the job of deleting extra liquid in her lungs. I want her to receive as few drugs as possible even though she has already been pumped with so much. Within the first hours of her life, she received antibiotics because of where and how she was born. Her tiny gut was stripped of healthy bacteria. She gets an x-ray almost every day, sometimes twice a day if her numbers drop too far. That is so much radiation. Somehow I will balance out these physical weights that have been thrown on top of her in the first weeks and months of her life. All of this I can't control, but later I can. She will be more my daughter then.

A friend called me in the afternoon when I was sitting next to Cosette. I did not answer, but I texted back saying I was at Cosette's bedside. I told her that Cosette's ventilator had been changed and it was hard to see her looking uncomfortable. She told me that she sensed Cosette was uncomfortable and not adjusting well to the change. She asked me if I had considered other children's hospitals. No, it had never occurred to me. Should it? I know she did not mean to upset me, but it was a hard thing to hear. Have you considered doing something that you cannot possibly do which might be better for your daughter whom your body has failed? I cried and cried. I told Ben. He was so mad. I told my Mom. She was very mad. I did not tell either of them who said it. That didn't matter. Their anger did not make me feel better.

Our pastor came to visit me and Cosette and to pray for her. He said Cosette does not know fear and anxiety. She's just sleeping.

CARING BRIDGE POST | October 11

Taking one day at a time is truly the path for us right now. Yesterday was a difficult day. Cosette's ventilator had to be changed because her lungs were showing signs of collapse. She is now on a ventilator that gives her short puffs of air so that she does not have to do the work of inhaling and exhaling. Her chest cavity stays full. She moves slightly because of the oscillator ventilator. It was hard for me to see and is still hard for me to see today, but it is working for her. I remind myself that what looks like suffering to me is not how she experiences it.

Today the doctor had encouraging things to say about Cosette. Given her history (being born in a car at 23 weeks) she is doing "amazingly well." There can always be changes and I will move forward cautiously optimistic, but I know it is important to celebrate good reports. I'm walking a line of wanting to celebrate her birth and also reeling from the trauma of it. I like using the giant water cup and the socks they gave me at the hospital even though they are a reminder of a terrifying night, but they're also attached to her birth which is a glorious thing. The doctor also told us that the respiratory therapist at the ER that night taught him how to perform intubations when he was a student many years ago. That RT used to work at UVa and now works at Martha Jefferson. They don't see emergency cases like ours there so it had been a long time since he had intubated a baby as small as Cosette. He did it quickly and perfectly. I feel very grateful he was there that night.

I am feeling gratitude for many things: all of the meals we were given this week; the selfcare I was able to do thanks to some help from friends; the kind, generous, thoughtful parents of my students who put together an amazing assortment of comfort gifts with my days spent at the hospital in mind (Ben and I thank you so much); the visits from our priest who came on day one and has supported us since; my sister visiting last weekend; the steadfast, honest, diligent friendship of Ashley and Mary; and of course for my mom, who has been at the hospital every day.

Saturday, October 12

My baby shower was supposed to be today. The weather is perfect. A gorgeous fall day. The mountains by the community center would have been stunning. My mother-in-law is arriving this afternoon to visit for one week. The trip was planned so she could attend the shower. Now instead she will help with Henry and see Cosette in the hospital. She will stay with us at our house. We still have a guest room because I didn't make it into the baby's room yet. Because he is coming back tomorrow, it is good that these changes haven't been made. I am not worried about having a guest in the house. I will be sad and will do my hospital routine the same as always. I think Ben's mom understands that. She is a very thoughtful, compassionate person. I imagine she wants me to feel my feelings at home and not act a particular way for her. I don't think I could even if I wanted to.

BABY JOURNAL | October 13

Happy two weeks of life, my dear. You are very cute. Everyone calls you a rockstar and feisty. Your breath is being supported by a new machine so you have time to grow. Your lungs are very tiny. Today you should be getting out your IV line. That's a big deal. You are doing so well. You love my milk which is great. I love your name so much. It will be fun when we can start planning for you to come home. It feels so long from now, 14 weeks or so. You're 26 weeks tomorrow. It will be wonderful to watch you grow. I can already see the difference in your pictures from two weeks ago. I sit by you every day wishing you strength and peace.

Monday, October 14

This morning I was upstairs getting dressed and brushing my teeth, all the things that take more time than I would like these days, and I was listening to Ben and Henry downstairs talking about waffles, birds outside, the day ahead. And then Henry said, "The baby isn't here. Baby is at the hospital because she's too small."

"That's right," replied Ben. "She's too small to come home yet. But she will someday, then she'll meet you, her brother."

"I'm the sister and she's the brother."

"No, the other way around. She's the sister. You're the brother."

I wasn't crying. I was okay. I was able to escape the house without making a scene.

A priest from church came to give me Eucharist today. We met in the lounge, which was thankfully empty. The lounge is cold and dark. Sometimes there are televisions blaring at a very high volume. I never go there. She told me about how she worked as a chaplain in a NICU at one time and how each day can bring a new challenge. When she held my hands and we prayed together for Cosette, I cried. My heart aches like it is stuck in a deep well of heavy, thick liquid. I am weighed down by the viscosity. Nothing cuts through it. I am so scared of what is to come. It hurts so much to be me at this moment.

CARING BRIDGE POST | October 14

Cosette is two weeks old and 26 weeks corrected. That's the word used to describe what week she would be if still in utero. She has gained some weight and looks a little fuller in her face and body. She is at full feeding amount for her weight and seems to agree very well with my milk. She does not need an IV any longer because the milk through the feeding tube is giving her what she needs. The big area of concern is her lungs. She was given something today to help dry out extra liquid. We'll hope to find out tomorrow that it helped.

I'm entering the third week of spending 6-7 hours each day in the NICU. Of course there's nowhere else I'd rather be right now, and when I step off the elevator on Cosette's floor, I feel a sense of relief knowing I am close to her again. But the days are deeply depressing and anxiety-producing. Alarms are going off all of the time and we witness the hardships of families with babies near ours. It's dimly lit, there's no fresh air, and so the day passes outside while I sit leaning into Cosette's isolette bed, trying not to let any light in so that she can sleep in as much womb-like darkness as possible.

Today she had many cute poses to show me like having both hands tucked under her tiny chin or a hand flung up over her forehead. All of the nurses describe her as feisty and a rock star. I like those descriptions, but she's also just my little baby who is now starting to look at me and reach toward me. But a layer of plastic separates us. It's painful to think of the past and how nice it was to be pregnant; it's scary to think about the future, and yet the present is very difficult, too. I started a journal for Cosette when I first found out I was pregnant and wrote in it a few times a week about how I was feeling and things I wanted her to know about being pregnant with her. The first entry after her birth was hard to write, but I'm doing it, and I write in my own journal which helps. I listen to music sometimes to dull the alarm sounds. And I lean in every few moments to see my precious girl and remind myself that she's a miracle. All of this hardship for her, me, Ben, and those close to us, is all a small price for what we will get in return, which I pray each day is a life spent together.

Tuesday, October 15

There's a lot going on here today. Cosette is doing okay, though. She got a diuretic again to help clear out some liquid in her lungs. She's receiving oxygen better now. The overhead lights were on when I got here and she was looking pink with blonde fuzz and eyebrows. She had her eyes open yesterday but so far not today. She's getting very cute. It feels scary to trust that she will be alright. Will I worry about her forever? Maybe all parents do anyway. The adrenaline has decreased some. Last night I felt very sad. I didn't cry though. Ben held her on Sunday which was nice. I felt protective while he was doing it. I think I will have lasting anxiety from this experience. How could I not? I'll just have to work through it. It's hard to remember the day we came in here for the first time. Susan was the nurse. I was in a wheelchair. She made it sound possible for Cosette to live. There was so much in those first days. Social workers and doctors. We ate in the cafeteria on that Monday. I haven't done that since. I had my phone out on the table in case the NICU called while we were away for those thirty minutes. I watched hospital workers eat lunch while looking at their phones, having normal days. I cried a lot. That night. The shock. I will work through that for a while. Maybe forever.

I am standing in the lobby by the large windows near the elevators. A baby in Cosette's pod had an emergency. They were doing rounds and a large group of doctors and students were at his isolette when it happened. I'm not sure if it was a coincidence that they were there or if they were trying something different with him. A loud alarm went off and nurses ran to put up screens around the area. Someone brought a screen for me, too.

"You don't need to see what's going on," a woman told me. She was an administrator in business attire. Blonde with a kind face. "I mean, you shouldn't have to see, you have your own worries." She pointed her head toward Cosette.

"Thank you," I said. "Should I leave?"

"No, you don't need to leave."

I saw the woman who runs the sign-in desk talking urgently on the phone. She probably had to call the baby's parents. I imagined a scene like this happening to Cosette and them calling me. I started to feel nauseous. I checked on Cosette, then pulled her cover tighter around her box. She was asleep. She looked peaceful. She had no idea what was going on a few feet away.

A social worker I have seen often came up to me. "It's a code red. You're going to need to go. No guests are allowed in the pod when there's a code red."

"Oh, okay," I stammered. "The other woman said I could stay, but I can definitely go."

The administrator walked up to us. "She doesn't need to leave her baby," she said to the social worker. "If she wants to stay, she can."

The social worker shrugged. She wasn't going to argue in front of me.

I have been in the pod when babies are having surgeries performed at the bedside. They pull a curtain around them. The lights get very bright in the whole pod and the nurses and doctors doing the surgery wear scrubs and masks. This was different, though. The lights were bright, but everyone in the pod seemed tense. I glanced to the corner where the baby was and thought again about the possibility of this being Cosette. I stood up and checked on her again. Asleep.

"I'm going to step out," I said to the blonde woman who was standing next to the screen she had put up by me.

"Of course," she said.

As I walked past the sign-in desk, a woman dashed by me, throwing herself against the sink to wash her hands as quickly as possible. The mother. That could be me, I thought. But it's not me.

I've been waiting in the lobby for two hours to be allowed in again.

Today two parents from the Waldorf school sent me the same article. One came through Facebook so it was one of those articles that pops up and then lots of people see it in their feed even if it's not new. I waited until I got home to look at it. I almost didn't because I have not been looking up anything about premature babies and that has felt like the right thing to do. The article was about the benefit of playing flute music for babies in the NICU. At this point, Cosette cannot hear music because she's in her isolette all of the time, but in addition to feeling like this good thing was not accessible to her, the article was also hugely upsetting. It listed all of the terrible side effects of premature birth, including a shorter than average lifespan if they do make it out of the NICU. Hearing problems, vision problems, learning challenges, depression, a wide range of mental illnesses. I cried. I told Ben. He got mad. It didn't make me feel better. People are trying to connect, but it is possible to help in the wrong way and that's just an inescapable fact when emotions are so high. I'm seeing Mary tomorrow morning for tea before I go into the hospital. She will understand.

Ashley sent me a care package made for NICU parents. The best part is a pack of milestone cards that I can put by Cosette and take a picture. It's exactly the right thing for me in terms of a coping gift because it feels like checking boxes. As I use one, I can place it in the back of the stack. And I can also look forward to what is coming. There is one for every week starting with 24 weeks and one for every pound from two pounds to seven pounds. Things like *Off the ventilator!* and *No more IVs* and *First breastfeeding* and *First clothes* will be so great.

Thursday, October 17

Last night I broke down in hard, loud tears at the kitchen table while Ben and his mother talked in the living room. I was texting with a friend, describing to her how hard it is to leave Cosette each day, and I started to sob. I felt so bad for Cosette and for me. Ben got quiet and then came in and put his hand on my shoulder. His mom slipped by him and went upstairs to bed. It has been nice having her here, and it is good for someone else to see Cosette and sit by her. She prays for her, which I appreciate. I don't want to make her feel bad for being here; she's helping a lot by taking care of Henry this week so Ben can see Cosette at the hospital.

I went back to Dr. H today. I did not cry immediately when she walked in this time. That's some improvement. I still cried but was able to speak clearly about things. She said she has friends who work at UVa and they were able to tell her that Cosette is doing really well. That was nice to hear. I asked her more questions about what happened to me.

"Preterm labor is a mysterious thing," she said. "Unfortunately we don't know a lot about it. You experienced no physical damage and weren't sick, so if you want to have another baby in the future, you could. You are at a higher risk of having another premature baby just because you've had one, but that does not mean you will."

"But could my body just not do it? Like follow through to the end? Was I missing something? Could the placenta tear again? Like, is that a recurring problem women have?"

"The placenta had indications of an infection, but there's no way to know if that happened before or after the birth. Since the birth was so fast, it seems that your body decided the only way for Cosette to live was to leave. And so far, that's been working for her. There is no way to know why the placenta got a tear. But it is absolutely not something you caused."

I am not sure if that line will ever truly land. Not something I caused. Maybe not mentally nor willingly but physically my body did cause an early birth. I told Dr. H about what the UVa attending said about the respiratory therapist who was there on the night of Cosette's birth.

"Yes," she said with a smile. "He most likely saved Cosette's life. He used to work at UVa and trained tons of doctors over there on how to perform intubations. He works at Martha Jeff now for a slower pace. In fact, he had just come to see me before your calls started that night saying what an abnormally busy night it was in the ER."

It was strange to think about other dramatic things happening there that night in addition to us. It's also weird to think about how I will never meet him or talk through what happened in the car with the doctor who told me to push. It is all locked up in a memory.

Ashley said I should have a beer to calm my nerves. Guinness can be helpful for breast milk supply, they say. It's hard to think about drinking, because people don't drink when pregnant and I still want to be pregnant. I don't want to do things that pregnant women are not allowed to do. Ashley said maybe I would be ready for an October Halloween beer. Maybe.

CARING BRIDGE POST | October 17

I t has been a fairly stable week for Cosette. I got to hold her twice which was good for both of us. She gets very calm when I hold her. They can wean her oxygen a little because she gets so relaxed. It's quite a process to get her out of her isolette and back in, but I'm getting more used to it. They have to give her breaths by bagging her for a few moments while they move her ventilator and I barely breathe during that time. When holding her, I have to stay absolutely still because she is positioned in a very precise way and her breathing tube can't move. Sitting motionless for 1.5 hours couldn't be easier though when the reward is being that close to her. I know that becoming a parent can make one be selfless in ways they never imagined. I know that my own mother has acted selflessly time and time again in doing things for me. But I could never fathom such a huge shift in myself. Usually I am someone who likes things a certain way and would never tolerate seven hours inside without a break on a beautiful day. . . it's just not as important now. And so thank you for saying my words reveal that I am loving her well already because that means something to me. It's not necessarily that love equals selflessness, but love is so powerful it can change a person's way of thinking and being overnight. If it's that powerful, maybe she really can feel it in her tiny body when I hold her, look at her, and think about her when we are apart.

Friday, October 18

I saw Laura today. We met for smoothies at a place near campus. The craving for liquids and smoothies has continued since Cosette's birthday. I wrote to Laura the week that Cosette was born and asked how I could not be terrified after having sat through so many child studies at school where the child's birth story was discussed as a predictor and influence on the child. If a kindergartener was having trouble with transitions, his cesarean section birth might be brought up. Well, we didn't have that but being born in a car seventeen weeks early? That has to be much worse. It is hard to not feel she is doomed, and yet when I look at her in her little isolette, she seems like she could be totally fine and normal one day. She stretches and is feisty, popping her feet out of the blanket when they are tucked in, reaching for anything that's put on her head or over her eyes. She always tries to help the nurse during care time. I asked Laura in that message if she had anything comforting to say to me. I wanted a spiritual answer and she gave me one.

These "little" beings come as such deep mysteries and such profound blessings to us, if we are able to see beyond the mundane into the Truth of this reality. If we are to believe that each one of us chooses our families and our birth moments and much of what we encounter in life. Those of us who receive them into physical life can only do our best to meet them the way they come. So if there is comfort for you and Ben I would say that Cosette has a plan and she chose you two to help her manifest it, whatever it may be. In reality, the only thing that you are asked to do is to love her unconditionally, and it sounds like you're already on that track. If there's ever magic in this life it seems to me that it happens between a parent and child at birth. That meeting between souls, the recognition, the instant absolute devotion are the most beautiful moments in life. It's very tempting (and normal and traditional) to implore the divine to make everything turn out according to one's hopes and dreams, but we all know that things rarely turn out that way.

If I were to give advice, I would encourage you to pray for the courage and strength to be able to do what is asked of you, and pray that she has the courage and strength to meet the challenges before her, whatever they may be. People may encourage you to envision her as healed and healthy and perfect, and you may choose to do that, but if I understand Reality correctly, it's better to pray for acceptance of whatever is given to you. We are not alone in this life, in this work. There are countless angels, spiritual beings, ancestors who want to help us on our way. I feel sure that Cosette is being accompanied by people on the other side who dearly love her and want to help her get through this challenge. I can only imagine that your little girl is a tremendously courageous soul, especially being born on Michaelmas!

The Waldorf world is one I believe in deeply. It's not something I knew anything about before applying to work at a Waldorf school in 2008, but something resonated within me and I knew it was "right." Some of the spiritual aspects are a little beyond my comprehension or desire to understand, but when a master teacher like Laura talks about it, I can absorb and trust it. Everything she wrote was comforting, and I have been trying in the lowest of times, but also just when I am away from Cosette, to imagine angels hovering around her. I also imagine my grandparents and other loved ones, especially my two previous students who died tragically young, watching over her. I suppose this is similar to how people think about a newly deceased loved one joining other loved ones in heaven. Cosette is with us, but she's in an in-between world. She would not be alive without her breathing machine. And she is supposed to be inside the womb, not living in a world outside embryonic fluid.

Laura said I looked better than she thought I would. That was nice to hear, but I also wondered if I was displaying a more optimistic side than I actually feel. I decided it was mostly because it was nice to talk to someone outside of the hospital. I spend a lot of time quietly sitting next to Cosette or quietly driving or quietly pumping.

When I got home from the hospital today, Teddy was by the front door and there was blood around him on the floor. He had licked his sore so much that it opened and it was bleeding. I started to cry. It's just too much to hold in the sadness all day, then get home to see Teddy suffering. I held a towel around his paw until the bleeding slowed. I had the idea to email a veterinarian who is the parent of a former student because she has written such kind things on Caring Bridge, and I know she cares a lot for me and would like to help if she can. I sent her a picture of Teddy's paw and she said he needs antibiotics. She's going to come to the house and give him a shot. I am so grateful to her.

Saturday, October 19

Today was the last day of my mother-in-law's visit. We all went to the apple orchard this morning and took a hayride. I drove separately from the others so that after I could drive directly to the hospital. But before we left home, something bad happened.

I have to keep all of my breast milk in 2.5 ounce plastic containers that have attached lids which snap on. They're called snappies for that reason. I filled two containers from a 1 a.m. pump, and also had two from last night and two from this morning. This was the first time I was taking six containers to the hospital. I felt proud and was glad I was making so much. The lactation consultant suggested I try power pump sessions for a few days in a row, which meant I would pump multiple times in an hour and do that for many hours a day, and I really did not want to do that so having six containers felt reassuring.

All four of us were downstairs getting ready to leave. I was reaching for the milk containers from the fridge and two dropped from my hands. They hit the inside of the fridge as they went, the lids popped off, and the milk emptied on the floor. My 1 a.m. milk was gone.

I whispered, "Oh no," then started to weep. Ben's mom took Henry outside. Ben tried to comfort me. There was nothing to say. I told him to leave and I would meet him at the orchard. I was devastated. I called Mom. She tried to talk me down from it. I still feel the ache many hours later.

When I got to the hospital, I told Beth, Cosette's nurse for the day, what happened. She told me that she once left a whole cooler of pumped breast milk outside in her car on a hot day and it spoiled. She said many women have a spilled milk story and the saying *Don't cry over spilled milk* was not created by a woman who has pumped milk.

Today a friend came to the hospital before seeing a UVa football game. We sat on a bench outside the main doors. The air was crisp and perfectly October. It was really nice to see him, yet when it was time to go, I was eager to get back to Cosette. She needs me by her and I need the same. If I am close to her and can see her little chest rising and falling, I feel calmer. I have my journal with me at the hospital today. I am going to hold her soon.

CARING BRIDGE POST | October 20

I will begin by saying Cosette is doing very well right now, but there have been some scares in the past two days. Yesterday, during skin-to-skin time, Cosette's oxygen levels dipped to dangerous levels. Several nurses, respiratory therapists, and others moved Cosette back to her incubator and manually breathed for her. Once she had been put back, Cosette's oxygen returned to normal and she seemed stable. The frightening fallout of this was that no one could tell us why her oxygen level dropped. We were assured that it was not because I was holding her.

At 3 a.m. this morning, Cosette coughed up her breathing tube and was re-intubated. Her breathing tube was too high and was causing a cough reflex that pushed it out. There is no doubt this is what caused the oxygen issues earlier when I was holding her. The change of position, being held, combined with the misplaced tube resulted in a low level.

There is a cloud of uncertainty that surrounds each new day. Cosette is doing well, and we are so happy to see her growing and developing: she's getting bigger and pinker all the time.

BABY JOURNAL | October 20

You are gaining weight, almost two pounds. Can you believe you were ever that small? Your face is filling out and you have blonde fuzz on your head. It's a rainy Sunday here, chilly. Your dad and I are going to put up Halloween decorations tonight. I wonder what we will dress you as next year. Your first Halloween and Christmas are going to be spent at the hospital, but I'll come see you, of course.

You are very strong and make big poops so you need a bigger diaper now. I'm glad you like my milk so much. You're three weeks old today! It has been hard, so hard to see you struggle or to leave you at night, but I would not trade it for anything, except maybe you still being in me. But we have this. We're doing well considering it all. I had a dream at 3 a.m. that you couldn't breathe and in real life you had self extubated. You're okay now. We are still very connected. I love you.

Monday, October 21

I am still processing what happened on Saturday afternoon while I was holding Cosette. And what happened Sunday morning when I went in and was told she had coughed up her breathing tube overnight. The nurse mentioned it like I already knew.

"She had quite the night," she said.

"What?" I said. "What do you mean? What happened?"

"They didn't call you?"

"No." My eyes darted to Cosette's isolette. It was covered. She was in there, right?

"Oh, I'm surprised they didn't call you. It happened late on the night shift and everything is fine now so maybe they figured there was no reason to bother you."

My thoughts raced to the nurse who had told me a few days ago that on this rollercoaster everyone gets a call in the middle of the night. *It will happen, trust me, and it will be okay.* That's what she said. I wanted to tell her she was wrong. She was trying to be comforting but that type of preventative fear/wisdom is useless to me. I will be upset no matter what, it is not going to be less in that moment because I remember someone telling me it was going to happen.

And now here I was, sort of in that moment, but not really because no one had called.

"What happened?" I said again.

"Cosette spit up her breathing tube. Christine noticed her numbers dropping, came over and saw Cosette foaming all around her mouth. Sometimes there's enough mucus and lubrication in the throat that they can cough so hard, they push the tube up and out."

"There was time when she had no oxygen?" My heart was beating faster and faster as the story hit.

"Just a few seconds. They bagged her, pushed the code button, and the intubation team was here immediately. They intubated her and she's been fine. She has shown no signs of distress from it. They took an X-ray, too, which they always do with a new tube to make sure it's in the right place. I saw an X-ray from yesterday, and it looked like the tube was too high."

"Could that have been why she started to crash when I was holding her yesterday?"

"Oh yes, definitely."

Well, that was good to know anyway. If any part of this could be good. That meant it wasn't something I did or a product of being held. She was not stressed out. She couldn't breathe correctly because of her tube. Holding her when that happened was one of the scariest moments of my life. Her numbers kept dropping and then steadying, then they just kept going down. No one was paying attention to us because of alarm fatigue and so I sent Mom to get someone. Then suddenly everyone was there because her numbers were so low. They fiddled with the tube, no change. The nurse disconnected the ventilator and started bagging her. I began to cry, but I was trying not to move because Cosette was on me. I turned my head to the left so they could have enough space to bag her on my right shoulder. Then they decided to take her off of me. I didn't even put her down myself like I usually do. They took her from me, put her in the isolette, got the cover down, and continued to work on her until her numbers rose. I stepped back. Ben was still there. He held my hand. I looked at Mom with a tear-filled, strained face. She was teary, too. I think because it was scary to see this happen to Cosette but also because she feels the pain of what I'm experiencing, just like I feel Cosette's pain. She wants to take it from me, shield me from it, but she can't. I was supposed to have a normal pregnancy, no one could have predicted this. The first shield of protection broke weeks ago.

Last night, Ben and I called to talk to Cosette's night nurse. We have started calling every night. There is usually a new voice on the other end of the line, but sometimes it's someone who is familiar with Cosette and that comforts me. When the voice sounds very young or she mispronounces Cosette's name and says Casette instead, it is harder for me to get to sleep. I will the hours by until I can get back to the hospital and watch out for her. But last night it was Christine who loves Cosette and signed up to be her primary nurse when she works nights. My guess from her voice is that she's been working in the NICU for a long time.

The first time we talked to her she said, "Your baby is just the most darling, cutest baby we've had here in a long time. Maybe ever. I just love her to pieces. She's so feisty and sweet. I wrap her up after first cares, and she pushes her tiny feet and arms out a minute later. But don't you worry, I get her wrapped up nicely on her belly and then she just sleeps and sleeps."

I like Christine. She makes me feel safe. We always call before I go to sleep around 9:30 p.m. so last night we talked before any of this tube stuff had happened. She knew about what occurred during the day though. "These things just happen sometimes," she said. "Just remember it's not your fault and don't let it keep you from holding your baby. It's the best thing for her. The absolute best thing. Your girl's a fighter. She's going to be just fine."

I wish I could talk to Christine and ask what happened. Maybe she'll work again tonight and we can talk to her. It's strange to have a movie scene in your head of a terrifying event that happened to your child. Like you'll never really know what it was like to be there or what was said or who intubated her.

The doctor came and told me that the tube had gotten too small for her. It wasn't down far enough to meet her lungs correctly. It was good they found this out before she was working too hard and strained her lungs. I admire all of the work they do at the hospital, in this NICU, but at times I feel like there is too much left to chance.

I went to see a new therapist for the first time today. Her name is Ruth. Laura recommended her to me. She didn't want to know much about my history, little about the birth itself. She said she wanted to help me with my present emotions rather than sorting out past feelings. The birth affects my feelings every day, but I understand her perspective on treatment. *What can you take from this*, she asked. *What have you learned, what good has there been?* She is an older woman who works from her house, which makes things feel cozy and very separate from the hospital. I can conveniently walk there from the hospital. She has a soft presence, like a relative who wants you to feel held yet also has pointed questions for you that cause you to cry. I like her. I'll see her again.

She had me lay on a massage table for a part of the session. She worked to calm my nervous system and turn my chakras in the correct directions. My heart was turned off. My voice was turned off. That seemed accurate. She asked me questions about Ben and how he is dealing. She warned me that habits can form and I need to communicate with him even if I feel like I cannot handle another person's emotions and struggle. Ben and I mostly talk about the hospital and Cosette. We don't talk about ourselves. One big thing we have in common currently is not having much self awareness.

When the parent/vet/friend came to give Teddy his shot, she said the tumor looks worse than it did in the picture I sent to her. She said it's definitely a tumor, not a callus. She thinks amputation is the best choice. They'll need to take an X-ray to make sure it has not spread in his body, though. If it hasn't, they can remove the paw. I just want him to live. I cannot lose Teddy right now.

CARING BRIDGE POST | Tuesday, October 22

Cosette is doing fine since her too exciting of a night over the weekend. The doctor told me today that they don't really know how she got her tube up and out and that she wouldn't put anything past her abilities. They all joke about her being a stinker and trouble maker and tell me to watch out for this one when she's a teenager. And I think to myself *Bring it on, please. Let her be a teenager someday.* The breathing tube is keeping her alive and so I know she needs it now, but the day it's removed will be one of celebration. It looks so uncomfortable and I know she has a sense of it being not right, especially now that she's tried to get rid of it. Each passing day is one day closer. For the present time, nutrition is the most important thing for her so that she can grow and get healthier lungs. She's not two pounds yet, but she's nearing it. Her length measurement is 12.4 inches. She continues to kick her legs and enjoys having her hands up by her face, resting on her head or chin, or even folded by her belly. When I change her diaper each afternoon, she wiggles and stretches bigger than usual, and in that brief moment of no diaper, seems to enjoy the freedom. Today when I put a swab soaked in my milk into her mouth, she not only sucked on it like she has before but also reached to touch my hand with her fingers. I haven't held her since what happened Saturday, but I hope to tomorrow.

The NICU continues to be a difficult place to be and on days like today when the intensity is high for other babies, I wish I could crawl into Cosette's isolette with her and close it all out, as well as protect her further from it. But even in those hard hours, I continue to be met with connections that remind me of stable life outside. Cosette's nurse from Saturday is friends with the head of school at the school where I work. She came back to check on me today. An eating specialist who will work with Cosette in the future is the neighbor of a good friend and parent of a previous student of mine. I met for a break today with someone else who falls under that same title and works in the hospital. And another parent is a lactation consultant and helped me during that first incredibly hard week. My precious cat Teddy has been in need of special vet attention in the last few weeks and a friend and parent of a previous student has helped him which has in turn helped me. While driving near the hospital today I saw from afar two people who work in the church office and have sent us kind messages. Seeing them settled me. *Thinking of you* cards and a string of hearts containing messages from previous Waldorf colleagues line a shelf in our house. The connections really do help, and it is powerful to be reminded how much we touch each other's lives in small and big ways.

Wednesday, October 23

Cosette is swaddled because she keeps pulling at her tube. She is determined and feisty and all those things, but I also hate to know she's so uncomfortable. Rounds just happened. She is doing fine. She's almost two pounds. It is still hard to register that her birthday is in September. She is a Libra. I looked up the star sign briefly but it does not feel important. Maybe someday in the future it will.

The milestones will happen and this will continue on and then she will be home with us. I feel like she is going to be okay. I love her so much. I slept more last night.

Teddy's paw is much worse. It is bleeding often and a lot. His surgery is scheduled in November but I contacted the vet office to see if it can be moved up. I will take him to the animal hospital on Tuesday morning, drop him off, she'll take an x-ray and then call me. That call will determine if he can live as a three-legged cat or he will die soon from cancer.

My brother-in-law hired someone to come to the house to clean my car. It is very kind of him to think of this as something I would want. It's too much of a hassle to take it somewhere and wait for it to be cleaned. The interior of the car still smells like iron even though Mom scrubbed and vacuumed it a few days after Cosette was born. She said a lot of blood had soaked into the cushions. I do not remember seeing blood or feeling like I was losing blood. I am ready for the car to smell like chemicals instead of iron.

Thursday, October 24

At rounds today the nurse practitioner explained to me that Cosette's metabolic panel revealed low levels in some areas that meant she could be getting an infection. Infection is the scariest word in the NICU. Infections can mean death. If they are unable to be treated, they can become too strong for doctors to help the baby combat.

"We don't know for sure but we will need to start treatment in case it is an infection. If we wait, it could be too late. We treat all infections aggressively here."

"What kind of infection?" I asked.

"Urinary tract. It could be. We will take a sample from her urethra and let it sit. If it doesn't grow a culture, we'll know she doesn't have an infection. The low red blood count could be from an insufficient supply of blood because she's not making her own yet, so we'll do a blood transfusion as well."

"Both today?"

"She'll get one dose of antibiotics and then the transfusion after that. And then another dose tonight. They need to be spaced out."

"That's a lot for one day."

"It is." She nodded sympathetically. "We will know in 48 hours about the culture. If nothing grows, then we stop the antibiotics."

"Aren't antibiotics really bad to take? Like for her gut and because she already had them when she was born?"

The NP looked at me without blinking. "An infection could be much worse than any side effects an antibiotic might cause down the road."

I nodded. She meant death. She meant do this if you want her to have a road.

"The process for getting the sample is a sterile procedure so we will have you step out for a little while."

I stood next to Cosette's isolette, her little body looking the same as each day, yet was there something bad brewing inside of her. An enemy? It didn't feel like it. I thought she was okay, no infection, but I have very little trust in my intuition right now. It's not like I would ever say no to treating her. I don't even know if they would listen to me. She is "institutionalized" after all. Maybe they would call Child Protective Services.

I looked at my baby and started to cry. At the beginning of rounds when they first started to describe her numbers, I did not comprehend where the conversation was going. Now it was sinking into my stomach and the back of my forehead. My poor baby. Drugs and a transfusion. I hated seeing the transfusions happen. The sac of blood, the IV. Now she would have a PICC line for a couple of days, which carried its own risk of infection. Any opening on the skin could become the site of an infection. My mind spiraled with the load of information from the past ten minutes. I had come in that morning like any other morning. This was the NICU rollercoaster. I never know if the day is going to turn rotten and full of heavy tears. I race to get there to find out everything is okay and some days it just isn't.

The nurse told me Cosette must be swaddled at all times now to keep her hands out of her mouth. Being swaddled sometimes seems to calm her but not all the time. She likes to stretch and touch her face. They say babies like to touch their heads while in utero. And now she's not allowed to have her hands above her hips. It is said with a chuckle, oh her straight jacket, oh she's so feisty she needs to be tied down. It is not funny. She's being constrained against natural inclinations and movements.

While Cosette had the sample taken, I pumped. And then I waited in the foyer of the NICU. I stood by the television screen that has Then and Now pictures of babies who have been in the NICU. The Then pictures look like Cosette. The Now pictures look like normal babies and toddlers. They list their likes and dislikes. One boy with thick glasses likes pizza and puppies. I wonder if Cosette will need thick glasses one day. The pictures are very encouraging. I stood under the slide show and watched it repeat over and over for thirty minutes. Finally I left the NICU and stood by the large windows that look over downtown Charlottesville. There's a world out there in which people do ordinary things. Someday that will be me again.

CARING BRIDGE POST | Saturday, October 26

It was a difficult couple of days but hopefully we are coming out of it. On Thursday, Cosette began receiving antibiotics to ward off a possible infection. She also received another blood transfusion due to being anemic. The blood helped with the symptoms she was having and this morning they stopped the antibiotics because the culture did not grow anything. Of course it is a relief for her to not have an infection, but it was hard watching her receive such powerful medicine as a precaution. It is what needs to be done though. On Wednesday night, Cosette tried to wedge out her breathing tube so now she has to be swaddled so that she can't stretch her arms. Again, it is what needs to be done and sometimes she looks comforted by it, but at other times she seems to be pushing and straining against it. Tomorrow, at four weeks old, she will receive another head ultrasound, which is another breath holding moment for us.

I have not been able to hold Cosette for over a week, which has been very difficult to accept each day when I ask. The NICU has been full and busy and those are not the right factors for helping me get her out for holding. It seems promising for today. She needs more opportunities to wear all of her pretty hats that have been knit for her by her adoring fan club.

BABY JOURNAL | October 27

You're another week old. Twenty eight weeks corrected tomorrow. They thought you might have an infection this week but you didn't. That was a hard day. They took a picture of your brain today. I think you're going to be fine. Better than fine. You're 2 lb 2 oz now. Good job! You eat all of your milk and poop a lot. Dad and I laugh when we change you because it's so much and you keep going once your diaper is off.

I think I'm going to change your room to the green painted room, at least while you're in a crib. It's brighter and warmer than the other room. Cozy for Cosette. I would start getting it ready now but you're going to stay in our room for a while. It rained really hard here this morning and then got sunny. It's warmer out than usual for October. It is dark in here, but I don't mind. You're in here. I want to be where you are.

Monday, October 28

This morning I went to school to see my students. I waited by the library and the kids came to me in two groups, the fifth grade and then the fourth grade. David came with them. They very proudly told me how they had all just washed their hands. No germs that could go to Cosette. It was very sweet to see them and I felt happy. There was no risk of crying. In fact, my face felt so strange, like it had not smiled in a long time. The only other time I have felt that is after a meditation retreat when I hadn't smiled in ten days. Those first interactions with people are incredible. This did not feel invigorating like that but it did feel nice. The kids asked about Cosette and I asked them about language arts class and Halloween. They asked me if I was dressing up as anything and I said not this year. They know I did last year and how much I enjoy it. One child asked about Teddy because they had seen on Caring Bridge about how he is not well. I said he is having surgery to help him. I hope that is true.

When the forty minutes were over, I was ready to leave. I was exhausted by the intensity of the interactions. And it was time to be at the hospital. The kids turned away easily, yet David seemed sad to say bye not knowing when he would see me again. I couldn't be sad about this. There were too many other things I am sad about, but it still felt like something, if not sadness. Maybe wistfulness. My friend, my friend who spent the month of September with me as a pregnant woman. I imagine it must have been hard for him to think of the trauma I went through and have no way to connect or help. Someday will I return to that life where he and I sat on the library steps saying bye to our students each afternoon? I don't know. The idea of returning to work while Cosette is still in the hospital is terrifying to me. Six weeks of leave means I go back to work the second week of November. I will be at school for November, December, and January until she comes home. Then six more weeks of leave and return to work at the beginning of March. My maternity leave was supposed to be from the end of January through spring break in April. I will miss a whole extra month of time at home. It pulls at my heart to think about it this way. I feel like I have already lost so much, then to have work/monetary constraints adds to the depression.

When David and I spoke on the phone over the weekend about me visiting today, he said colleagues were donating some of their sick days so that I could stay away longer. My mouth really hung open at that thought. There was nothing better anyone could say to me. I need to be there for Cosette and get her through this time.

Before I left school today, two friends came to wave and smile at me. Joy brimmed inside of me to see them. People are so powerful. No one has any idea the hell I have gone through but that's okay. I don't need to feel separate from them forever just because I am living this isolated experience that cannot be shared. Someday things will be normal again, and I want to be a likable person then. I want to be remembered and allowed to return to my old self. I cannot talk now, but I will again, and I need there to still be people who want to listen and tell me things about themselves. I hope smiling and waving is enough.

I spoke to a birth trauma specialist on the phone last week and she told me that Cosette knows when I'm there and knows when I'm not. She said when I go back to work I should tell Cosette that I must spend time with the kids who she remembers hearing when she was in my belly. I need to go to them during the day, but then I will return to her. It was comforting to hear that a specialist believes Cosette knows me, her mother, is there for her, but also devastating to imagine her sensing me leaving. That moment I walk out each day is the absolute worst. She asked if there is an option to room-in, sleep there with her. I cannot imagine sleeping in the NICU, but no, it is not set up like that. The suggestion of something that could be good for Cosette that I cannot physically do is hard to swallow. I circle back again to: not talking to outsiders is safer for my stress level. And yet she is an expert on helping moms like me and babies like Cosette so I will persevere and schedule an appointment with her.

I feel a warning rise in me when people tell me I should seek out a parents of preemies group whether in person or on social media. Or I should talk to other mothers who had babies in the NICU for long stays. I have no desire to do that. I have no energy to hear anyone else's story. Maybe someday I will want to join a group or commiserate with others but not today, not yet. I am having this experience on my own and Cosette is doing remarkably well. I do not want to hear from others who have babies who are not doing well. I know most who are born as early as Cosette have major difficulties. Do not tell me it might happen or how lucky I am that it hasn't. I want none of that. Maybe I am missing out on something helpful, but for now I am trusting the repulsion. It is easy to say I have no intuition left, that it was trampled when I thought Cosette would be fine and she wasn't, but I do still have gut feelings. If a wise voice is there, then I need to listen to it. There was the night I dreamt she couldn't breathe, and she coughed up her breathing tube. I woke in the middle of the night and was so scared for her. The cord is not cut. The line repeats in my head.

CARING BRIDGE | October 28

Cosette will be one month old tomorrow. If you'd like to light a candle and make a wish for her, we would love that. The ultrasound results were good. The focus for now is decreasing the amount of help she gets from her ventilator and continuing to grow. We're very excited to see her pass the two pound mark.

Tuesday, October 29

Today is many things. It is my dad's birthday. It's Teddy's surgery. Cosette is one month old today. And I see Ruth again this afternoon. By the time I see her I will know if Teddy can have surgery or if I will need to say goodbye to him soon. If the cancer has spread, no surgery will happen. The drive to the vet this morning was very emotional. Teddy hates driving in the car and this ride was long because it is not his usual nearby vet. I want so badly for him to be okay. I also know an amputation is going to change his life and will be a hard recovery. There was nothing uplifting to think about on that drive. I cried so hard when I left him there. I took one last look at him with four paws and walked out the door in a flood of tears.

I am in the hospital now waiting for the call. I think I'm going to hold Cosette soon which means I won't be able to look at my phone for two or three hours. Mom will be here and can answer.

We have been here for a whole month now and have probably had twenty different nurses. I do not like to complain about things because I am grateful for everything they have done for Cosette, but this is one thing that really aggravates me. Every time there's a new nurse they ask about her story, how was she born, did it really happen in a car? It is a roller coaster here, they tell me. All of that is annoying, but I can deal with it. What makes me upset is when the nurse does not know things about Cosette. She doesn't know how to swaddle her just right or does not clean her mouth like some others do or feeds her late. Some of them are more laid back and that makes me nervous. My favorite nurses are the most attentive and the ones who tell me they have small children and treat Cosette the way they would treat their own child.

I saw the director of the NICU in an elevator recently and he gave me his card and told me to write to him if I have any questions. I will write and ask if we can request a primary nurse for Cosette. Even if she had the same person a few times a week that would be better. There are multiple babies in B-pod who have primary nurses. I do not understand why Cosette only had Christine sign up for her on night shift. They all seem to like Cosette a lot. She's adorable and easy to take care of. Seeing some of the other babies and the equipment hooked up to them and even hearing their parents talk to the nurses makes me feel like we are a simple case comparatively. There is little I can do for Cosette beyond pumping and holding her when they can assist in getting her out. If I can organize consistent care, then I will try to do that.

As I returned to the hospital after my appointment with Ruth, there was smoke billowing into the sky around the area. Traffic was blocked from going into the parking garage. I turned in the opposite direction and got a single open spot in a nearby lot. I texted Mom. *There are fire trucks and the garage is blocked. It smells like smoke and it's coming out of the parking garage. What's happening in there?*

She replied: *Nothing in here. I'm with Cosette. All is normal.*

They can't evacuate her. She has to be able to stay in there.

No one here looks worried. The walls are cement and very thick. If there's a fire in the garage it's probably a car fire and they'll take care of it quickly.

I walked toward the hospital entrance. This had to happen on the day of Teddy's surgery. He was getting the surgery at least. Ruth had just calmed me down and now my nervous system was revved again. My baby was in there. People stood in the dropoff circle staring up at the garage. Two fire trucks had placed their ladders against the outside of the garage and hoses were being used. Giant clouds of white water sprayed into the third level.

I was about to ask someone what had happened when I heard a parking attendant say, "Someone was smoking up there, started a fire, car caught it. People never learn. You can't smoke there, dude, no smoking by a hospital."

I had seen visitors and patients smoking in the garage. Mom told me patients often wheel themselves out of hospitals to the garages because they're not allowed to smoke inside but have such a powerful addiction they need to find somewhere.

What level is your car on? I texted Mom.

I'm at the Battle Building.

That's the garage next to the main one where we both usually park because it's easier to access. It means walking the pedestrian bridge between buildings, but ultimately it's faster. Things one learns when going to the same crowded place for months.

The fire alarm was going off inside the hospital, the main lights were muted and emergency lights flashed from the ceiling. A recorded voice over the intercom said, "Please exit the building. Fire located on level 3. Please follow signs to the nearest exit."

Everyone was walking around like normal. The check-in people at the front desk sat in their chairs unphased. I went toward the elevators like usual and made my way to the seventh floor. Even on the seventh floor the alarm was sounding and emergency lights were flashing. How could this not be heard inside the NICU? It was a protected island of a place within the hospital but how could it be 100% protected with vulnerable floors under it? I pushed the button to be let in, and the door swung open after a few seconds. I told my name and signed in. I could see Cosette's isolette from the window. There she was, undisturbed.

When I got to her, Mom said, "The announcement just started here since you last texted." I moved the blinds to look out the window. The side of the fire truck was barely visible. It looked like traffic was starting to move through better. Things were calming down.

"Some added chaos there for you?" Rachel asked me. "I thought I smelled a little smoke when I was in the break room."

I nodded and stared in at Cosette. I put her isolette cover around either side of my head and held back tears. She was fine.

James went with me to pick Teddy up from the vet after his surgery. I was scared to see Teddy for the first time with only three paws. It was more intense than I had imagined because they shaved his back and the area around the missing paw. There were visible stitches, and Teddy was obviously very confused and upset. He was trying to hobble around in his cage on three paws. He also had a cone around his neck to keep him from licking the stitches. He got the cone off within seconds of being in the car. It was good to have James with me. He had been with me when I picked out Teddy from the SPCA. Our cats lived together during the two separate times we shared space. James took care of Teddy over holidays when I would fly to see my sister's family. He did that even after we broke up. I remember feeling jealous that Teddy got to spend time in James's apartment when I didn't.

I have Teddy in the bedroom with me now. He's insisting on being on the bed so I piled quilts on the floor in case he tries to jump down. He is very medicated and keeps moving around in circles. I know it was for the best but he is so miserable. I think I underestimated how intense this recovery would be for him. He is not supposed to go down stairs for two weeks or move around a lot for that whole time. I will need to isolate him to one room and visit in the morning and at night when I get home. It's just two weeks. It will be okay. And then I will have my loyal friend back again.

Thursday, October 31

Some years have felt more like Halloween on the day than others. The years I hosted big parties were very fun Halloweens. Ben and I had one at my old house before we moved. This year, the first year in our new house and new neighborhood, does not feel like Halloween. We put up a few decorations last week mostly for the sake of Henry who is spending Halloween with us.

I spent the day in the hospital as usual. A nurse made a sign for Cosette's area that said *My first Halloween.* The words were written over a cut-out pumpkin pasted onto black paper. The sign was laminated; all of her signs are laminated which is considerate of them. She has an *I'm one week old!* sign and ones for me and Ben saying when we held her for the first time. I look at those signs every time I hold her.

Some of the hospital staff were dressed up. It seemed like select people in the NICU volunteered to be a part of a group who dressed up as characters from Toy Story. I was making one of my many trips out of the NICU to the bathroom and back into the NICU again when they were arranging themselves for a photo. A friend sent it to me a few hours later because she saw it on Twitter. It was strange to see the team on such a public forum like that. People follow the UVa NICU. I live the UVa NICU.

I got to hold Cosette today and we put a tiny pumpkin hat on her that Mom crocheted. Only the side of her cheek is visible, then the tall hat, but it was Cosette's tribute to Halloween for the year. She will have a bigger pumpkin hat next year.

I did not dress up tonight. Ben bought a full body dragon suit, that could also be elaborate pajamas, to wear with Henry who was also a dragon. It was drizzling in the beginning of the night and we all went out and walked down the street to watch Henry get candy. It was fine. I didn't cry. I had imagined doing this same scene while pregnant. Six months pregnant. But instead my baby is in the hospital and I'm getting thinner by the day. After about thirty minutes, it started to pour and got very windy. Umbrellas turned inside out. Mom and I went back to the house and then she left soon after to get home before the storm elevated. Halloween is such a big deal where my sister lives and I know my mom has had a great time trick-or-treating with my niece and nephew. She is here though and of course I'm glad she is, but I also regret that she had a depressing Halloween because of me. Next year will be different. We will take Cosette out dressed as something cute and we'll refer to it as her first Halloween. She will be nine months corrected then, and already one year old.

Friday, November 1

This morning I went to the dermatologist to get a mole checked. I have reached my deductible for my insurance so it seemed like a smart thing to do. Apparently moles are affected by hormones so a slight increase in size is not a concern. When the doctor saw my Care Partner wristband she asked if I was a patient at UVa.

"No," I stammered and started to cry. "My baby is in the NICU. She was born very early."

The doctor stopped examining me and sighed. "I'm so sorry. How early?"

"At twenty-three weeks."

"Very early." She was standing close to me, and I could see all of the lines on her forehead crease in concern for me.

I nodded. "She's doing great though."

"That's wonderful." She looked at the nurse who was also in the room. "You know they should not make you wear something like that for everyone to see and ask about. You'd think they could have a more discreet system set up."

It is not something I had ever thought about. It is my wristband that I wear every day and do not take off. I shower with it and sleep with it on. It is always there. I felt bad for the doctor that she stumbled into that trap. I quickly stopped crying.

But there were more tears coming. At the hospital, I asked Mom if she could watch Henry for a little while so Ben could come up and see the baby, and she said it wasn't a good day for that and started to cry. I was so surprised.

"What's wrong?" I asked. I was sitting in one of the large blue recliner chairs they bring for when I'm holding the baby. No one else had needed it so it was still there.

"I wasn't going to tell you because I do not want you to worry, but I'm still just so upset I can't help it." She was crying and rubbing tears away from her cheeks.

I put my hand on her shoulder feeling my body go stiff. Had someone died and she didn't want to tell me? Was she sick?

"When I was driving home last night from your house in the storm, a tree fell right in front of my car, like directly right in front of it. I slammed on my brakes and stopped just in time. Braking was almost not enough, though. I would have been crushed. It was a huge tree that blocked the whole road. Cars behind me stopped and turned around to go another way. I did that too but I only made it a little while before I had to pull over and throw up. My hands were shaking the whole ride home."

"Oh, Mom," I whispered. "That's so scary. I'm so sorry that happened. You should have spent the night. I'm sorry I didn't make you do that."

She nodded. "It's not your fault. There was no way to know. The thousands of times I have driven that road. But I called your father this morning and told him I am serious about selling the house. I cannot drive that far on that road every day once the baby comes home."

My dad had returned to their apartment near my sister about a week ago. He had come in to see Cosette twice. Once during her first week and once before he left. I know he cares about me and her and wants her to survive, but he also has a lot of his own body pains that distract him. He went to the apartment because his arthritis feels better in the warm climate. Mom usually goes back in August or at the latest September to help with the grandkids, but not this year.

"I think you need a break," I said. "This has all been so much. You should go see the kids for a week. We're okay here." I tilted my head toward Cosette.

"I can't leave yet," she said. "Maybe later in November."

"You should go there for Christmas, too. Christmas won't be anything here."

We have Henry this year for Christmas, and Ben's parents are already scheduled to spend it with us. They still will and the four of them will have a nice time, but Christmas is not happening for me this year, not with my baby in the hospital.

"We can talk about that later," she said. "I'm sorry to get so upset."

"It's very upsetting. It's okay to show that," I said. Have I been so fragile that it seems like no one else should express feelings around me? I have not been asking Ben how he is feeling. He doesn't really ask me either. I imagine we agree that we are both sad and trying to get by.

In the afternoon, I met Ben at the Waldorf school for the fall parent conference with Henry's teacher. At the end, I asked his teacher if Henry mentions his sister at school.

"No," she said, "but we don't ask him about her either. If he wants to talk about her, he can, but we do not want to pry into something like that."

"That sounds right," I said. "Thank you."

Ben added that Henry talks about her a lot with him and at home.

I spoke up. "It's probably still confusing for him. He hasn't even seen her in person, just you FaceTiming while at the hospital."

Everyone agreed with that.

"We're not sure what will happen when Cosette comes home. We hope it is around her due date at the end of January. Henry may miss some school around that time."

"We totally understand," his teacher replied. "Just let us know how we can help."

Cosette will be so vulnerable when she comes home, away from the hospital and all its devices and precautionary measures and specialists. Henry perpetually has a cough during the winter. My mama bear instincts are already working to protect Cosette even though it is months until any of that will happen.

The day ended with me bringing Teddy out of his room because it seemed like he was lonely, and I thought he was doing okay enough to be in the living room with us. But I was wrong. He somehow got himself on top of the upper couch cushions, something he never does and probably only did because he is still feeling effects of the drugs, and he fell. He fell on the soft cushion of the couch and landed on his wound. He screamed. I have never heard Teddy make those noises before. Such excruciating pain. He wailed and wailed and stayed motionless on the couch. I texted my vet friend and she called me. She could hear Teddy screeching in the background. She and her husband were at a Halloween party, but she told us to bring Teddy to the vet hospital and they would give him more pain medication. He will stay overnight there and we can get him tomorrow. Ben, a saint, took him for me. I stayed home with Henry sleeping upstairs. This was our Friday night.

CARING BRIDGE | November 1

Cosette had a good week. She is doing well on the decrease of help from the ventilator. We would like to see her gain weight more quickly and the doctors will be revisiting that topic on Monday. We got to enjoy a nice snuggle today.

Even though she's stable, each week is full of emotion. This week happened to have the added event of my cat getting surgery. As a friend put it, lots of things are demanding my love. At the hospital, it has been difficult to have so many different nurses, almost a new one every day, because they aren't familiar with Cosette and sometimes do not make her as comfortable as I know she can be. The work of trying to soothe her through asking someone else to make a change for her can be heart wrenching. Someday I will get to care for her directly. We have been told that she will have a consistent care team in place soon since she has been there for a month and has more to go. It is hard to think about this NICU journey only being one fourth of the way done, but as always, the next thought is I am grateful we get to have a journey at all.

CARING BRIDGE | November 2

Cosette's ventilator was changed today to a different one, the one she started on originally, which is a great step toward breathing on her own. This vent allows her to take breaths and helps her along in a more natural way, whereas the other one gave her about 900 breaths per minute in short puffs. It was a very happy moment when the doctor said she was ready to make the switch. They will watch her carefully to make sure she is doing okay with the adjustment, but so far today she did well. She has gained some weight too; she's 2.3 lbs. One of my favorite times of day (and I think hers too) is when I give her milk on a tiny sponge. Each day she clamps down on it with more might and sticks her tiny tongue out to indicate she wants more. I hope that these are signs that she will be a good nurser in the future.

BABY JOURNAL | November 2

You had your first Halloween. We put a pumpkin hat on you and I got to hold you. You're getting bigger, and it feels easier to pick you up and hold you. You have a lot of blonde hair, too. I am sitting by you now and you're laying on your belly. You are so, so cute. We are here every day for you. This week was hard because our cat Teddy had to lose his leg. He'll be better by the time you come home, though. I'm prepping your space for you and thinking about taking walks with you. It will be so nice to wear you against my chest in a wrap. My dear baby. We're going to be a family.

Monday, November 4

I am in my last week of maternity leave. The people at work have been so kind to me. I will be working Mondays, Wednesdays, and Fridays until Cosette comes home. Tuesdays and Thursdays are covered by the substitute who has been there during the past six weeks. He was supposed to be my sub from January through April but was able to step in early in October. I'll never know all of the effort that went into making things run smoothly at school while I have been at the hospital every day. I think that's the way it needed to be.

I am here with Cosette. We would be 29 weeks today. Ruth is recommending I keep talking to Cosette as if she is still inside me, kind of like what the cranial sacral therapist told me early on. I feel very close to Cosette but that also makes it hard to see her struggling. I am looking forward to her being removed from the ventilator. They have weaned her but are stopping that today to give her a rest. I do not want to rush anything with her, but I want that tube out more than anything. It looks so uncomfortable. A nurse warned me that after the breathing tube is gone, the next step to assist breathing will hide Cosette's face more than the tube. She said sometimes parents are disappointed by that. I cannot imagine anything being worse than this.

Every so often I worry about what comes next after we go home. Will she have vision problems? Brain issues? Continued lung problems? Some premature babies leave the hospital still on oxygen. I think about it and then the thoughts fade and don't return for days. It is not worth worrying about right now. She'll be my girl no matter what.

Teddy was more calm yesterday and this morning. They gave him more drugs. He's been sleeping on a mattress on the floor in Cosette's future room.

Ben and I are doing okay. Life has changed in a striking way but normalcy has even found us in this period. I imagine time might move faster once I am back to work. I'm dreading not driving directly to the hospital every day, but I have always known I would need to go back to work before she came home, and if that is happening, it means time is moving along. I feel like this NICU segment of my life will be held onto in an odd way, that I may feel an attachment to the trauma. I think I may be a very anxious parent because of this. I will need to work on that. Or maybe small things that would have bothered me won't because we've had this giant, overarching challenge that trumps all others.

BABY JOURNAL | November 6

You are getting your breathing tube taken out tomorrow! We're so excited. You changed to a different ventilator yesterday and are ready for no vent that quickly. I'm so proud of you. I am going to hear you cry! I cried when the doctors said you could be extubated tomorrow. My little girl! Today when I was holding you I felt you poop. My hand was against your diaper. It was very funny.

Thursday, November 7

She is getting extubated today! I cried because I was so happy and surprised when they told me. Please have this go well. We are also moving pods which is exciting. Moving away from B-pod is a significant step. She doesn't need as intense care and maybe we can have more privacy. Today is a major victory. I have been waiting for this for weeks and weeks.

CARING BRIDGE | November 7

Cosette was taken off her ventilator today! She is now on non-invasive ventilation and has prongs in her nose. She has to wear a small elf stocking cap and a contraption around her chin and lip to keep it in place, but she no longer has anything down her throat. When the medical team told me yesterday that it could happen today, I cried my first tears of joy since her birth. And more today when it was taken out. I have known that she really hated that tube and it is a relief to know she does not have to resist it any longer. She's still going to be uncomfortable at times, but it won't compare. She did well for the rest of today on the new breathing assistance, but they will know for sure after 72 hours of watching her and doing lab work. There is a chance she will have to be intubated again, but her response today did not indicate that is needed. We will hope. We're moving through the stages. One step closer to home.

Friday, November 8

The new pod is much nicer. Our spot is so roomy compared to where we were before. The extubation went well and it was a very joyful day. I am so glad this all happened before I had to go back to work and before Mom leaves for a few weeks. She and I were both there by Cosette's side for the big moment. The RT said "One, two, three," and then he pulled the tube out. The tube was shorter than I expected and the whole process was fast, but there were many people on hand in case help was needed. Yesterday and today have been very stressful because they are watching her closely to see how she reacts to the decrease in breathing assistance. They did a few x-rays and so far they look good. But I'm holding my breath, a lot. Even though she has been fine for 24 hours, it does not mean she is in the clear. Just like with her first vent, she did well on it until she didn't. Until she tired out. That could be happening to her right now. All I can do is sit by her and do her cares every three hours and pump and listen to what the doctors tell me.

BABY JOURNAL | November 9

You did so well getting your tube out. You seem more comfortable. You have to wear a head apparatus but it's got to be better. You're breathing mostly on your own now. I'm very proud of you. We moved to a new pod, too. It's bigger and quieter. Changes feel good. We're moving on up. You weigh 2.4 lb now. You'll keep gaining and we'll get you strong. You are already very strong. I love you!

CARING BRIDGE | November 10

Today was the longest and one of the hardest days we've had yet. I return to work tomorrow. Please think of us, pray for us. Our little girl is strong. Send her even more strength.

Monday, November 11

Cosette had an apnea episode yesterday that lasted 75 seconds. So long. We all stood there waiting for her to start breathing again. The nurse had to flick Cosette's tiny heels and rub her chest hard, stimulating her brain to do the work of breathing. It was terrifying. It was like we were watching her die. But she didn't die. Her feeding tube was also in the wrong place, which was discovered on Sunday morning when I was there. The feeding tube is how she exhales air when she is not eating. So since it was too high up, she was not able to breathe correctly. Someone put it in wrong. An x-ray showed it way up her throat instead of down by her stomach. It also means food could have gone to her throat instead of down further. The new pod is so much nicer but now my memory for this spot is standing by her isolette watching the red numbers flash.

Going to work today after all of that was very rough. I hardly slept last night. I stayed at the hospital until 8 p.m. and was wound up when I got home. I texted a friend at work in the morning to tell her that yesterday was really hard and asked her to spread the word to others to not ask me about Cosette because I might start crying. I ended up not seeing many other adults. The kids were very excited that I was there. David helped them make cards to put on my desk that all stood up and spelled out *We're glad you're back* on one side. They drew cute pictures on the other side. I felt embarrassed to be there going through this huge life event while knowing I didn't really want to be there but had to be. But I also started to feel like my old self with them. There was also a small sense of guilt for enjoying it. A thought came to me today that having work and colleagues with whom to connect will make it less bad if Cosette doesn't make it. We feel far from that happening now, but I still think about it. I could still have a purpose in life with my job if she never leaves the hospital.

When I called for an update during my lunch break, Cosette's nurse said she had more apnea events, and she wouldn't be surprised if Cosette was intubated again by the end of the day. It was an awful thing to say to me over the phone. I had never met this nurse before and was not looking forward to it. I sat in the closet of my classroom, pumping and crying.

CARING BRIDGE | November 12

Thank you so much for all of the comments and love you sent our way. Sunday and yesterday were very difficult days, but today was better. I thought things would feel easier after Cosette was extubated and so it was especially hard to not have that be the case. On Sunday when I arrived at the hospital, her nurse and I discovered that Cosette's feeding tube was half the length it should be. Someone had taped it to reach the back of her throat instead of her stomach. No one could tell how long it had been that way. Her belly filled with air because she vents out air, or sort of exhales, through her feeding tube when she is not eating. But a distended belly can also mean infection or that she was not doing well without a breathing tube, so there were a lot of distressing questions floating around. On top of that, she had several apnea episodes, which means she stopped breathing and her heart rate plummeted. We witnessed one of these on Sunday afternoon that lasted for an excruciating length of time. When these events happen, the nurses stimulate her and suction her mouth and throat. Since Sunday, they have learned she mostly has these episodes when she needs to be suctioned. She did not have any today while I was there. In fact, I got to hold her for two hours which was very nice. The medical team feels that she is doing well on her non-invasive ventilation and just doing well overall. It was heartening to hear after a few days of uncertainty. It does not mean the message won't be different tomorrow, but we had today.

They're also increasing the volume of her feedings because she hasn't gained weight in the past week and a half. Some of that has to do with getting extubated, and she had to miss a feeding to get another blood transfusion on Sunday night. Please think pudgy, fattening thoughts for her. As she gets bigger, she'll make more lung tissue and will be able to breathe more easily.

The apparatus she wears now to keep prongs in her nose covers most of her face and head. Sometimes it makes her eyes swollen and puffy. It's hard to not see as much of her and she still pulls at it like the tube, but I know she is more comfortable. Our main hope this week is multiple days when no one suggests she needs to be reintubated.

Going to work was difficult on the heels of Sunday and little sleep, but my students were happy to see me and very sweet. I am working Mondays, Wednesdays, and Fridays until Cosette comes home, which I can manage due to a generous donation of sick days from my colleagues. I saw today how crucial it is to have that time with her. I knew it was important, but I felt it deeply today.

BABY JOURNAL | November 12

I got to hold you today. It was very nice. I got very warm because you're so toasty. You made a giant poop in your diaper while I was holding you. We had a few hard days adjusting to the new way of breathing but today you are doing great. I am so proud of you. Your doctors say you are a star and should set an example for other premature babies. All of your nurses like you a lot and fawn over how cute you are. My precious Cosette.

Thursday, November 14

Today our pastor visited me and Cosette. It was nice to sit with him in the bigger pod spot. I told him how Ben said he feels like sitting by Cosette can be a spiritual experience, like seeing life restored and coming forth from the tomb. And I said I don't feel that way. I am not angry at God, but I don't feel much of anything. I just don't think about it like that. Ben's mother said early on she believed Cosette was going to be okay. She prays a lot. I want to believe her. Our pastor said it does not matter that I don't feel anything. He said this is the time to let others hold me. It is great that Ben can fall back on his faith, but I should not feel guilty or flawed for not feeling that way. He reminded me that this is all harder on me than it is on Cosette. I like thinking about how she will never remember any of this.

Saturday, November 16

Mom left today to visit my sister's family. I am glad she is making the trip and getting some time away from here. She cried saying bye to Cosette. I did a little too. Cosette is doing well but she is on breathing support so of course there is always a chance something could change. I felt in those tears the fear of Cosette dying while she is away. Mom has visited almost every day. She knits and crochets while she sits by the baby. Nurses and doctors and chaplains comment on what she's making. She will be away for two and a half weeks. The biggest change here at the hospital for me will be that no one will sit by me while I am holding Cosette. Mom would try to be here when I was holding her in case I needed water or if something happened and I wanted her to get a nurse. Now it will just be me. It will be scary at first, but I will get used to it just like everything else.

Sunday, November 17

Things at the hospital are always so busy. I have spent the day here, seven hours now, and they fly by. I held Cosette for two hours which was great.

She was very calm. We just need her to get bigger. The apnea events have decreased since last weekend, but they still happen often. A very scary alarm triggers and her numbers on the screen turn red and flash. Sometimes they jump right back on their own, but other times she must be stimulated to start breathing again. They say this is a trait of her prematurity and it's all about the brain. Her brain will learn how to do this consistently on its own and not take little rests where it totally stops. At this point, with these breathless events happening many times a day, I cannot imagine her coming home. She has taken caffeine since she was born to keep her brain alert and remembering to function. The wean from caffeine happens around 36-38 weeks, which is when the brain is supposed to know how to take care on its own. I hate thinking about her being on caffeine. It is the opposite of a healthy, natural birth. I only need to look around to remind myself we are very far away from any of that. Here we're in survival mode.

I am allowed to hold Cosette every day now. The new spot in H-pod has made holding her feel more private. I also get a little scared to do it alone because there is a curtain around me and it feels like I need to yell to get someone's attention. In B-pod we were constantly surrounded by people. The curtain is also odd because it means I can pump by her bed, and yet it's flimsy and doesn't quite reach the wall. When the lactation consultant is around, she brings me a pump or sometimes I use a cordless one that Mary bought for me. It was a very expensive and generous gift. It can be difficult to use, but it has been helpful when I am worried about missing rounds if I go to the pump room or after work when the last thing I want to do is leave Cosette. We have a big spot, but it's in a walk-through area for staff. People are constantly walking by. But I have no modesty in this place. I am on the path of least resistance.

A few times Cosette has cried while I am holding her, which is hard because I'm still getting used to hearing her cry. At first her voice was scratchy from the intubation, but now she really cries. One time she had junk in her throat which was why she was crying. She's my baby. I love her so much. She is almost 2.5 lb. The weight gain is coming slowly.

BABY JOURNAL | November 17

You are seven weeks old today. I would have been 31 weeks pregnant tomorrow. You are doing really well. Breathing is getting easier for you. Now you just need to get bigger! They are giving you more of my milk now. I spent the weekend with you because Dad and Henry are away, and Mom Mom left yesterday to see your cousins. It is very nice to hold you for two hours and have you snuggle against me.

Cosette is seven weeks old today. She will be 31 weeks corrected tomorrow. Yesterday the doctor moved her from the ICU group to the ICN (intensive care nursery). This won't mean changes in her care, but she shifted to this label because she is stable. That is always a good word to hear. Last week we moved physical spaces within the NICU. Cosette was transferred from the most active pod to one that is quieter. We no longer have days spent with bright, overhead lights on during bedside surgical procedures. We have more space to sit too, and there is a curtain which offers a small feeling of privacy. It has been a big improvement, and I'm grateful Cosette does not have to listen to as many alarms.

Cosette is doing better with her breathing and having fewer apnea events. Although I miss seeing her face and head (when they take the little hat off once a day she has so much blonde hair!), her NIPPV (non-invasive positive pressure ventilation) system makes it much easier to get her out of her isolette to hold her. It now takes one or two people to help move her versus four. So I have been holding her every day. There are still issues that arise which make her uncomfortable and affect her oxygen intake and heart rate, but I've gotten more used to things happening and it being okay after. It is really important to me to not feel scared of holding her. This week her medical team will discuss moving her to CPAP (continuous positive airway pressure) which is a step closer to breathing on her own. It will still involve the same headgear, just no reminders to her to breathe. Cosette is doing well on getting enough oxygen; her weakness is with opening and closing her lungs. As a premature baby, she did not have surfactant in her lungs yet. She was given doses of it when first admitted, and the ventilators put pressure into her lungs to make sure they open and close correctly. The bigger she gets, the better her lungs will be able to do this on their own. That's why gaining weight is so important. The volume of her feeds has increased; we're still waiting for her to gain weight more steadily.

Going back to school was fine last week. I am able to focus on work when I am there and feel fairly normal with the kids. On the days I work, I am beyond exhausted by 8 p.m. when I get home after visiting the hospital. One of the hardest parts is fitting in seven times to pump throughout the day. I have to freeze all of my milk at home now because I filled my allotted space in the hospital freezer. It's hard to stay inspired and watch my home freezer fill with milk. I question if she will consume it before it expires. When it all feels like too much, I remind myself this routine is not permanent. This is a stage and already within this stage there has been so much change. Cosette and I are both very different than we were six weeks ago, three weeks ago, a week ago.

We have a lot to be grateful for. A few nights ago, I was putting a few pictures in Cosette's baby book and thinking about her looking at it years from now. I feel and hope that a theme of her life, of our life together, will be gratitude.

Monday, November 18

They tried her on CPAP today, but she did not like it. I learned this bad news during my lunch break. I cried in the closet, again. The attending on Friday said they might try it on Monday, but the doctor over the weekend said she thought it was too soon. I hoped that message would get through to the weekday team but it did not. Ben and I both weren't there when they tried her on CPAP. On the phone, the nurse said she was on it for less than a few minutes because she started to crash immediately. I hate that this happened to her, especially when we were not there. They put her back on NIPPV right away.

We are going to move holding her to every other day to see if it helps her gain weight. That's her big goal now. Last week I held her every day, rushing in after work to pump and then hold her. I read that babies who are born at four pounds between 36 and 40 weeks can go home. That's so small. I hope I feel prepared when it's time to take her.

Cosette has had some really great nurses in H-pod. There are three who are good friends and have worked in the NICU for a long time. One is very funny and she says the most outrageous things. She makes me laugh hard which is unusual these days. Another, Liza, is someone to whom other nurses come for advice. That makes me feel really good, like she is an expert and knows exactly what is right for Cosette. She has a lot of opinions about what is good for Cosette and gives her loads of attention. She told me yesterday that Cosette can wear clothes soon. She must be able to regulate her body temperature on her own first. They'll stop heating her isolette and see what she does. She cannot expend energy keeping up her body temperature because she needs those calories for weight gain. If she is able to do it without too much effort, then the next step will be an open crib. That sounds so wild to me, having her out in the open. Only babies under a certain weight are in isolettes in the NICU. Term babies who go there are in open beds. If they do not require oxygen help, then they're in a bassinet. Cosette will never be in a bassinet while here. Once she's off oxygen, she will be going home or else she'll go home with an oxygen tank. It is scary to imagine her sleeping in the pod exposed to ordinary air and hearing everything going on in the room, all the conversation and alarms. She appears safer in her isolette.

Of course last night I went home and bought her clothes. It felt strange to put *premature baby clothes* in the search bar. A short time ago, I was searching for organic baby clothes for 3-6 month babies because my family typically only has very large babies at eight pounds or larger who are too big for the newborn size. And now I was looking for clothes that would fit a baby under five pounds. There are not many, but I picked out a few. Nothing organic. That feels point-less now that she's had all of the drugs and sleeps wrapped in blankets that are washed in hospital soap.

Liza said that Cosette is over the hump. She would not say that if she did not strongly believe it. She is going to be okay. I am letting myself trust that now, finally.

I felt good and smiley at school today. Maybe life can be normal again in some ways while this is still going on at the hospital. A parent has been making me delicious lunches. It means one less thing I have to think about at home, and I am always very hungry when it's time to eat. I need to eat well for pump-ing. People are so kind.

Tuesday, November 19

Cosette had more apnea episodes today. They say it could be from the stress of trying CPAP yesterday. I'm not supposed to hold her as much. Last night, she had so many events. I think they said 25. I asked if they would consider intu-bating her again at this point and the answer was no. A cranial sacral therapist came to see Cosette today. I hoped she would be able to look at her and say pos-itive things or help her with some cranial sacral work. When she arrived, I was holding Cosette. I knew I didn't have long because of what happened the night before and because she would need her drops soon for her eye appointment.

But what I didn't know is that they were going to come to take an x-ray of her lungs because of all of the events. The therapist came and then moments later the tech arrived with the portable x-ray machine.

I started to cry. "It wasn't long enough," I said, holding Cosette more tightly, knowing it would probably be a few days until I could hold her again.

Cosette's face contorted in a cry and she whined.

The nurse said, "See, you're upsetting her. She can tell you're upset."

I put Cosette back in her bed and we both stopped crying. I swallowed it down.

The cranial therapist said, "I don't agree with what that nurse said. It's okay for Cosette to know you're upset. She's going to learn all sorts of emotions. Feel what you feel."

I know she's right and it was good to have someone there who is not a part of the NICU world. The rest of the day was very hard. The eye exams are terrible. Cosette screams and writhes while one nurse holds her down. The ophthalmologist pries open Cosette's eyelids with an instrument and then shines a very bright light into her eyes. The drops they give numb her eyes so it doesn't hurt, and they say she is only screaming like that because of the bright light and not wanting to be constrained, but it looks like torture. When it looks like and sounds like torture, it is hard to believe it is all okay. I worry these eye exams will imprint traumatic scars on her body for a long time. I haven't felt that way about other things that have happened here; I feel like she may just not remember any of that, but the eyes, it is different.

I have started calling the NICU in the morning before night shift ends to talk to the nurse about the night. We also call around 9 p.m., but they don't know much then, and I have often left the hospital only an hour or so before that. Sometimes Ben and I will be watching television, and I'll get tired and just want to go to sleep, but then my brain switches into call NICU mode. I escape for a little while, but then very much want and need to be in the world where she's sleeping in her isolette fifteen miles away.

CARING BRIDGE | November 20

Today is Cosette's 56th day in the NICU. It is also two months to her due date. We might be halfway through with our time in the hospital, but there's really no way to know. She could come home before then or possibly after. Acknowledging that we've made it halfway is uplifting, but a simultaneous thought is: "It's only halfway?"

She has gained weight this week and is 2.7lbs. It is difficult to imagine bringing her home right now because she is so small. Yet as I bond with her more and more, it gets easier and feels more urgent to have her with me as much as possible. I held her today for almost three hours, our longest time yet. We're both more relaxed which makes it possible for me to sit still for so long. We've built stamina. I tell her about our family, her relatives, our house, pets, what her room will look like, and what kinds of things we will do when she comes home. I tell her about all of her pretty clothes that people have bought for her or her Mom Mom has sewn and how I will carry her on me as much as I can when she's home with us. I sing to her and make up lyrics to songs. She seems to like that a lot.

They tried to move her to CPAP on Monday, but she didn't respond well to it. After five minutes, she was back on NIPPV. Unfortunately, that weaning caused her to have a scary number of apnea events that night. They returned her settings to where they had been when she was originally extubated and may try to wean her again this coming Monday. Hopefully a week of gaining weight and strengthening will have helped her. She had her first eye exam on Tuesday. So far her eyes look fine, but it's really too early to see damage. She will have an exam every Tuesday now. Premature babies are at high risk for retinal damage so it is something they watch closely. Our main health focuses for Cosette are gaining weight, lungs that can open and close well without the help of a machine, positive growth of capillaries in her eyes, and resistance to all infection. As always, thank you for thinking of our baby girl.

Thursday, November 21

Ben has a cold. He cannot visit Cosette until he stops sneezing and coughing. After those symptoms subside, he will need to wear a mask and won't be able to touch her. It's unfortunate this happened while my mom is away because now no one will be with Cosette during the day while I am at work. It's just Friday and Monday and Tuesday because of Thanksgiving. Hopefully Ben will be better by then. I am terrified of getting sick myself because then Cosette would have no visitors. I am extremely careful to wash my hands and use hand sanitizer constantly at work. I use alcohol wipes on all of the door handles, sink faucets, dry erase markers, and light switches in my classroom as soon as I arrive. I wipe the keyboard of my computer and even do some surfaces in David's classroom. Overall, the students have been healthier this fall, which might have something to do with these protocols I put in place. If we are sitting in a circle on the floor and a kid coughs, I hold my breath. I am taking many preventative vitamins and herbs and Ben is sleeping on the couch.

Saturday, November 23

I am so tired after work when I get to the hospital, but I want to give Cosette lots of attention.

Usually when I arrive I have to pump because it's been since noon when I did it last. If I go to the pump room, I put my head back and close my eyes. Sometimes friends text me. Ashley, Mary, and others. A friend I made through my Waldorf school trips has consistently checked in. He says wise things. I feel honored that he wants to text me and send me encouragement. He's someone who makes me feel like I'm doing something right with my life and my personality because he wants to know me well. He and I were in touch a lot when one of my students was ill. It has been a year now since she died. I think of her often. She must be an angel now. When a thought about her pops into my head, I sometimes tell her mom because it means she is still very present.

BABY JOURNAL | November 23

We're moving right along. Eight weeks tomorrow, 32 weeks on Monday. You gained weight this week and are almost breathing room air. You just need help opening and closing your lungs. I held you on Thursday for almost three hours. It was great. When I sang to you, you calmed down right away. I love you, little one.

Tuesday, November 26

The Thanksgiving program was held today at school. It's the biggest choral production of the year. The kids sing songs, parents and grandparents come to watch, and then everyone departs for vacation from the assembly. Last year was my first one at this school and at the end many of the kids and parents crowded around the teacher I had replaced because he was back to watch. A friend noticed me standing by myself and came to talk to me. We said a few things about the upcoming break and then laughed as we quickly departed from the room without anyone noticing, trying to focus on the positive part of being somewhat invisible.

This year I was very emotional before the program even began. It was hard to be at work two days in a row. I expected to be at the hospital in time for Cosette's eye exam but being at work two consecutive mornings was more difficult than I anticipated.

My students gathered in the kitchen that opens into the assembly room. They stood eagerly waiting for their turn to go on stage. The preschool children were singing. I could not see them but hearing was enough to melt me. I started to cry big, painful tears. I turned away so the kids couldn't see. Finally that ended and my students filed on stage. I leaned against the sink, not visible to anyone in the assembly room, and stared at the posters on the wall. I couldn't stop crying though. When I thought I had it under control, my face would scrunch again. My friend saw and came to stand next to me. She put her arm around me.

"Do you want to leave?" she whispered.

"No," I shook my head. "I just want to stand here."

She nodded.

"You can go in," I said. "Go watch."

"No," she said, "I want to stand here."

She stood next to me for the next fifteen minutes as we listened to the kids sing their songs, some happy and some melancholy. I stopped crying and felt worn out.

She said, "You should go before it ends so you can get ahead of the crowd."

She was right. I did want to do that. I couldn't see anyone right now. "Will you tell David?" I asked. "Tell him I was upset, too. Don't just say I left early."

"Got it. Don't worry." She squeezed my hand.

"Thank you."

"I'm making a huge Thanksgiving dinner on Thursday and there's no way we will eat all of it. Can I bring you some at the hospital?"

"Really?" I looked at her and smiled. Her sweetness broke through my sorrow.

"Yes. Okay, I'm doing that."

We hugged and I left. I walked across the parking lot toward my car which was parked down the street to make space for parent cars. I kept my head down and walked fast. To my baby I went. Someday she might be singing on a stage like that. She will stand by her classmates and no one will ever know how painful the beginning of her life was, how unlucky she was. She will sing in a sweet little girl voice, and I will cry for all of the right reasons.

CARING BRIDGE POST | November 27

Cosette will be two months old on Friday. There haven't been any changes with her health this week. After declining a bit after the CPAP trial, they're letting her rest and grow without pushing forward. She passed the three pound mark, but a lot is liquid weight because she started retaining water after having lung distress. They decreased the volume of her feedings to help with that and we hope her puffiness will decline as the week goes forward. We are enjoying long holds and hearing about the changes that will start happening for her as she is now 32 weeks adjusted.

Friday, November 29

Thanksgiving was yesterday. I went to the hospital in the morning and the nurse who always manages to make me laugh was Cosette's nurse for the day, which was a treat. A night nurse made her a *My first Thanksgiving* turkey sign. It's sweet, but again like Halloween, this is not really her first. Her first will be next year with us at home.

We were supposed to meet friends in the afternoon for a special lunch. I wanted to be back in time to hold Cosette when she got fed at 3 p.m. She gets fed every three hours, and I can't move her to hold her while she is being fed through her feeding tube because it can cause her to reflux and that causes dips in her breathing. So my option was holding her at noon or at 3. Some days I hold her at 6 p.m. after work.

But the lunch plan fell through because we drove to a historic tavern place that Ben wanted to go to and it was very crowded. Line out the door. They said it would be an hour wait. There was no way I could make it back by 3 p.m. So we went to the grocery store and got food from the hot bar and took it to our friends' apartment. It was fine, nothing special, but I wasn't really looking for special. I'm looking to spend time with Cosette, hold her as much as possible on my non-work days, and get through this. I would like a pass to not care about much else but Cosette right now. She's my world. Ruth encourages me to connect to nature, go on a wander in the woods, and try to have some in the present moments with Ben. I know she is right.

UVa beat Virginia Tech today in football. It was a huge deal. Nurses were watching it on the computer in Cosette's pod. I could hear the last few minutes of the game and felt excited too. It was a rare moment of camaraderie and feeling like a normal person amongst them.

Ben came to the hospital after he dropped off Henry with his mom. When it got late, Ben texted my friend from work and asked if they still had leftovers. She was excited to hear from us. We drove to their apartment down the street from the hospital and they came outside with bags of food. She and her boyfriend were so bubbly and happy to see us and it made me feel that way too, even if briefly. We don't know them that well and have not gotten to spend much time together outside of work, but they seem like such fun people. I hope when all of this is over we can hang out with them. When Cosette is ready for Mom to babysit, they are at the top of my list for socializing.

Now it's the day after Thanksgiving and Cosette is two months old. She looks good. Very pink and less swollen. Ben held her today which was nice to see. She looks comfortable as I sit by her and write. Liza told me about something that I'm going to start doing. There are small cut out fleece hearts that I can put in my bra and wear around all day. Then I take it out and put it with Cosette so that she can smell me. She has one too, and I take that and carry it and we keep swapping.

I am tired. I'll go home soon and eat and workout, then pump. Always pumping.

BABY JOURNAL | November 29

Dear baby, you're two months old today! I'm so proud of you for being strong and doing so well. We've had many long snuggles over the past week. Up to three hours at a time! You seem to really like it. You only need room air now but still require help opening and closing your lungs. We'll get there. A girl who is twelve years old came into the hospital yesterday. She was born at 23 weeks and three days, two days younger than you. She seemed great. She was coming there to be grateful on Thanksgiving day. Maybe we'll do that together on a holiday. I love thinking about our future together. Right now is okay too because you seem more content and less uncomfortable. Keep growing my dear and I love you!

CARING BRIDGE POST | December 1

Cosette seems to have successfully transferred to CPAP (a type of breathing support) which is a big accomplishment. She failed a test on it two weeks ago, but yesterday she was more ready. She gained weight in those two weeks (now 3 lbs 6 oz) and has come down a lot on how much oxygen she requires. She did well overnight on it and was staying strong today. She doesn't appear to be laboring to breathe on the new mode of support, but they will lower the pressure of air she is receiving tomorrow; hopefully she will remain fine on that decrease. The hat and mustache are still a part of CPAP so no relief from that yet, but this is a step toward wearing just a nasal support of oxygen that will get taped to her cheek. She is so handsy, always wanting to pull at everything on her. I do hope she can leave the support on her cheek when the time comes so that she can have her hands free and by her face which comforts her. Today when I arrived, she was wrapped in a small sleep sack instead of just swaddled in a blanket. It was light green so she truly looked like a sweet pea in a pod. It felt funny to unsnap the buttons since I've only ever known her to be in a diaper.

Yesterday when the doctor was deciding if it was a good day to try CPAP again, she asked me what I thought. I said I knew she was getting stronger and passing the 1500 gram mark which would probably mean trying again. It was a conversation I have been thinking about a lot. Even though I am well into adulthood, sometimes I still catch myself feeling like other adults are more of an adult than me. Like when did that crossover happen? There have been interviews in front of a roomful of parents whose kids I would teach for five years, losing loved ones, buying houses, getting married, and yet that moment of asking me what I thought should be done next for my baby and having an answer. It felt like something new.

Standing alone making decisions for a baby's lung health is an experience I wish for no one. I am finding it more and more difficult to genuinely interact with people. When I smile that is real but answering the question *How are you?*. . . It is very hard for me to verbalize how I am. And really I don't think many want to know the truth nor do I have the energy to give it. Today Cosette stopped breathing while I was holding her because the tube of her machine got disconnected somehow. She wasn't getting air and her nose was stuffed with prongs, so she couldn't breathe through those either. She just had her mouth open silent. It took a while for a nurse to come over. At the end of the hold, she coughed up her feeding tube and I held her arms down and tried to soothe her while a new one was put down her throat and she wailed. A few other things happened too, but that's enough to show my Sunday is not typical. I power through, no tears today through all of that, but as I step away from her, I feel the ripples of shock that I absorb in the moment. Not every day is like this, but more than half are. I think more than anything I want to be accepted as abnormal. There is nothing normal about this experience and I know it doesn't end when she gets discharged; there will be a lot that comes when she is home too as a small baby who spent four months in the NICU. But the highlight of my day is holding her and looking into her eyes, and those moments will continue to drive me. I know all of the hard work is worth it, of course, but I also need to be good for her when she comes home, so I am trying to figure out how to do it all.

Monday, December 2

While I was at work today, Ben sent me a photo of Cosette wearing clothes. Her first outfit! Liza decided it was time. It was a gray onesie with little, colorful gumdrop circles on it. She looked so adorable, sleeping with her CPAP mustache and holding a pacifier to her lips. She loves her pacifier these days. She can't always hold it in well, though, so sometimes I stand for a very long time holding it in her mouth. Some nights I feel like I can't leave until she is asleep and the pacifier helps with that so I'll lean over her isolette for an hour holding in that thing. Anyway, first day of wearing clothes! I was very excited to get to her after work and see for myself.

Liza is so wonderful and has signed up to be Cosette's primary nurse. We found out that nurses weren't signing up for Cosette because she is too easy of a case. They like to have more medical procedures to do to stay busy and use their skills. It's understandable, but I'm relieved there are also nurses like Liza who want to help a baby and her family get to the finish line in the best way possible. It is very comforting to know that she will be taking care of Cosette a few days a week from now on. Being away from the hospital is more tolerable when I know Liza is there. She also calmed me down about the apnea episodes. No one is threatening re-intubation these days so I am just trying to get more used to it. She dips, the alarm sounds, she comes back up. It's going to happen. I try not to watch the screen when I am holding her in order to anticipate when they are going to happen because there's not much I can do to interfere. I close my eyes, I sing to her, I talk to her about Lyle and Teddy and her bedroom. I often think about me and her sitting on a blanket by the reservoir near our house and looking at the clouds. We pick out animal shapes and giggle.

I asked Mom to make a chain of Christmas fabric rings for the month of December. We had a tradition of doing this at our house growing up. At the beginning of the month, it hung from the knob at the bottom of the stairs and spiraled up the railing. It got shorter and shorter as excitement for winter break increased. I have hung the one Mom made for Cosette near her isolette. I will take off a ring every day, counting us down to Christmas. I'm not really trying to make Christmas special for her, she doesn't know what is happening on that level, but the idea of visually seeing the month get smaller feels good. Once December is over, it's January and that might be her last month in the hospital.

Ben goes to the hospital in the mornings as often as he can. Sometimes he goes after work too because he can only stay for a short period of time. It's a lot of driving and parking and elevators. We connect every night around 9 p.m. when we call the NICU. One of three receptionists picks up, and I say, "Hi, I'm calling for an update on my daughter, Cosette Fraser-Morris." And the voice on the other end says, "Yes. Baby ID?" And then I recite the six digit number that I have memorized. Ben says it so fast now when he calls that I think sometimes they have trouble following him. I picture them looking up her name in the big binder of babies and then looking over at the ID to see if it lines up. We call every night but they always pause and look it up. I think that's fine. I like that they are being careful.

"One moment please," she says. Then we hear a pulsing tone that can sometimes last for many minutes. Occasionally we need to hang up and call again because the line discontinues or it seems like we've been forgotten. Sometimes we get connected and the nurse will say it's the wrong pod and send us back to the receptionist. Unless it's been a bad day, I usually just want to know who is with her overnight and connect with them briefly. Who is caring for my baby when I can't? Is she comfortable, fed, warm? We talk to the nurse and then I will myself to sleep and pass the time until I can go back to the hospital.

Tuesday, December 3

Today was a hard day. It's a Tuesday which means I spent the day in the hospital. I arrived at 9 a.m. after pumping and doing all the things at home I need to do that have slipped to the side since I am never there. Liza was Cosette's nurse. Tuesdays are eye doctor days, which is always bad, but it's better to be there for it than not. I cannot hold her after she's had the exam because she's more likely to drop her vitals due to the stress of it. So I held her with her noon feed and hoped the doctor would not come until close to 3 p.m. He was in the pod at 2 p.m. so I put her back. Liza tried to distract me while the exam was happening, but I still cried. I cry at all of them. The doctor is very kind and I trust him. He seemed to look at her longer this time. I shifted my weight back and forth on my feet and grabbed at my fingers.

When he was done he pulled his goggles down and looked straight at me. "There has been a lot of growth here, not the good kind. She has a massive amount of ROP that has appeared in just the week since I last saw her. We need to get in there fast and stop the growth of those vessels. All of this retinal development was supposed to happen in the womb and because it's happening out here instead it's not going well."

I was crying. I kept looking at him as he talked. He made consistent eye contact and stayed very calm. He would be a good politician. I saw Liza in the background make a gesture that would match the word dammit. She had been trying to distract me but she knew this was a real possibility. More than I did. Cosette has been doing so well and beating all the odds, I figured she would beat this too. In my plan, she would not have anything longlasting wrong with her.

The doctor told me about two options: an injection into the eye or laser surgery. If the injection did not fully work, she would need laser surgery later in addition. Laser surgery right now has a higher risk of doing permanent damage. The obvious choice was the injection.

"I'd like to schedule the procedure for first thing tomorrow morning if that is okay with you. She will need an IV to receive medication to help her body regulate itself during the procedure and also numb her from any pain. The procedure itself is very quick and she will not feel anything, but it is an intense blow to the body. Here is some literature about the procedure that you and your husband can look over tonight."

My thoughts were whirling around in my head. Tomorrow morning I will be at work. I should be here.

BABY JOURNAL | December 3

Here we are in December. Thirty-three weeks. You're nine weeks old. Tomorrow a doctor is going to help your eyes so that you can see well. Your eyes have not been able to form correctly since you're not inside of me. This medicine is supposed to help you. The next day you get your first vaccines. It's a lot this week. You're wearing clothes, too! Little onesies. You look so adorable. I held you in my arms today and was able to look at your face. It was very nice. I love you very much and will take care of you the best I can.

Wednesday, December 4

decided early this morning that I had to be at the hospital for the procedure. It all went fine. Cosette was very tired today but had no other serious reaction. She was supposed to have her first round of vaccines, but they're going to do it tomorrow instead. Yes, please. That is way too much for one day.

I went back after work and sat by her. I hate that she has a PICC line again. Hopefully they will take it out soon because she doesn't need it. When I called the NICU at 5:30 a.m. this morning, the nurse told me that Cosette's bedspot was moved within the pod. I do not like that. She had the best spot in that pod, separate from the others. The thing about H-pod is that it is mostly for older babies, six months and older, who are going to be there for a long time. They are not just there growing like Cosette. They have older baby germs. I heard a boy near her got a flu shot which means he is six months old. Now she is in the middle of all of them. Their parents have brought in stars for the ceiling and other big decorations. The kid right next to her has flashing Christmas lights above his bed. And there was country lullaby music playing for the three hours I was there tonight.

There are thin curtains that don't pull fully around Cosette, so there is less privacy to pump. Her isolette is directly next to the nurse's station. They can pay close attention to her, but it feels like everyone is on top of me. The reason she was moved is because her previous spot has a setup for a special procedure that a baby needed. There was a lot of activity at that old bedspot tonight. One of the main attendings was talking to the parents of the baby and explaining what he was going to do. He did some sort of procedure right there with his white collared shirt on, sleeves rolled up. It was odd to see an attending do anything like that because they're usually advising others and mostly talking and typing on the laptops they wheel around the unit. For some reason, it felt like this family was VIP. After the doctor did the procedure, they took the baby off CPAP and he breathed on his own fairly well. They will probably be gone in a few days and their scary time in the NICU will be a memory and something that felt very long. They may refer to themselves as NICU parents and go to the reunions.

Ben picked up Mom from the airport tonight. He took her to our house. She was supposed to come to the hospital first, but I was exhausted and left before 8 p.m. They sold their house, so no more windy roads in the dark. She's looking for an apartment near us. That will be so much better for helping with Cosette at home. I feel bad that I cannot help her pack, but she understands. All of my time that is not at work is spent at the hospital.

People at school understood about me coming in late this morning and they covered for me at the last minute. I got to school by 10 a.m. Work is generally going okay. I'm not winging it exactly, but I am certainly not prepared in the ways I used to be. I don't think it is affecting the kids at all, more just me feeling a little guilty. Thank goodness for David. I am pumping in the closet during all meal/recess times so I have to close out all of the kids and he watches them. Mood-wise I feel chilly, like I'm a shuttered house experiencing my own personal tornado, dropping in and out of their stable, normal days.

CARING BRIDGE POST | December 5

On Tuesday during Cosette's weekly eye exam, she was diagnosed with retinopathy of prematurity, an eye disease that causes abnormal blood vessels to grow in the retina and can result in blindness. Yesterday she underwent a procedure to reverse ROP. It involved injecting a medicine into her eyes to destroy the bad vessels that had grown. The ophthalmologist will continue to see her every week to track the new growth of healthy blood vessels. In 93% of cases that are given the type of treatment that Cosette received, the ROP does not return. In the remaining percent, it returns most typically in about ten - twenty weeks from now. If that happens, she will get laser surgery and another injection of the medicine. In very few cases, blood vessels do not regrow at all. It was not a difficult decision to make, to get the treatment, because it's her best chance to have vision, but it was still very hard to put her through such a procedure.

I don't feel a constant feeling of guilt anymore as I did in those first weeks, but when the doctor said multiple times that this is because the retina doesn't form well outside of the uterus, it's like being hit in the chest. This setback regarding her eyes was a reminder to me that although she is progressing and is looking bigger and chubbier every day, there are a lot of unknowns about her future health. I understand that everyone's future is unknown, but it feels more fragile with Cosette because she is not starting from the common ground shared by most. Yesterday she was very inactive due to the drugs she received and the stress to her body, which was hard to see after so much recent development. Today she was more active and wore a onesie with a sheep pattern.

She is doing well with her respiratory progress; she's breathing 21% oxygen which is the percentage in room air, so now she is just reliant on air pressure to open and close her lungs. She was weaned slightly on that pressure on Monday and will be again most likely this weekend.

Friday, December 6

One of my favorite nurse practitioners talked to me today about respiratory syncytial virus, known as RSV. It's a very common, very contagious respiratory infection that most babies get before the age of two. In most children, it presents as a common cold. For a baby like Cosette who has lung disease of prematurity, it could be lethal. Premature babies are given a powerful injection once a month during the cold season, October - February, called Synagis, which is supposed to mitigate the severity of their symptoms. The NP gave me a pamphlet about Synagis to take home. I read it and was horrified. It stated multiple times *This is not a vaccine. This does not prevent RSV.* It said the only way to be entirely safe was to not get it. They listed the biggest risks and the first one was having a sibling who is preschool aged. We will need to do everything possible to keep Henry from getting sick.

Sunday, December 8

Tonight I went to a program at church called Lessons and Carols. I thought it was going to be geared toward little kids. I was surprised to find that it was more elegant than a children's program. Candles were lit along the main aisle, casting shadows against the walls and faces of the many people gathered. The choir sang beautiful songs and parishioners read Scripture readings related to Advent and Christmas. The music was so touching. Our friend sang a solo in one that was so poignant it made me cry.

When I arrived at the church, the choir was gathered in the main atrium so I had to walk between them to get into the nave. A lot of our friends are in the choir.

"Karen!" they said with a mixture of surprise and sadness and happiness. They were glad to see me; I haven't disappeared yet.

I sat near the back in my own aisle. Ben was supposed to come after tutoring. He had picked up Henry in the afternoon to start our week together. The end of this week is our one year wedding anniversary, Sunday the 15th. Mom is coming over on Saturday night to put Henry to bed so that Ben and I can go out to dinner. I'm looking forward to that. Ashley got us a gift certificate to a fancy Belgian restaurant.

Sitting alone, I hoped no one else would sit with me. Right before the program began, the mother of the former student who I saw the day I was in labor sat in the aisle behind me. I had not really thought about it until that moment, but I wonder how surprised my student was when she heard I had my baby the day she saw me. I told her I wasn't feeling well, and then I had a critically premature baby. I should write her an email. I did not want to talk to her mom. I knew I would cry. Crying to beautiful singing is one thing but generally crying in a big group of people while speaking, no. I ended up leaving during the last song so that I wouldn't be there when everyone filed out together. I walked back to the hospital parking lot in the dark feeling cold and sad.

CARING BRIDGE POST | December 8

Cosette had a good weekend. She weaned down to the next level on CPAP and is doing well. She's got one more level to go before she can start trials on a small amount of oxygen through her nose. She will be glad to be rid of her CPAP gear. She loves her pacifier and we hope she's strengthening to succeed at some breastfeeding tries later this week. Her temperature wean in her isolette has gone well, too. She's regulating her temperature on her own, so she will be moved to an open crib soon. It will be very strange and wonderful to see her outside of the isolette. I imagine it will be much easier to change her diaper when not reaching my hands through tiny portals.

Monday, December 9

Cosette was moved to an open crib today. Ben sent me a picture while I was at work. She appeared so small in the big bed. Dressed in a pink pajama suit against stark white sheets, she looked so sweet and vulnerable. The day could not move fast enough.

I arrived at the hospital after my workday and was very excited to hold her. There she was in her open crib looking so tiny in her new digs. I could touch her so easily. She is still connected to machines that track her vitals and the air support, so I can't just pick her up. Her nurse today was someone who acts like it is a chore to answer questions. I don't care though. I mean it does not prevent me from doing what I am going to do with Cosette. I told the nurse I wanted to hold Cosette and she said she needed to do something with another baby and then would be over to help me. The baby she went to assist is in isolation which means the nurses have to put on gowns and gloves when they go near the baby. There are many babies in this pod who are like that, at least three of the seven. I think they all have tracheostomy tubes. That is a very scary idea to me. They get those when they have been on breathing support for too long and it's going to wear out their lungs. So they make an incision in the throat and put the breathing tube in there instead. They have to be cleaned, and I've heard nurses teaching the parents how to clean them, too. When I listen to stuff like that it makes me grateful Cosette does not have anything like that and also terrified to have another child in case that one did need something like that.

The nurse took a very long time with the other baby. At 6 p.m. Cosette would start her feeding and I wouldn't be able to move her. I watched the numbers on the clock increase, feeling the tension in my chest rise. I would only get to hold her for an hour at this point. I felt so powerless. Here was my baby, so close, we've been waiting for each other all day, and now I cannot hold her. I started to cry. I turned my back to where the nurse was so she couldn't see. At one point she called over saying she would be there soon. She must have suddenly remembered she told me she would help. My tears were hot and salty against my cheeks. I didn't have any tissues.

Finally, she came over. "You can really start doing this yourself, you know." She could sense I was upset. Was that comment to make herself feel better? Like she wasn't responsible for my pain because I could be doing it without her?

"I can? No one has said anything to me about that."

"You just need to grab all of the wires in one hand, move the vent to this side, and be careful to keep her head still."

I nodded. That was not going to happen tonight. She helped me gather Cosette into my arms and then guided me backwards into the large chair.

"Do you need anything else?" she asked kindly.

"She'll get fed at 6 right?" I choked down more tears at the thought of putting her back so soon.

"Yes. Why don't you just hold her through the feed?"

I looked at the clock. 5:15 p.m. The feeding was given to her over the course of one hour to prevent reflux. Then she needed to stay still for at least thirty minutes more after that. I would need to help her fall asleep after putting her back in bed too. So I'd be home by 9 at the earliest.

"Okay, I'll do that," I said.

She walked away seeming satisfied with this resolution. I looked down at Cosette, my arm already stiff beneath her to make sure her head didn't move, which would cause her nasal prongs to slip out. I had my girl. Everything was okay.

BABY JOURNAL | December 9

You're ten weeks old and 34 weeks corrected! You moved to an open crib today! You're doing very well and are moving up the stages. Clothes and a crib happened very close together. I read books to you today. You could hear me and look at me better. The nurse said you got more alert when I was there. This week we may try breastfeeding, just putting you there and seeing what happens. Next steps are off CPAP and moving to a quieter pod. I am always greedy for the next step of progress to get you more comfortable and closer to home. It is going to happen one of these days. It's hard to leave you there at night. I want you with me always.

CARING BRIDGE POST | December 10

Cosette moved to an open crib yesterday. She is doing well so far in regulating her temperature. Today we removed her CPAP gear and took some pictures. She loves having it off. Her head will get back to a more rounded shape once she does not have to wear the CPAP hat, and her cheeks are red from the adhesive, but she's looking pretty adorable to me.

Thursday, December 12

Cosette moved out of H-pod. I am so relieved. It was getting really bad there. I told her nurse today that I was very eager to move pods.

"Have you told anyone that you want to move?" she asked.

"I have mentioned it to the team in rounds a few times, that I'm worried about all of the stimulation in this pod."

"Yea, your mom was here yesterday during a really terrible day."

Mom had not mentioned anything. She probably didn't want me to worry. Things were calm by the time I got there after work.

"Alarms were going off all day and there were some serious procedures." She raised her eyebrows toward the opposite corner of the room. "The team wouldn't be the ones to instigate a move. You need to tell the charge nurse."

"What about Liza?" I asked. "We'd lose her. She would stay with her other baby in here."

She shrugged. "I think moving may be more important. You'll be more comfortable. I think her other baby is leaving at the end of the year. Then she can join you."

I nodded. It did feel important, even though I loved having the consistency of Liza caring for Cosette.

The charge nurse today was Cosette's nurse the day Cosette had to be taken off of me and bagged. She came to talk to me less than an hour later.

"I have a few spots to show you," she said. "Let's go on a tour. But don't tell others I did this for you. Most people don't get to pick."

I laughed. "I don't talk to anyone else here."

I had only ever seen B-pod and H-pod. The others were a mystery. First we went to G-pod, which is a small but cozy pod with a handful of bed spots. It is one narrow hallway with curtained off spots on either side. The walls are yellow and it not only feels warmer temperature-wise but also more cheerful. Only two nurses work in the pod at a time. There are windows at the end of it. The spot available was second from the window; natural light was in sight. The bedspot itself is very small, though, only room for one chair. Ben and I are hardly there at the same time anyway. I saw the others too, but they were in D which is a dark, windowless area that feels colder than the rest of the NICU. I was surprised how many spots are back there and it was very strange to see so many parents sitting by their babies. I have a feeling many of them are shortstay cases, not supercritical like in A,B, and C and not longterm like in H. I decided on the first spot in G.

I helped the nurse collect Cosette's things such as her clothes and her signs from the wall behind her crib, and also all of my pump stuff. Someone came to help wheel Cosette through the hallway. It doesn't feel like this is the last place she will be in the NICU but maybe second to last. There is something called J-pod where parents stay overnight with their baby before discharge, like a test run before going home. A nurse told me about J-pod when I was worried about Cosette's apnea episodes. She said they would never send her home with apnea like that. With apnea she also has to wean off caffeine, get it entirely out of her system, and then not have an episode for seven days.

I like the new spot but it was hard to leave Cosette's nurse.. I would've liked to have stayed with her for the remainder of the day. She even gave Cosette a quick tub bath in her bed while we were waiting to move. The new nurse in G-pod this afternoon was fine. She was very welcoming. I made sure to write on Cosette's new board that she owns her own clothes. Some babies there use the hospital's clothes. I prefer to use our own and wash them in no dye, no fragrance detergent. I take the dirty clothes home every day and bring them back when they're clean. A green plastic bag hangs from one post of Cosette's bed and the nurses know that's where to drop the dirty clothes at night. They usually change her clothes in the middle of the night when they take everything off to weigh her. At the beginning of Cosette wearing clothes, a few items immediately went missing. Someone put them in the hospital hamper instead of the green bag, and we never saw them again.

I saw the baby specialist this morning before going to the hospital. She has worked with NICU babies a lot in the past and has written papers about them. We only touched on everything that has happened, but she did try to help me reintegrate into my body. She said it's very important for Cosette's nervous system that my nervous system be balanced, and that Cosette can sense things in me even when we are not touching. That is a huge responsibility. But I also like to think that we're still connected. Babies can sense a lot in a room or from their parents even when they are not as tiny and new as Cosette. This is part of why I want to do this work now, so I can be okay for her in the present and the future. My heart is also going to race sometimes when I'm holding her, though.

This whole experience has been hard in so many ways; as an introvert it has taken an energetic toll on me. I get very little alone time. I haven't sat and read a book in a long time. I am trying to fit in exercise. It will all be different when she comes home. No more trips to the hospital every day. But this is my life now. I am one of those people whose life has changed dramatically in having a child. There is a lot of purpose in it though, I think.

Friday, December 13

Last night when we called the NICU, the night nurse had surprising news to tell us.

"Cosette seemed so uncomfortable in her CPAP gear. She kept trying to pull it away from her face, and when I took it off to clean her skin and massage her head, she was breathing fine. She was so happy to be free of it. I paged the NP and asked if we could try a nasal cannula. She came and assessed her and said to try it. She's been on that for an hour now and is doing great."

I was shocked. And of course ecstatic. No mustache and head gear is huge. The attending doctor on Thursday said they would do a high-flow trial in a week or two. He explained he didn't want to push her, which I usually agree with, but he also hardly sees her. This nurse observed Cosette and made a call. I may never meet her, but I loved her cheerful voice and how much she cared to help my baby.

I was so excited to get there today to see her. Ben sent me a video this morning and she looked adorable, cooing in her way and looking around with wide eyes. She looked more comfortable even in the short video.

She weighs four pounds now. They have weighed her every night that she's been in the hospital. Weights go up and down and fluctuate within a week. It felt like it took forever for her to hit two pounds and then two to three took a long time, too. Four came more quickly.

We're going to start breastfeeding trials soon because she is 34 weeks. Technically a premature baby is one who is born before 37 weeks, but babies born at 34 or 35 weeks can nurse and go home just fine. Of course Cosette is not like a 34 week old baby who was just born simply because she is 34 weeks now. The trials of the last eleven weeks do not disappear. But at four pounds and on the nasal cannula, she can try to start nursing. I am very excited for this next step. It feels like ages ago that a speech therapist talked to me in B-pod about someday working with me and Cosette on nursing. Speech therapy covers the area of food and eating, everything mouth related. I think that Cosette will be able to nurse. She loves her pacifiers and sucks on them so strongly.

CARING BRIDGE POST | December 14

Cosette had a big week. She had her first bath, transferred to a quieter pod within the NICU, reached the four pound mark, and she moved off CPAP to a nasal cannula. She was supposed to be on CPAP for another week before starting nasal cannula trials, but in a surprise move on Thursday night, she went on it and has been doing well. She looks so much more comfortable and it's easier to hold her. Today her feeding tube will be moved to her nose, and we will start steps toward nursing.

Last night while holding Cosette, I overheard the day shift nurse tell the night shift nurse all about Cosette from the beginning. On the day of her birth, after being intubated, Cosette received chest compressions for thirty minutes before her heart began to beat. We've been through so much and there is much more to go, but I know how important it is to come back to that fact whenever things feel hard. We almost didn't have her with us, but we do. Looking through pictures of her from day one until now is really incredible. She has come so far.

Sunday, December 15

Today is our anniversary. Ben and I went out to dinner. A nurse from the NICU was seated directly next to us with her partner. I wondered if she recognized us. Ben and I both had our green Care Partner wristbands on. If she did notice us, she pretended not to, which was fine with me.

Rachel was Cosette's nurse today and she helped me give Cosette a bath. This one was longer than others she has had. We put Cosette in a tiny basin of water and soaped her body, then dried her off, dressed her, and put her back on her bed. In the bed, we washed her hair and dried it. It's very important that she does not get cold. But her clothes got wet during the hair wash so we had to redress her. Even though she only has the nasal cannula now, she still has three leads on her belly that track vitals, as well as the cord that connects around her foot. So getting dressed is not simple. It was all kind of funny though because Rachel made it that way. I laughed so much. It's truly amazing how individual personalities and demeanors can affect your whole day and outlook. A bubbly, sociable nurse means a nice day. Mom was there and took lots of videos of the bath. Ben was at church and then with Henry before taking him back to his mom. The next time Henry will be back with us is for Christmas.

Rachel gave me a little scrub brush to use on Cosette's head. Cosette loved it. For the body washing part, she wasn't so sure she liked it, but the head part she seemed to enjoy. She looked around with her eyes open wide. It is so satisfying to see her take pleasure in something. She made little squeaky sounds in her throat. She can definitely cry audibly now, as she did with her bath, but she doesn't do it often. Despite everything, she seems like a fairly content baby. I think she is very pleased to be on the high-flow air far away from intubation.

The baby next to Cosette, the one with the window view, seems to be more sick than Cosette. She is getting surgery this week. Her mother is very concerned. I hear the mother talk to the nurses a lot. She is vocal about her fears and hesitations about what comes next. When she walks past our spot, the scent of smoke accompanies her, which bothers me because Cosette is not supposed to be anywhere near secondhand smoke. I wonder if anyone took that into account when we moved to this spot. When I smell it and I know the nurses smell it, I feel like we may not be in G-pod for very long.

Another baby in G-pod was born at 35 weeks but she is under four pounds. Or at least that's what I think I heard them say. She is very, very small. Her parents are Mennonites and I have seen them and their friends by the baby's bed spot for weeks. They were here while we were still in H-pod. The mother was kind to me in the pump room. I noticed once that she had only pumped a very small amount of milk and I felt badly for her. Maybe more will come in for her. One Sunday there were about twenty young Mennonites in the lounge. They were singing worship songs. It was beautiful and I felt envious of all the uplifting support. It is not the first time I wished I was a part of a tightly knit group like that.

Tuesday, December 17

Cosette latched on briefly today. It was such an odd, good feeling! Her little mouth nibbled so intently. The lactation consultant with whom I have become friendly came by to check on me. I had told Cosette's nurse I did not know what I was doing and didn't know how to get Cosette in a good position, so she called for help. Over the weekend, the nurse had said, "Give nursing a try!" and closed the curtain and left me there looking down at Cosette who was looking back at me with big eyes. She has lots of long wires connected to her and her head still needs to be held in a certain way. I got frustrated, which I know is not something the baby is supposed to feel from me. So today was better. Help is good.

The lactation consultant took pictures of Cosette at my breast which felt a little funny. It was reminiscent of the feeling in H-pod where I used to pump next to the flimsy curtain which barely separated me from a busy hallway. There have been many times where my body has seemed to be more of a tool than anything else. It's okay, though. I'm just happy she is interested in nursing. It will be a while before she actually takes any milk, and when she starts doing that she may choke and sputter a lot, but the nuzzling signs she gave today with her hands close to her mouth are positive ones. I'm proud of my little girl. I think she would have been perfect at all of these things if she was born on time. These skills are all stored inside of her ready to come out and shine.

Our nurse today, who was our nurse yesterday too, is very anxious. She does not have the type of faith in Cosette that I do. Cosette has apnea episodes every day, but they have increased this week probably from the adjustment to the high-flow. They seem to happen most often when one of us is holding her. Cosette gets so comfortable and relaxed that she forgets to breathe. Yesterday she had one on Mom while I was at work. The nurse told me about it when I got there in the afternoon.

"She was turning blue. It was really bad," she said. "I had to interject and flick her feet a lot. I put her back in her crib after to observe her."

"She has needed stimulation for some of her episodes," I replied calmly.

"Yea. Well, this one was really bad."

If Liza or Rachel had said this I would be alarmed. But this new person doesn't know Cosette very well. So of course today Cosette had a couple of dips while I was holding her, and the nurse dashed in like Cosette was dying. That is the worst reaction someone could give. It has taken me months to not have that reaction and now someone is acting like I should be more concerned.

Wednesday, December 18

I left work early even though it's Wednesday to be there in time for Santa's visit to Cosette. I put Cosette in a special red outfit that Mom bought her. Liza played Mrs. Clause. She had been hyping it up for weeks. Liza took Cosette out of her crib and held her so a photographer could take pictures alongside Santa and an elf. Cosette slept through the whole thing. She looked so tiny being displayed in front of the adults in costume. She is tiny, but I am small too, so I don't think about her being abnormally small. She is a very little person currently.

CARING BRIDGE POST | December 18

At 35 weeks adjusted, Cosette is busy gaining weight and learning where her food comes from. She's also frightening her parents a few times a day with apnea episodes. She has had more of these with each big transition; we hope she grows out of them soon. Santa visited the NICU today. Cosette slept peacefully through it.

BABY JOURNAL | December 19

Yesterday, Santa and Mrs. Clause visited you and held you for a picture. You slept through it. I've been holding you a lot and you're getting interested in feeding. We are in a new pod, mostly quieter. I miss Liza, your primary nurse, but it was the right move. You're 35 weeks adjusted. I wish you were in me still for Christmas. But here we are together. It will be very nice to be home away from here in February. I miss you at night. You are looking very cute all of the time.

Friday, December 20

Liza was the charge nurse today and she came to see me. I told her that I was having trouble with a nurse who was making me too anxious and upset. The tears came fast. Liza pursed her lips and apologized. I think we will probably be moving pods soon.

Mom left for my sister's yesterday morning. She is going there for Christmas, which makes perfect sense. Christmas here will be dismal.

Ben and I went to see the new Star Wars movie last night. He really wanted to go and had gotten free tickets. I was so paranoid of germs and flinched anytime someone coughed in the giant theater. The movie was fine. I did not follow the plot entirely, and I left for a long period of time to pick up our food. The kitchen was a mess, and I ended up just taking food that looked like ours that was ready to be picked up. Being among all of the people out on a Thursday night having fun, I felt like they would understand that I needed to eat. If they knew I was a nursing mom whose baby has been in the NICU for twelve weeks, they would approve of me taking the unlabeled food.

Ben's parents are arriving in Virginia tonight. They are staying at an Air BnB that is owned by my friend from work. I think it's good that they will have their own space, and Ben can take Henry there to see them. The house is close to the hospital which is convenient, too.

The Mennonite baby is sick. They were told they could go home in time for Christmas. I heard them say a few days ago, "What better Christmas gift could we ask for?" But apparently overnight the baby had a lot of apnea episodes, like a staggering number, so they have to assume she may be sick. She could have a UTI, just like what they thought Cosette might have had. They are more common in baby boys but girls still get them. The baby had the same procedure that Cosette had months ago when I stood in the lobby for a long time. The nurse had trouble getting the urine sample, and the baby screamed and screamed. I held Cosette close. She kept sleeping. In times like those, when everything around us is mayhem and she's asleep, I try to join her in that calm place. I squeeze my eyes shut and hum softly. I take us to that grass by the reservoir where we will look up at the sky and trace animals in the clouds.

Saturday, December 21

Henry woke up this morning and threw up. Ben took him to the Air BnB to get him out of the house immediately. Ben will not go to the hospital today or tomorrow to make sure he is not sick.

Today is the first day of winter break. What a joke. There is no break for me. People at work kindly tried to say how good it was that I would have two weeks to spend with Cosette. And that's true, it is good, but it is not a cheerful thing. The hospital is a miserable place and cuddle time with Cosette is not what I think people imagine it is when they wish it for me. It's wires and screens with alarms and loud background noise. I know what a cuddle is and that's not it. But I smile and agree with them. What's the point in acting grumpy about it? That just makes everyone feel worse.

Ben's parents came to see the baby in the morning. They left their house before Henry got there to make sure they didn't pick up anything from him. They said kind things. I glowed while presenting my girl to them. It was tight in the little bed spot for the three of us to stand.

But later in the day, Cosette was moved out of G-pod. Liza was the charge nurse and made the move happen. I was sad to say bye to the chipper yellow walls and the view of the window in the distance, but knew I needed to be somewhere with less anxiety.

Liza picked the spot and she thought I would like it because it was much bigger. But I don't. It is in D-pod, the dark, cold tunnel one. A nurse told me they refer to it as the dungeon. The hospital helicopter takes off and lands right above it. The smell of fuel filters into the pod every time that happens and the walls shake. I hate it there.

Sunday, December 22

Cosette is 35 weeks today and she weighs five pounds. The progress from four to five pounds felt very fast compared to previous growth. She is looking fuller and healthier each day. The high-flow air has been really good for her.

Things are difficult for me right now. I hardly see any sunlight in a day. I should probably take more breaks. But it is so hard to leave Cosette in the dungeon alone.

BABY JOURNAL | December 22

You are five pounds now! You're doing such a great job at growing bigger. Your legs, arms, face, and belly are all chubby. You're twelve weeks old today. Your due date is just a month away, four weeks. I think you'll need to be in the hospital past that but the end is in the future. We have come really far. You're almost three months old. It's hard to believe. I am eager for our normal life to begin.

Monday, December 23

Cosette is doing well. Her whole body is very chubby. I can get her out of her crib by myself now, which is pretty amazing. I hold her all day between cares and pumping. The pumping riddle is a hard one to solve because she's supposed to try to eat with me, but then I don't want to give her up to pump right after she tries, but that's when my milk is ready. She's so cute, I never want to put her down. We have come really far. Twelve weeks. She's not going home in four weeks but maybe in six. We could be ⅔ done right now. That is much closer than we were in October. Once we hit January, it will start feeling more real.

Thirty-six weeks adjusted today. I could have been starting my maternity leave now with winter break tagged on to make it longer. Eight months pregnant. Maybe someday in the future I will know what eight months pregnant feels like. That's hard to think about right now.

Tuesday, December 24

The most amazing thing happened today. During rounds, the attending doctor asked if I liked being in D-pod.

"No," I said. "I'm not trying to complain, everyone here has been so good to us, but it's awful back here. It's depressing to see no natural light. It's cold and I'm worried about Cosette not being warm enough at night. Liza was trying to help by giving us more space, but G was better."

The doctor nodded and said, "Everyone wants a window. I wish I could give everyone a window."

"Yes, of course." I blushed and laughed softly. Had I come off seeming ungrateful? We moved to talking about Cosette's progress. No changes for her, stay the course.

About ten minutes later, the same doctor came back to me. "Ms. Fraser-Morris, would you be interested in moving to a private room? I think Cosette is stable enough. We have a handful of NICU rooms over by the PICU and they have floor to ceiling windows."

My mouth fell open. "Seriously? Of course, yes. I would love that."

"I can't make any promises, but I'll work on it."

I smiled largely at her. "Thank you, thank you so much."

It was a Christmas gift. Although I did not expect it to happen today but maybe tomorrow, on Christmas.

Mom was a nurse and she had warned me that different people often work over the holidays. And by different she meant less experienced or from different floors. Occasionally, Cosette had a Peds floor nurse or PICU nurse who had little experience with the NICU but was still a good nurse. They took instruction from me well because they needed guidance. I didn't mind giving it. At this point, Cosette is stable enough that I am not worried about them doing something majorly wrong that will hurt her. It's not like it was in B-pod where she needed to be suctioned often or things like that.

A few days ago, I started to see nurses on the floor who had been training in October, shadowing other nurses. Now they are on their own. Cosette's nurse today, who will also be here tomorrow, was a shadow of one of Cosette's nurses back in the first week of H-pod. Cosette was having a hard time with apnea then and this nurse was not acting with much certainty. She seemed scared too. At first it felt scary because she was on her own with Cosette, but it turns out she was quite attentive and good with her. She's young, younger than me, and wanted to chat some which was fine because it is Christmas Eve and I have been alone a lot. She told me that she was going to see her boyfriend tonight and he has two children, which has been challenging. I told her I have a stepson and agreed that it can be hard.

I left around 4:30 p.m. to walk to church. I was planning to return to the hospital to stay until 7 p.m. to see who was spending the night with Cosette, and then I would be home before Henry went to bed. I told Ben I wanted to help Henry write a letter to Santa. Ben did not do much Santa stuff when he was growing up, so I feel like it is up to me to bring in some magic.

Church was very difficult. I missed Cosette so much. Seeing all of the families together dressed up made me feel like I was in such a different world. I met Ben and his parents there; I was coming from the hospital, entering from a separate world. I am an island floating into everyone else's normal routine, and then I float back to Cosette. I feel like I'm treading water when I am outside the hospital. Inside the hospital it can feel like drowning, but at least it is familiar and she's right there for me to look at. I held it together until we sang Silent Night. The lights were dim and everyone had candles to light from each other. It was beautiful. I have been singing that song to Cosette when I hold her because it's a lullaby and I know the words. Bringing those moments with her into this moment at church without her, singing about mother and child, I cried and cried. Ben noticed and put his arm around my shoulder. It was poignant and painful, something I will always remember, singing that song and longing for her to be with me.

I walked back to the hospital. It was very cold. It felt like Christmas Eve weather. The tears started again when I started to say goodnight to her. As I walked to the elevators, tears streaming down my face, I saw one of the other trainee nurses now working her own shifts. She was headed in for the night. She smiled at me and I gave a weak wave back. She didn't try to talk to me; I am sure she made the connection about why I was crying. I am a mother leaving her newborn baby alone on Christmas Eve night. This is one of the hardest things I have ever had to do.

I stopped crying shortly before I got home. I helped Henry write his letter.

He was enthusiastic about it. Ben and I ate the cookies he left out for Santa, and I made sure to leave some crumbs. We brought our presents out to place under the tree. It looked very nice and full.

I have a very specific memory of being sick on Christmas Eve when I was about six years-old. I was on the couch with my mom and I had my head in her lap and she was stroking my hair. We both gazed at the tree. I was sad and felt bad but also safe. That's what I wanted to give Cosette tonight, assurance that even though it is Christmas and she's unwell, she is safe with me. And I can't, I just can't, because I am here and she is there.

Wednesday, December 25

I tried to be present this morning with the others and I think I was successful. I wanted to see Ben and Henry open their gifts from me, and I cared about what Ben's mom would think of the things I helped him get for her. Some of the ideas came to me very close to Christmas day. It was hard to think about buying things for others until it was only two weeks away. I knew I would feel embarrassed if I skipped it entirely. My favorite for Ben and Henry are matching pajamas that say Papa Bear and Little Bear respectively. I got some that say Mama Bear and there are a pair for Cosette to grow into that say Baby Bear.

When it got to be 10:30 a.m., I started to move toward leaving for the hospital. They began making waffles with my family's waffle iron that my mom offered to us and Ben accepted. I know he'll only use it a couple of times, but it was cute that he wanted it. We used it a lot growing up. A giant fluff of carbs does not sound appealing to me now, but I can see wanting to make them for Cosette one day.

Our agreement was that I would be back by 4 p.m. and we would eat dinner soon after. Cosette certainly did not know it was Christmas. It was just an ordinary day to her and so it was to me while I was with her. I sang the two carols I have been singing all month to her -- Silent Night and Have Yourself a Merry Little Christmas. I probably sang both of them five times each over the course of the day. In H and G-pod they probably had music on, but in D it was crying babies and a lot of silence. Big groups of families came in to see some babies and that made me nervous about germs. I held my breath as they walked by our curtain.

It was the same nurse as yesterday. She was pleasant and I asked about her Christmas Eve with her boyfriend and his kids. She said it went well but that it was a little weird. She asked about my Christmas morning. I was vague in my response and said it was nice. How can anything be that nice while Cosette is here?

This morning I said *Merry Christmas* to Ben when we first woke up. There were tears behind my words. That's how it feels to me. Unmerry and sad and yet still Christmas. It is only one day of the year but it's an emotion-filled one and there is no way to fully reduce that unless we were not celebrating at all. On a Thanksgiving many years ago, my dad was in the hospital and we all skipped the day. It was fine, no one cared that much. We made some Thanksgiving type foods a few days later. We all agreed and it made it easier.

Throughout the day in the hospital, I kept waiting for word about changing rooms, but it did not happen. That would have been a great Christmas gift.

Thursday, December 26

My in-laws came to the hospital in the morning to say goodbye to Cosette before they left town. They were meeting Ben and Henry for brunch at a restaurant across the street. We were in dark D-pod where there was more space but it is a depressing place to present Cosette. The overhead electric lighting was intense and she looked washed out. They said she looked great, though. She is doing much better than she was even just weeks ago.

"I'm about to do her cares. You can watch if you like," I said.

"I'd love to see that," said Ben's mom. "I remember seeing you change her diaper and give her the swab of milk when she was just a few weeks old."

"I do those same things just a little differently now and no one helps me."

Cosette was slightly fussy getting her diaper changed and the cords still made things complicated, but I am sure I'm more efficient and confident than I was in week two. *My baby came really early, my body went wrong, but look at me now, look at us now.*

Ben came into the hospital after he parted with Henry. We spent some time together with the baby, then I walked to Ruth's for therapy.

When I got back, I was met by Ben and a nurse wheeling Cosette's bed down the main hallway outside of the NICU.

"What's happening?" I asked while reaching for my phone where I saw a *We're moving!* text on the screen.

"We're going to the new room," said Ben. "Wait until you see it. It's in J-pod. They already took me in to make sure we're okay with it."

I put my hand into Cosette's crib to touch her. It was strange to see her in the big hallway. She looked so tiny in a new environment. We were led to a door by the elevators that I had seen before but had not given much thought to. The nurse flashed her badge in front of a scanner and the doors opened toward us. As we went down the hall, I could see into individual rooms. Each had a sliding glass door that separated the room from the hall. A curtain was pulled halfway on most and all the way on one.

Then we turned into Cosette's new room. It was 5 p.m. and almost fully dark outside. The lights of the city could be seen below us and far into the distance. The windows stretch from the floor to the ceiling, just as the doctor had described, and are about twelve feet across. It is a huge amount of glass, an expansive view that looks over the hospital dropoff circle, the Emily Couric Cancer Center, the parking garage, and many buildings and homes past that. I could even see the steeple of our church. It is a beautiful view because of the lights, but also because it is our city and it's a view. We went from no view to one of the best of the city. It gives us an image of the outside world while we are inside with Cosette. Entering that space, our separate worlds are taking a big step toward blending into one.

The room is bigger than our living room at home and has its own private bathroom with a shower.

"For when you stay over," said the nurse who saw me investigating the shower.

"We can stay overnight here?" I asked, my voice slanting up in amazement.

"Of course. It's like a hotel room but in the hospital. They'll bring you new towels every day."

The nurse was getting Cosette's machines hooked up on the wall. There was a couch and two big recliner chairs.

"Does the couch pull out to a bed?" asked Ben.

"I think so," she said. "They can give you sheets. It might just be for one person."

It was hard to wrap my head around the idea of staying over in the hospital. The screens, the lights, the beeps. Would it actually be sleep?

Our nurse finished connecting Cosette and then had to return to her other patients in D-pod for the last hour and a half of her shift. It was far from here and she couldn't be away long from her other patients. She had been new to us that day, a PICU nurse, moved to our floor because of the holidays. I liked her a lot; she was jovial and exuberant. That is rarely my mood in the hospital, so it was helpful to be met by my opposite.

The dayshift nurse who had Cosette's no longer empty room came in to meet us. "They moved you here now? So late?" she questioned.

We shrugged. Um yes?

"Is she getting discharged soon?" she asked, as she scanned Cosette's ankle tag which brought her info up on the computer.

"No," I said. "Not soon. Next month we hope."

The nurse was reading the screen. "She's still on high flow? We don't usually have babies on high-flow in J-pod. This unit is for patients who are preparing for discharge."

"I was asked a few days ago by one of the NICU attendings if we wanted a private room, she didn't say much more than that. She did say Cosette was stable enough to be here."

The nurse grunted. I was defending Cosette but that did not feel good. If this nurse did not think Cosette was ready to be here, then was it dangerous? At that moment, Cosette had an apnea episode. After it was over, the nurse said, "Does she have those often?"

"She's gotten much better recently. That's the first one today."

"Well, I'll get her 6 p.m. feed ready. Do you have breast milk?"

"Yes, yes." I showed her the refrigerator drawer containing four 2.5 oz containers of pumped milk. Our dayshift nurse had brought those over first.

"Are you planning to stay tonight?"

We were supposed to go to a friend's Boxing Day party. It was at her new, big house that I really wanted to see. I was looking forward to being with my friend and around people who were feeling festive. I thought maybe I would have a drink. I was nervous about it, too, the chance of getting very sad out in a group, but I had talked to both Mary and Ruth about it and they had encouraged me to go. We could always leave early. This friend hosted a Boxing Day party every year on the 26th, but I had never been in town to go. That was not the only reason I wasn't staying overnight though.

"We didn't know this was happening today. We don't have any of our things. Pets at home." I trailed off.

She didn't respond. I started to hang up Cosette's signs on the wall by the window. I noticed her first sign, her name sign, was missing. I knew where it was. I told Ben I was going back to D-pod to get it.

Her recently vacated spot was bare with no bed, no new baby yet. It had only been twenty minutes and needed to be cleaned. Her sign was on the oddly placed window between her bed-spot and the one behind us. There was no reason for that window except that it made the spots less private. I had put the sign there to block the view. I was so glad to be leaving this pod. It had felt like we had been there several weeks even though it was only one. As I made my way back to the lobby where all of the pods came together, with the screen scrolling through the before and after pictures, I wondered if I would be back in this area at all. Could I go to the pump room if I wanted to get snacks? I would definitely be able to pump in our private room. Everything was changing. We were leaving NICU central and moving up.

I was crying by the time the dayshift changed to night shift, and I was ready to admit we had made a big mistake. Even this great thing I wanted, the private room, was not right. Cosette would not be safe enough. She was all alone in a giant, echoey room, so the beeps were louder for her little ears, and if something bad happened no one would know. When we left at night, she'd be totally by herself. At least in the other pods, there were always multiple nurses and respiratory therapists filing around.

I texted my friend at 7 p.m. and told her we were not coming to the party. I was exhausted from the change, the crying, the doubt, the regret. The only way I got out of there was because the night shift nurse said Cosette seemed fine and capable of being in J-pod. She said she would check in on her a lot and imagined she would just sleep soundly through the night and would be ready to see us in her new, bright room in the morning. Ben and I drove home in our separate cars through the dark, winter streets. I listened to melancholy Christmas songs and tried to have faith that all my good feelings weren't disguised mistakes that would later cause fear.

CARING BRIDGE POST | December 28

Cosette will be three months old tomorrow. We received a wonderful gift this week of a private room at the hospital. One wall is all windows; Cosette got her very first dose of natural light yesterday. At first this move was stressful because it is difficult to imagine her being behind a closed door all night alone, but the advantages have outweighed this.

Time off from work has meant shifting into a stream of eleven hour days at the hospital. That was extremely hard when in a dark, windowless pod. I am working on breastfeeding Cosette so it's important that I am there for as many of her feedings as possible, so I arrive by 8:30 a.m. and leave around 7:30 p.m. In this new room, we do have the choice of staying over, which I may do on work days in January when I can't be with her during the day, but for now sleeping well seems a high priority. Her alarm settings for her oxygen saturation are very narrow right now because she is on less support. They say you can tune the alarms out to sleep. I suppose I will find out if that is true. Breastfeeding is going very well so far. She's still getting her regular feeds through the feeding tube, but that may have to change soon because she got a lot of extra snacks directly from me yesterday.

Christmas at the hospital was very difficult. Leaving Cosette alone on Christmas Eve night was heart wrenching. I tried to remind myself it felt like just another night to her and the sadness was only in me, but yes, there was an immense amount of sadness. I went to church and imagined having her there with us next year. One of my many efforts to stay healthy involves not hugging people so that I don't potentially collect germs. That's been an awkward thing to tell people in the moment and I do of course miss that comfort. Someone asked me this week how I would describe how I feel and since I couldn't find words she suggested some. The one that stuck was burdened. I feel burdened by the nonstop needs and fears that have not eased in three months. When I am holding Cosette, though, it is a small break from that feeling because I am offering her the best medicine, and I'm not at risk for getting sick while sitting there with her, and we can be at peace. So I hold her as much as possible.

Another thing that has helped me feel a little lighter is moments when I can help strangers in the hospital. I try to offer directions to those who appear lost, and one night I drove a mother and her son around the hospital garage until they could find their car. Interacting with kind nurses offers relief, too. On Christmas Eve and Christmas, I spent the days with Cosette, and being able to interact occasionally with a warm-hearted person helped to decrease the loneliness that can surround us on holidays that have good, family-filled memories attached to them. On Christmas Eve, a doctor asked if we would want a private room, something I didn't know was possible, and that was a present in itself even though it didn't happen until the 26th. The doctor didn't need to go out of her way to do that but she did. I hope making that happen for us made her feel as good as I did driving strangers around the parking garage.

BABY JOURNAL | December 27

We moved to a private room last night. I hope you're more comfortable there. You're more alone, though, which is hard. Today it will be nice to see natural light. I'm excited for you. Nursing is coming along. You are doing a great job. You're five pounds five ounces now, newborn size.

Sunday, December 29

Each morning when I arrive to Cosette's room, she's usually still asleep. There is a button that opens the one giant screen that hangs over the window. I push it and she continues to sleep but slowly starts to wake. I need to try to breastfeed her before they connect her to food at 9 a.m. Mostly they still feed her while she is breastfeeding so she thinks she is getting full while sucking, but they've encouraged me to start trying before the food begins, too. She coughs and sputters often when she tries to nurse and sometimes stops breathing momentarily. It is very scary, but I'm also more used to it. I am not going to stop trying just because of these isolated events. We have not started with a bottle yet but that will come soon. She must drink a bottle before she can be discharged. Cosette will not be a baby who can survive just on breastmilk. She needs the fortification that comes in formula. I understand this and yet also wish it could be different. I still catch myself thinking maybe she will be a special case and not need the formula, but I need to remember she is already a very, very special case.

I feed her and hold her while she gets fed, which usually goes until 10 or 10:15 a.m. While she's being fed through the tube, she usually falls asleep. She will sleep all the way until the next feeding session if we hold her. If Ben is there, he can take over after her food has settled in her belly. And then I pump. We start her cares -- change her diaper, take her temperature -- at 11:45 a.m. and then it's time to eat again at noon. And we do it again until 3 p.m. and then decide if she's eating in her bed at 6 p.m. or being held for that feeding. When Ben is there, it's easier for me to leave at 6 p.m. because we either go together or he lingers behind until she is asleep. It is very difficult to leave her in the big room by herself when she is still awake.

It has been nice to spend this time with Ben, just the two of us with Cosette. Often we're reading or lying quietly with our eyes closed. I have been working on reports I need to write for my students before Cosette comes home and I start the second half of my maternity leave. In these rooms, we get food vouchers for three meals a day. I receive them as a nursing mother. We have ten dollars to use per meal so Ben and I can both use them. It has made a huge difference. It is a pleasant perk to go to the cafeteria and pick out a chocolate milk or a breakfast sandwich. I am careful being in a public place with all of the germs coming in and out of the hospital. We are constantly washing our hands and using hand sanitizer. I have not gotten sick since before I became pregnant and I don't plan to in the last month in the hospital. January is peak flu season. Obviously, it would be tragic for Cosette to get the flu right now.

The weather has been unseasonably warm. I go for runs in the afternoon which feels great. Since I am arriving at the hospital earlier and staying later, it's essential to exercise while there. A nurse was so amused by me one day for doing yoga in the room while Cosette slept. She said it was great to see me taking care of myself and being healthy. She said she has never seen anyone exercise in one of these rooms. We are definitely using the private space for all its worth. Everything changed with this room move. Ben's commitment at the senior center is over, and he has full availability to be here for this whole week ahead of us with no other obligations but to be with Cosette and take care of each other.

Tuesday, December 31

Today we say goodbye to 2019. It was a challenging year from start to finish. 2020 just sounds better, a more even year, a year when Cosette will be at home except for a few weeks in the beginning. Things have to be better because of that. We will have a party for her, people will meet her, we will be like normal parents of a newborn.

We have decided not to stay overnight in the hospital tonight. We considered it, bringing in the new year with Cosette, but it would mean Ben sleeping on the floor and both of us being very tired tomorrow. Ben stayed last night and he barely slept, mostly because of all the noises and light. Every time her feeding is over, a loud beeping sound goes off. He said some of the neighboring babies had the really loud alarms go off, and they basically sound like they're in your room. It's best for us to go to bed at a normal time and get back here in the morning for her. Someone sent us 2020 glasses made of paper as part of an advertisement for a company. The eye holes are at the zeroes. They're cute. I took a fun picture of Ben wearing them holding Cosette. He looks happy in the picture. We've been having a good week together except for when we leave her at night. That is hard no matter what.

BABY JOURNAL | December 31

It's almost 2020. You are three months old. I spend all day with you now. Last night Dad stayed overnight with you. You are doing a great job with breast-feeding. You tried a bottle last night, too. I love you!

Friday, January 3, 2020

I went to see the baby specialist for a second time today. I went with an intention. I needed to go through the night of the birth with someone. No one else has asked me questions about it or wanted to review it with me. I can understand that. Hearing the play by play of a trauma is not something you do with just anyone. She is trained to help with such things. She had me lay on the table, and as I spoke, she held my arm and then moved to other parts of my body to provide grounding. She told me to pause, breathe, and come back to the room. She told me to look at her bookcase and tell her something that stood out to me there. This is a method for grounding that I can use in the hospital too -- look around and identify five things in the room. Notice color, smell, textures. That type of observation can help me ground when it feels like I'm headed into fight or flight.

Going through the birth night was hard but it needed to be done. I hope it will help me stop thinking about it so much, especially when I close my eyes at night.

BABY JOURNAL | January 4

It's 2020, a new year. This is your year! It's going to be a fun one for you. Everyone is cheering you on. You're eating well and will be 38 weeks soon. You're six pounds!

CARING BRIDGE | January 4

2020, the year of Cosette! She weighs six pounds and has been moving right along with breastfeeding. She has not progressed much with the bottle though. They say it's different with every baby, some do better at the bottle because it is easier mechanically but others do better at the breast.

Breastfeeding is safer for her pacing-wise. Some babies go home only breast-feeding, but they have to prove themselves by gaining weight. Unfortunately, this isn't possible for us because I have to go back to work on Monday for three days a week. I will stay overnight at the hospital the night before work so that I can wake up every few hours to feed her, but she will still miss the daytime feeds. This is something neither Ben nor my mom can help with. One of the hardest things to accept with Cosette's early birth is that we will miss the 12 weeks of maternity leave at home together. She's similar to a newborn baby learning to eat and is awake more, but she has a mom who immediately has to go back to work. I get six more weeks when she comes home, which we have been told will most likely be the last week of January or the start of February. I feel happy about this but am still in a breath-holding place. I'm not sure when or if that will ease.

One of the big advantages of our new room is that we have our own bathroom with a shower so I've been going for runs for a break in the afternoon, especially on these warm days we've been having. It is very strange to run around the campus of UVa, which is full of so many 15-year-old memories. I am running through dorms I stayed in when I was 18, now with my hospital band on my wrist. The passage of time and intersection of past and present selves is a very strange experience when in the midst of such an intense period of my life. The outdoor break has been great for me though. The private room has really increased the positive charge of the days.

Monday, January 6

Today marks Cosette's one-hundredth day in the hospital. The only reason I've counted is because there's a *100 Days in the NICU* card in the pack of NICU cards that Ashley sent me. I marked it on my calendar a while ago. And now here it is. After spending two weeks straight with Cosette, returning to work was very difficult. Now that we're in the new room, I can take showers here and get free breakfast from the cafeteria. I decided to stay overnight last night so I could be here in the morning before work. But the nurse convinced me at 9 p.m. that I should go home. She had taken care of Cosette the past many nights, and said Cosette wasn't waking up to eat and was just getting the tube. There was no point in me being there. So I drove home, went to bed, woke up at 4:45 a.m. and drove back to the hospital in time to feed her at 6 a.m. She ate a little but mostly it was nice to be with her and not go from Sunday night to

Monday afternoon without seeing her. I will plan to do this each day this week. Maybe next week she'll be ready for more overnight feeding tries, and I can stay over. It's only a few more weeks. I can do anything for a few weeks. Honestly, I am nervous to stay over. If I do not sleep at all, it will be very long and upsetting.

At work this morning, I tried to be chipper but it was sad to share that my "break" was spent in the hospital every day all day. The kids went on trips, saw family, and did fun Christmas traditions. As they should. I hope that I am giving them an example of resilience. Maybe one day they'll reminisce about their elementary school teacher whose baby was in the hospital for four months and she came back to teach some during that time. And she was okay. She was emotionally stable and still present. I hope that's what they remember.

I put the little 100 Days card next to Cosette as she slept in a cute sleep sack and took her picture. These pictures will be meaningful for my entire life.

Today is also my niece's birthday. Mom is spending the night with them to celebrate and flies back tomorrow. She'll be moving to her new apartment in a couple of weeks. The time for Ben to be here with me and Cosette all day has ended. There is a lot happening, though, and as I predicted in December, January feels different and better. We're just working on Cosette eating on her own. I think soon she could do fine breathing on her own. She definitely still needs the help while she's learning how to eat because she coughs and sputters and loses her breath. She's trying hard, though. My little, smart fighter.

Tuesday, January 7

I am very glad it's not a work day for me. It's snowing! It started in the middle of the morning and has quickly covered the street and sidewalks. It came down faster than people expected. We have a beautiful view of it on the seventh floor. The tops of the buildings are blanketed in white fluff. Mom flies back tonight. I hope it has melted by then. Schools were not closed this morning because nothing had dropped at 8 a.m., but at noon they started telling parents to come pick up their kids. Ben had to leave to collect Henry, and it took him an hour to drive what usually takes ten minutes. Ben was supposed to be here for Cosette's eye exam today. But it doesn't matter how hard she screams and how much it makes me cry to witness these exams, I can do it. They eventually end, then we get a two week break until the next one. They've been every two weeks since soon after she got the Avastin eye injection. She'll have an exam on the 21st and then, who knows, maybe we will be home by the one after that on February 4.

I'm glad Mom is coming back. Ben and Henry will pick her up and bring her to our house for the night. Then she'll go to the hospital tomorrow but also continue packing her house. She moves out in just a few weeks. It is very strange that I will never go to their house again. The last time I left it, I was pregnant. It will be someone else's home soon. I never lived in that house, but I have memories from there, all good ones like trying on my wedding dress, playing with my niece as a baby, playing house there with James for a night one winter when my parents were away, several Christmas celebrations, and many trips to the big lake in their neighborhood that was perfect for summer dips. Another chapter closed.

BABY JOURNAL | January 9

You're doing great. Being back to work is hard for me, but we're doing it. I say goodnight to you around 8 p.m. and wake you at 6 or 9 a.m. I love you!

Friday, January 10

Today is mine and Ben's first date anniversary. On Tuesday, January 10, 2017 we met in person for the first time. Ben and I started talking in October of 2016 but lost touch for a bit after the election. Then he messaged me through Facebook on New Year's Eve. I was at home but I waited until the next day to reply to him. I was not going to be that easily accessible. I was having a night on my own and had already turned down a late invite to a nearby party from a different online guy. I was determined to enter 2017 sober and refreshed. Ben and I ended up talking on the phone a few days later. His voice was friendly and he came off as modest and slightly self-deprecating, which was a new trait for men I met online. We eventually set up a first meeting. I had gotten a cut on my lip and treated it with an ointment that I was allergic to so I was very self-conscious about it. I thought it looked gross and on my lip of all places. I almost put him off longer because of it, but finally decided to tell him about it. He promised not to stare and to remember that it would go away soon.

When I opened the door to the coffeeshop where we had agreed to meet, he was right there at a big table facing the door with all of his stuff spread out. He had a book in his hands and he kept it open while looking at me for a moment. He smiled, then shut the book and started moving some of his things to make space for me. I sat down without ordering anything and we talked. He made me laugh. He got up to refill his coffee and rolled onto his heels while he waited at the counter. I carefully observed this new person in my life.

We stayed there for about an hour, then went next door for Mexican food. I had never been inside the restaurant even though I had been living in the town for years. It was mostly empty, probably because it was a Tuesday night. The joke had been that I would not commit to dinner until having the coffee date. Like I would not get stuck at a full dinner with someone I didn't want to be with for another minute. Too many bad experiences had taught me this.

"So I made it to dinner? I'm doing okay?" he asked, half playfully, half serious.

I nodded. "You're doing okay," I said and smiled shyly. It felt good to have some control in the situation. I had only met one man over the past ten years who did not reciprocate my interest if I was interested. He and I went out a couple of times before he told me he didn't think it was going to work out. I asked if he wanted to be friends instead, sort of desperate for English department friends after moving to Charlottesville when my MFA program was over in Roanoke, and he said *No, I have enough friends already.* Oh the dating stories! With Ben, I could tell that he liked me. I was wearing my staple winter go-out attire of the time which was black tights, legwarmers that went above the knee, and a skirt that didn't quite meet the legwarmer, and my brown tough-girl boots. I wasn't sure about him yet, he was a little wacky, but I was feeling good being around him. When I went into the restroom, I smiled at myself in the mirror and then frowned at my lip mark and took a deep breath.

Then there was the second date to the Thai restaurant. He made me feel special, like I was royalty, that I was a gift to be around.

He came to see me at my house the following night, Sunday. I had off from work on Monday for MLK Jr. Day. It was romantic and lovely and we told each other how excited we were about each other. First date turned into three dates in one week. I was so, so excited about him.

I felt that feeling on our wedding day too. In the midst of dancing during the most planned, most looked-forward-to event of my life, I had a moment of being ready to be alone with him on our honeymoon. It was a surge of love and excitement. I felt that at the end of April, too, shortly before Cosette was conceived. Again, we were dancing, this time at an 80s Prom fundraiser. I was gleeful to look across at him and know he was with me.

CARING BRIDGE POST | January 13

Last week we passed Cosette's 100th day in the NICU. Today was 107. I haven't been counting every day, but I was aware of the 100 day milestone. She's 39 weeks adjusted; my due date was next Monday. She won't be leaving the hospital by her due date, but hopefully a few weeks after. Today she went to low flow oxygen support, which is a great step in her respiratory progress. It also means less stuff on her face. It's hard to tell which she'll do first -- breathe with no support or eat without a feeding tube. We're still working on breastfeeding but it takes a lot of patience. I usually get four or five tries with her a day and often one is really good, one starts well and then she gets overwhelmed and coughs and it's over, and a few she is too tired to try. They say it often suddenly clicks for premature babies and then they're successful, so we are eagerly awaiting that day. Ben is working on bottle feeding while I'm at work, and the nurses also try to give her bottles overnight if she gives cues of wanting to eat. With Ben she will take some milk but tires quickly. She needs to be able to take a full bottle in order to leave the hospital. Ideally she will mostly breastfeed but will have to drink two bottles a day to get necessary supplements for being born premature. There is no telling how long this will take; it's all on her schedule.

The rigor of my routine is exhausting to say the least. I'm waking in the middle of the night again to pump because currently Cosette drinks more milk in a day than I am pumping so I need to increase my supply for when she's ready to eat at home. I was filling my freezer with milk after giving the hospital a huge bin of frozen milk in November, and then shockingly last week I found out it had all been used. Talk about stressful. I still have more frozen milk from home that is being added to fresh, and when she is nursing more the supply should increase, but there's no guarantee. I wake up at 5 a.m. to go to the hospital before work to see if she wants to eat at 6 a.m. Then I go to work, and then back to the hospital until about 8 p.m. On Tuesdays and Thursdays, I am at the hospital from 8 a.m. - 8 p.m. The days right now are certainly less stressful and emotional than they were three and a half months ago, but there is no time for anything else. I feel a little lost in any moment of socializing because I have only this happening. There is no weekend, there's just this and it has been like that for over one hundred days now. I'm not complaining, just stating.

Cosette is adorably cute and we love spending our days with her. We're grateful for our room that allows us to be more peaceful with her, but of course we look forward to the day when she can be at home with us every day and sleep in a crib right by our bed instead of 20 minutes away. It's coming, it's coming.

Thursday, January 16

The nurse who told me not to stay overnight two weeks ago because Cosette was not ready to breastfeed at night, told me on Monday morning that I was out of milk in the freezer. What? She had to be wrong. I got the dayshift nurse to check, and then I got a lactation specialist to check. Months ago I brought in everything from my home freezer because the lactation specialist was worried it wasn't cold enough, and I felt like I was running out of space. Word was sent that I was to be given extra room in the freezer to store milk. It was more than anyone usually stored and would fill two shelves in addition to my own. Everyone made it sound like it was limitless milk. But apparently it was getting used quickly and no one told me. The reason no dayshift nurses had said anything is because I was pumping milk at the hospital and they were using that. But I was not there overnight and she was eating a lot, so the stored containers went quickly. This sent me into a panic.

I was told again to try power pumping, which means pumping every ten minutes in an hour for a few minutes each time and doing that several times a day. How am I supposed to do that when I was at work or when I was at the hospital constantly holding Cosette? The lactation specialist said I could always resort to the F word. She meant formula. I did not want Cosette on pure formula, after all the work I had done to pump and teach her to breastfeed. Breastmilk is on average 22 calories per ounce but could be as low as 18, there's no way to know. With formula I can make the calorie count of her bottles higher than 22 calories. But we also need to be careful because if it's too high it can be constipating or cause stomach discomfort. Cosette is past the risk age for getting NEC (necrotizing enterocolitis), but it is still out there as a terrifying thing that could happen because she was born premature. NEC is a stomach infection that is very, very bad. I have accepted that she will get some formula because she needs the calories and extra vitamins, but breastmilk is the most important substance she can consume.

I'm sad and worried about the milk. I've been trying hard to keep a good pump routine, but I feel like I just don't make as much when I'm at school. I use a different pump there too, not the hospital grade one. If I don't get everything out, then that can signal my body to decrease supply. I feel so angry sometimes that I have to go to work. People there try to be cheerful with me and I try to be back but I just want to scream that being there is hurting my baby. That's not explicitly true, but I have a lot of exaggerated feelings these days.

Friday, January 17

I decided this morning that I should stay overnight with Cosette for the first time. I went there like normal before work and realized it was the weekend, and we're getting close to coming home time, and that I should do this and see how often she will breastfeed. Mom went to the house before coming to the hospital and got things I needed to spend the night. I will try to go to sleep early because I know I will be up a lot. Right now it feels nice to be here with her. I don't have to call and ask how she is. I don't need to say goodnight to her and walk out the door, looking back over my shoulder twenty times to have a last look.

BABY JOURNAL | January 18

I have been at the hospital so much it's been hard to find time to write in this journal. You are doing great. You're on a room air trial and doing so well. I stayed over with you last night, and I breastfed exclusively for over 24 hours. You did a good job. It was great to see you with no equipment on your face. I'll miss you tonight, but we'll both get solid sleep and I'll return in the morning. I only have two more days of school, then it's all you. We are getting so close to bringing you home. Monday is your due date.

Sunday, January 19

The overnight on Friday went okay. I did not sleep very much, maybe five hours cut into pieces. I tried to feed Cosette so many times, more than I probably should have. She wasn't getting enough so she kept waking up. I was determined though. It felt good to hold her in the dark and then return her to bed, and I'd crawl back onto the couch. The nurse decided Cosette should do a room air trial at the same time as I was there. It was easier to move her in and out of the bed not connected to the vent. So Saturday felt like a victorious day because I had stayed over and she was breathing on her own. But this morning when we went in, she had the low-flow back on. Apparently she had an event overnight, and the nurse practitioner said to put it back on in the middle of the night. It was very sad to come in and see the tape back on her face. We got more details during rounds, and it sounds like it could have been reflux, but it is being logged as an apnea event. We are not sure yet if this means a new seven day countdown. To me, it means she's not ready to come home. She needed stimulation to breathe in the middle of the night. She is not ready to come home.

Monday, January 20

Today is Cosette's due date. She got an MRI today. It's something they do for every premature baby who spends a long time in the NICU. The discharge MRI. They took her out of the room in a transport box like the one she was in the night of her birth. I cried hard seeing her like that. Then I left and went to my appointment with Ruth. Mom went to Cosette's room so that someone would be there when she returned. About three-fourths of the way through the therapy session, Mom texted me that Cosette was back. It was just an MRI, but I felt so nervous about it. We are getting close to leaving and I do not want any surprises. Of course, no one ever wants bad surprises, but I feel like my whole body is braced for it.

CARING BRIDGE POST | January 20

Today is Cosette's due date. It's certainly hard to think about all of that we have gone through in the past 16 weeks that could have been avoided if she was born today, but it's also a relief to know she is officially full term. This does not mean she is similar to a "normal" newborn; there are still a lot of things that lie ahead due to her prematurity, but there's also reason to celebrate -- we're at 40 weeks!

On Friday, I stayed overnight at the hospital to try to breastfeed exclusively for 24 hours. She breastfed frequently but ended up losing weight, which means she's not quite ready for that. She also did a room air trial over those 24 hours (coincidental timing). She did really well on it, but overnight on Saturday she had an apnea event that she couldn't recover from on her own. It seems likely that it was from an obstruction while getting fed through her feeding tube in bed, not something that will be happening at home, but it still sets her back in terms of discharge. Hearing about that and her weight loss on Sunday morning was difficult, but the doctors and nurse practitioners here have seen it all and are very good at explaining what needs to be done next. Now that she is 40 weeks, there does feel like a small push from them to get her home, with suggestions like taking her home with a feeding tube and on oxygen. They also say they will not send her home until she can go safely. Because of the apnea event she had, she will be here for a while longer and my hope is that she can return to room air and lose the NG tube before we go home. I want her home and they say she can learn to bottle feed better there with the consistency of me and Ben, but I feel like the amount of stress the combination of those two things could produce might be too much for us. After four months of hospital life, a few more weeks sounds manageable. After four months of hospital life, putting a NG tube up her nose to reach her stomach does not. Since the 24 hour breastfeeding trial went mostly well, I'm feeding her all day in that way, and then she gets bottle tries and the feeding tube overnight. We did that yesterday and she gained a lot of weight, more than she's supposed to day to day, so she's balancing out from the loss. My hope is that she is fully ready to come home by the end of the first week of February.

Tuesday, January 21

I stay overnight every night now. Today I went to school in the morning to meet with the teacher who will be taking over for me full time next week. As we talked, I felt more and more like I am not going back in March to finish the year. That feels impossible. Three days a week has been hard but five days a week for three months? I would be missing so much with Cosette. We've had such a difficult time, then I would be leaving for the nice part. She cannot nurse super easily so she wouldn't be able to do that at school like I had imagined before she was born. I pictured nursing her in Mom's car in the parking lot or in a tiny room behind the main office. But she cannot nurse in the place where the sick kids go to lie down before their parents pick them up. She is vulnerable. She's just different from all ideas of how I thought it was going to be.

The parents and teachers have been so supportive. I worry about them thinking I am ungrateful, that I should be able to stick it out for a few months. The teacher I met with today said he does not want to finish out the year for me. That was disappointing to hear, but I understand. They could find someone else. The kids though. I think of them and the moment of telling them that I'm not coming back. But I actually can't do that now because I do not know if it is true. They would be told by someone else while I was on leave.

Mary told me she would quit if she was me. Some others have said that, too. A friend at school gave me the idea last week when I explained that Cosette needs me at the hospital to practice breastfeeding in order to go home. She said I should quit. Mom is pushing me in the resigning direction, too. I think she is nervous about taking care of Cosette so much over those three months since Cosette has special needs. That's totally understandable. She also wants me to have a break and be home with Cosette.

David came in while I was talking to my substitute, and I hinted that I may not be finishing the year with him. He looked sad but I am sure he suspects it. Everyone knows I have gone through hell. I will miss him but work is hard and it feels like a relief to not have to plan the remainder of the year past what I have already done. I am working on mid-year reports to make sure they are finished by the time Cosette comes home. It is many, many hours of work.

I was at school for about 45 minutes, then drove back to the hospital. I miss seeing Teddy on these days where I stay overnight so many times in a row. Ben is taking care of him. I'll be there soon. We're in the homestretch.

Wednesday, January 22

During rounds yesterday, the doctor said the first read of the MRI looked good. There is no reason to suspect something has developed since those first scans. She has not had any procedures done where she wasn't able to breathe. Of course, I think about the night she pulled her tube out, but they assured me a new one was in quickly. But this afternoon when I arrived after work, the nurse practitioner came in to see me, which is rare. If you're not present for rounds in the morning, you usually do not see anyone on the team unless there's something wrong.

Cosette does not have any brain bleeds or anything like that, but she does have an ectopic pituitary gland. The radiologist caught this on the scan. They were not looking for something like that, but it showed up because the scan was of her whole brain. An ectopic pituitary gland means it's slightly out of place, not exactly where it should be. There is no way to know how many people have this because a majority of the population does not get an MRI in their whole life. They do know people can have this and present no symptoms. But others do. It can affect the production of growth hormones associated with dwarfism. It can affect the thyroid and the overall functioning of hormones in the body that regulate many processes. It can potentially be a big deal. It can also be nothing. Cosette has no symptoms of anything being wrong but the endocrinology department wants to do tests. A nurse came in tonight ready to draw many tubes of blood before we even understood what was going on. It wasn't her fault, that was the order, but the NP hadn't even spoken to us yet. Cosette has lost so much blood over her time in the hospital, and this draw involves putting a medicine into her to see how she will react to it. It's a lot and I rejected the draw. I told the nurse we needed to speak with someone from endocrine first and this could wait until tomorrow. Cosette has no symptoms, there is no reason to rush into it. I feel like at the hospital when red flags wave on results, a certain department gets the message and clicks a button to request a test. There's no check on the person, in this case an infant, behind the result. Well, I am Cosette's person who will demand more knowledge before proceeding.

I know we'll eventually let them do the test and hopefully it will be a good result, but regardless they will now be following her out of the hospital. She will need blood draws periodically, every few months for years. Cosette may not be leaving with an oxygen tank or NG tube, but she will be leaving with the threat of a hormonal disorder and more visits to the hospital. Like I had feared, there was a surprise waiting for us. I feel very sad about this. I can't write anymore tonight.

Thursday, January 23

The NP came to talk to us again this morning. And then she paged someone from endocrinology to talk to us. Everyone acted like it was sort of above and beyond what was needed -- talking to the department who ordered the tests. I don't care what they think of me at this point. We have been perfectly amiable parents and well liked around here. One push back should not make a difference.

We let them do the test and the results came back quickly. Presently, Cosette has no abnormalities with her main hormones like cortisol and thyroid stimulating hormone. That is good news. But she will need to be checked again in a few months.

Liza was here today and she drew blood from a vein in Cosette's head. It's a prominent one that sticks out, and Liza was able to do it without causing Cosette to cry. She had to do a heel prick as well and she did that without causing tears, too. I wish Liza could be at all of Cosette's appointments in the future. I wish we could take her home with us.

BABY JOURNAL | January 23

I'm sleeping at the hospital now with you. Just a week or two more to go. You're doing so well. We passed your due date this week. I love you so much. You make great noises and open your eyes very wide. I can tell you are going to enjoy the world.

CARING BRIDGE POST | January 24

Cosette is doing well, but I'm having a hard time. I realize this site is about her health and journey, but it has been helpful to me over the last four months to write about my experience, and so if it causes me to stabilize then it's helping her, too.

Tonight is my fifth night staying over at the hospital this week. Cosette is not consuming enough in a bottle to only bottle feed overnight so I stay to breastfeed her. We need her to be on just bottles and breast with no feeding tube. She wakes every 1.5 - 2 hours to eat. I worked a few days this week, but today was my last day. I am starting the second half of my maternity leave even though she's not home yet. Getting such little sleep is hard enough on top of it happening in a hospital and working all day. It's bright in the room and noisy, of course. I sleep with earplugs and an eye mask on a couch in a sleeping bag. Opening a zipper many times a night to go to her, at times feels like a tear-inducing frustration. Cosette's main awake time of the day is from 5 - 9 p.m. I interact with her but that's also a time I'd like to eat and maybe do a thing or two like an exercise video off my phone or look at a book. It's not really possible. I can't carry her with me to the fridge to get something to eat; the cafeteria is seven floors away. Being alone here at night is very lonely. It's lonely because I'm alone trying to take care of a newborn who is fussy and prefers to be out versus in her bed, but it's also lonely because I'm having a very singular experience. I feel dismayed when people say it's great I get a maternity leave now to spend more time with Cosette. I understand it's said with good intention, but to me it feels like I am having this very hard, abnormal experience and when it becomes normalized in that way, I feel like no one can understand how hard this has all been. I think it's a kind thing to say to someone who is hard to say the right thing to. That's me. It's hard to talk to me right now. And not being understood feels lonely.

She cried for hours tonight and when I finally got her calm, my tears mixing with hers, I put her down in bed asleep, but her wires were caught under her back so I had to move them and she began to scream. I got her asleep again and just a few moments ago a respiratory therapist came in to listen to her breathing. I held my breath, knowing I would fall apart if she woke Cosette. I know there isn't that much longer here, and when I'm rested and she's doing well, that feels great. But now, when I am too weary to sleep and know she will be up again soon, a future where I feel at peace seems unimaginable.

As many people do before they decide to have children, I wondered how I would deal with the stress of a crying infant and choppy sleep. I feared it. And now I'm living that without the normal comforts of my home and coming off four months of consistent trauma. Now instead of wondering it as a hypothetical, I wonder it in the moment she's screaming, and my past self questioning and my present self experiencing become one somewhat vacant mind trying to get through it while also trying to do all the right things for my girl who is very real and very precious.

Saturday, January 25

Cosette is back on room air and doing well. All of the suggestions about taking her home on oxygen are now a thing of the past. Thank god. I always felt she wouldn't need it, and the breathing event was probably not apnea related, but it is reassuring to see her numbers so steady without any assistance. Her lungs, which were once so tiny and strained, are now much healthier and doing their job. The red marks from the adhesive which kept the tube in place are healing on her cheeks and upper lip.

Sunday, January 25

I'm having a hard time. I barely slept last night because I was up so much trying to feed Cosette, but she is not taking much from me. By the time Liza got here this morning, I was crying while holding Cosette in my lap. Liza made a new plan for us and sent me home. I'm back now feeling refreshed and eager to get my girl home soon. It's going to be such a different life when we are not constantly in the hospital. I feel like I have memorized every piece of vegetation on the side of the road to get here. It was strange to see the sunlight pour through the front windows of the house for the short time I was there. I have not been there in the afternoon since October. In rounds this morning, the doctor suggested discharge could happen this week. It's always a different doctor on the weekend, so they could have varying opinions.

BABY JOURNAL | January 26

You're on room air and eating well. You may come home this week! I've been making a video of your pictures from day one. Seeing where you were and how you are now, it brings me to tears.

CARING BRIDGE POST | January 26

Cosette's room air trial this weekend has gone very well, and we started a new plan yesterday after a very teary morning to supplement breastfeeding sessions with some bottles so that we are sure she's getting enough and can gain weight. We weigh her before and after breastfeeding to know exactly how much she's gotten which takes some pressure off me to predict. But she doesn't like getting weighed so often. Room air and gaining weight. . . they are hinting at discharge this week.

Monday, January 27

Ben and I were both there this morning when the doctor and nurse practitioner came in to see us. The doctor had a funny smile on her face.

"Cosette is breathing room air and she's gaining weight. She's drinking the bottles, and you seem to have a good feeding system in place. She doesn't need to be here anymore. So it is time to talk discharge."

Ben and I looked at each other and smiled. "Okay," I nodded."We agree. What day are you thinking?"

"Tomorrow."

"Tomorrow?" I coughed out the word. "But that's... tomorrow."

The doctor laughed. "Yes. She's ready. You're all ready. There's no reason for you to stay, and I promise we would not make that up."

My cheeks heated and I felt a constriction in my chest. But Ben looked more worried than me.

"What about the car seat test?" I asked. I remembered the Mennonite baby in G-pod who did the test and then got sick and stayed longer. I'll never know how much longer.

"Do you have it in your car? We could do it today."

"No, but my mom is still at home. She could go by the house and get it."

"Do that. You could do it tomorrow morning too, but it'd be better to get it done today."

The car seat test is what it sounds like. The baby needs to sit in the seat for 90 minutes to make sure levels don't drop. If she were to get really angry or not be able to breathe well in the upright position, she would fail. There was no reason to suspect that would happen to Cosette, but it is still one more box to check.

The doctor and NP said congratulations and left. Ben and I started going through all of the things we needed to do before tomorrow. I felt that surge of organization and preparation that I had not felt in a long time. She was coming home. Like really coming home, tomorrow.

Mom came with the seat. Ben met her in the parking garage to carry it for her. She did not seem surprised that Cosette was getting discharged tomorrow. Happy but not surprised.

Liza was Cosette's nurse today and will also be there tomorrow. That was good luck. Liza told me to go home and get things done. "Don't come back tonight," she said in her strict, playful voice. "Go home, do what you need to do, and have one last night together at home just the two of you. I'll be here with her all day. You can call me and ask about the car seat test. I'm sure it will be fine though."

So I left Cosette in her car seat in the afternoon looking adorably small. She held onto the chest straps like she was going on an amusement park ride. She looked all around inspecting the parts of the seat. I left the hospital earlier than I had left in a very long time.

I called Liza before her shift ended, and we also called Cosette's night nurse before we went to bed. She was giving her a bath. Cosette just had a bath yesterday. She gets baths twice a week.

"She's going home tomorrow, right?" the nurse asked.

"She is," I said, joy flooding my face.

"We always give babies baths before they go home. You get them delivered to you nice and clean."

My sweet Cosette is getting polished up and ready for her big journey tomorrow. It will be her first time outside, her first breath of fresh air, her first time in a car, her first time in our house and her crib. She will sleep here tomorrow night. Will I sleep tonight? Some hopefully! What about tomorrow night? Probably less because I will be listening to her breathing and being alert to all of her noises. That's okay, though. No beeps, just peaceful breathing of baby and her parents.

Tuesday, January 28

S he's here. She's in the house.

We got discharged right before noon, which is the goal at the NICU. I remember seeing that on the board in the main lobby, a tally of how many discharges they had before noon. Cosette was one of those numbers today. Her room at the hospital is empty. All of her signs came down, everything she collected over her four months was put into a bag and sent with us. Her tiny sunglasses from her first week when she had light treatment, her first blood pressure cuff, a tiny diaper to show the size she wore for those first weeks.

Ben and I were there before 8 a.m. Then he left a little before 10 a.m. to go to the firehouse to get the car seat base installed. The NICU recommends getting it done by firemen, so that's what we did. While Cosette and I waited, her doctors and therapists came in to say bye. Everyone was so happy for us.

Liza got Cosette a stuffed bear wearing a tuxedo to celebrate her special graduation day. She made a hat to go on the bear's head that says *NICU Graduate!* We took many hilarious pictures of the bear propped up next to Cosette in her bed. The bear is bigger than her. We took pictures of Cosette with Liza, too. I could tell this day was almost as exciting for Liza as it was for us. I imagine moments like these are a reward for her in a job that can often be sad. I am very grateful that she signed up for us and stuck with Cosette. It made a huge difference to create a relationship with a nurse like we did with her. The NICU had us fill out a form about our experience and that's the only "complaint" I put on there, about how hard it was in October to have a new nurse every day.

One of the best moments was when Liza took the leads off Cosette's chest.

Those are the stickers that hold the sensor wires down on the skin. She always had three on her chest. The only time she did not have them on was during a bath. She'll probably always have scars on her stomach and foot from the first leads she had when her skin was extremely thin. Taking them off was the last thing Liza did before we put Cosette in the car seat; she was no longer a patient once her vitals were not recording. The hospital was no longer responsible for her after that moment. She is all ours now. We got her in her seat, and I recorded a little video of Ben carrying her from the room out into the hallway. It's something I never want to forget. Liza led us to the main doors of the NICU and had us take a picture in front of the main sign. She went in and told another nurse to come out to say bye to us. She had not been one of Cosette's nurses since we left H-pod in December, but we remembered her fondly from our time there. She had been a big part of that rough transition onto NIPV after extubation. She was happy to see us and of course thrilled to see us leaving. She got teary, which was moving to me since it had been over a month since she had cared for Cosette. Rachel was there too and wished all of us well.

And that was the last goodbye, except for Liza. Mom went ahead and pulled my car up in front of the hospital in the pickup/dropoff lane. Liza went down in the elevator with us, and we all prayed there were no flu germs in the elevator car that could reach Cosette. Liza went outside with us, and Ben put Cosette in the backseat of the car. The plan was for me to sit with her in the back while Ben drove. I turned to Liza and started to cry. She was crying too.

"You've got this girl. Now it's your turn, you're strong, you've got this." She squeezed me tight in a hug.

I nodded against her shoulder. "Thank you," I said through heavy tears. "For all of it."

"You're welcome," she said. She clenched my shoulders one last time and then released me. I looked right at her and smiled. As I turned away, I saw Mom standing nearby also crying. She hugged Liza too. I got in the backseat next to Cosette and held her hand. She peered at me with her big eyes, knowing something big was happening.

Ben turned into the lane of cars exiting the circle. I waved to the hospital. "Goodbye, hospital," I whispered. Goodbye to our temporary home, our place that allowed our girl to live. I'm grateful, but I hope we never have to be there with her again unless we're coming to show her off to all of our superstar nurses.

I talked to Cosette the whole way home about trees, leaves, cars, and who she would be meeting at home. By the time we arrived, she was asleep. We took her out of the carseat and laid her in her crib. That didn't last long. She napped on one of us for the rest of the day except for when eating. It feels amazing to have her here. We don't have the camera set up yet to see her when we're not in the room, so I'm in here with her as she sleeps. I am exhausted anyway and know she will be up in about three hours to eat. It feels great to be in my own bed with her so close. It is what I've been waiting for and now it's here.

Thursday, January 30

Today is Ben's birthday. Cosette is a little bundle of unimaginable cuteness. We carry her around flung over a shoulder or cradled in our arms. The sleep sack she wears to bed makes her look like a small taco. When I get to pick her up from her bed in the middle of the night, it's like scooping up mashed potatoes, a soft, compact lump. I hope I never forget that feeling and what she looks like in these moments. She hardly ever cries, except sometimes when she gets hungry. The bottle still isn't the easiest thing, she gets finicky, but mostly we are doing okay. We hold her a majority of the day. She does not nap in her bed; she just sleeps there at night. I go to bed before her sometimes and Ben brings her up after she eats late. We sleep a few hours at a time, just like in the hospital. We are following all of the same routines which might be excessive. She may not need her diaper changed every three hours overnight. We're trained though. Why mess with a regimen that has worked?

Ben seems really happy to share his birthday with Cosette's coming home week. We won't see any friends or do much of anything special, but the general feeling here is one of joy. Mom has come to help each day too and she holds Cosette for one of her naps. Cosette is not like a newborn even though she recently passed her due date. We are not having the experience of bringing home a baby who is three days old. We don't need that kind of help. Instead, we're all just having a nice time. It feels like a reward for passing a test.

Ben asked his mom if she would come take care of Henry in February during the weeks he is supposed to have him so that he doesn't need to leave me alone with Cosette. Directly in flu and cold season, it's too dangerous to bring Henry into the house each day after being at school with lots of other four year-olds. Instead of that, his parents have offered to come get Henry and fly him back to their house for an adventure. He will visit with Ben's siter and her family and then with them. Ben likes this plan because it means Henry gets to spend time with his family. It's a long time for Henry to be away, but I think he'll enjoy all of the special activities they'll do with him.

BABY JOURNAL | January 31

Dear baby, you came home on Tuesday the 28th, one day before turning four months old. We made a video of the four months, which we will have forever. It is so great to have you here. We cuddle all day. Today we gave you a bath. That was the big event of the day. It is really nice to stay at home and not go to the hospital. You seem really comfortable too. We hold you most of the day, then we all go to bed in our bedroom. At first it was scary to hear you and not hear you, but I'm getting more used to it. I don't mind getting up for you at night. I hope you can change to all breastmilk next month. I have decided to resign from my job so that I can take care of you better. It will be fun in the spring and summer to take you out to places. Everything feels lighter and better now that you are home with us. I think we're all pretty content. You are very cute and lovable. I am glad for all of my days with you.

CARING BRIDGE POST | February 1

Cosette has been home for five days, and it has been blissful. We have been taking care of her for many months now and she's not really a newborn anymore (although her adjusted age is just under two weeks), so our transition home has been easier than returning home a day after delivery. We have our feeding schedule and know her signals. Ben and I didn't realize how amazing it would feel to not drive to the hospital each day, to be in our own space, and most of all to pick up Cosette and move her around the house whenever and wherever we want. Even when she was on room air in the hospital, she had wires to read her vitals. I'm enjoying doing skin to skin with her each morning in a fun shirt that she fits inside of, not something I could easily use at the hospital. Ben and my mom and I take turns holding her during the day, and then she goes to her bed nicely at night. I realize babies are constantly changing and things may get more difficult with her, but for this moment, this week, the ease feels like a reward for everything that has led to now.

We are prepared to stay isolated for the month of February, and under advice from our pediatrician Henry is going to wait until March to be with us again. Generously and lovingly, Ben's parents are flying from Washington state tomorrow to pick up Henry and will take him to their house for three weeks. He will get to visit his aunt and uncle and cousins, too. We have to take Cosette to her eye doctor appointment next week, but her pediatrician comes to the house which is great. I hope to take her outside on Monday when it will be warm for her first real drink of fresh air.

I plan to keep this site active until we have a celebration for Cosette in the summer so that I can invite everyone who has been following her journey and supporting us. I will post occasionally until then. Three hundred twenty-six people have followed Cosette, and her page has been visited over 7000 times. This mode of communication has been instrumental in getting me through the past four months; I am grateful. It's hard to believe it was just a week ago that I was feeling so desperate. If I had known then we had less than a week to go, it would have been easier to handle. That night really caused a breakthrough though because a new feeding plan was put in place the next day, which ultimately led to her gaining weight and going home. We were warned it would all wrap up quickly and that's how it happened. She is doing great, though, and there is no doubt that she was ready.

Tuesday, February 4

Cosette has been home for one week. It is wonderful to have her here and to be away from the hospital. We took her out for the first time today to go to the eye doctor. We kept her covered in her carseat in the waiting room and sanitized our hands constantly because we are wary of flu germs. It was awful there, to listen to her scream, but we got through it. So far her eyes still look okay, but the doctor said she has much growth ahead of her. Hopefully all of it will be good growth.

The privacy at home is amazing. And there is no rushing. Cosette sleeps and eats very well. She's adorable and seems happy. I'm resigning from my job so I can stay home with her. Otherwise I would go back in March. Once the decision was finalized, it felt like there had never been another possible option. This is where I belong now. This is where I am needed most.

Even though the hospital stay was four months, the ending felt fast. All of a sudden it was over. It's a relief and it has not been scary, but it is taking some mind adjustment. Now I have a baby. And I will not be working. I will find things in which to invest energy, maybe some tutoring and writing, or election related things. But I can also just enjoy my baby and being home. It's fun to watch documentaries and movies I missed over the past months while Cosette sleeps on me. She is a warm, comforting lump. One hundred twenty-one days straight in the NICU. We deserve a rest.

BABY JOURNAL | February 4

You have been home for one week. It's been smooth. You eat and sleep. We hold you. We went to the eye doctor today. I hope you get to have good vision. We're trying to make that happen for you. You are very cute, and I love scooping you up in your sleep sack and bringing you into bed with me in the middle of the night.

CARING BRIDGE POST | February 9

Save the date! We're having a celebration for Cosette on the afternoon of Saturday, May 30. All who have followed her journey on Caring Bridge are welcome to attend. Her baptism will be on May 31 during a 10 a.m. service at St. Paul's Memorial Church and anyone is welcome to attend.

Monday, February 10

I went to see Dr. H today for a checkup. I did not cry this time. It was nice to talk to her about Cosette being home and I showed her a picture. She is a very kind doctor. I asked about her thoughts on having another child and if she could tell me more about my risks of having a premature baby again. She said she was going to call in a referral to UVa's Maternal and Fetal Medicine department and have me talk to a specialist there.

BABY JOURNAL | February 16

You've been home for almost three weeks now. It's been great. You're 8.5 lbs and seem so content. We are hoping for good news at the eye doctor on Tuesday. I adore spending each day with you. It has been very cold out, so it's nice to stay in and cuddle. We watched your movie from the hospital again last night. You have come so far!

Wednesday, February 19

Cosette's pediatrician came to the house today for a checkup. She visited a few days after we brought her home, too. Cosette needed vaccinations, which was terrible to do in the house. Ben held her while the doctor jammed the needles in Cosette's legs. The doctor will come back in two weeks to give Cosette her Synagis injection against RSV. She had one on the day she left the hospital and will receive another one for the month of March. It will be shipped to the house, and then the doctor comes to inject it. I am glad Cosette will have one for March and that the insurance approved it. It's $2000 per shot without insurance.

CARING BRIDGE POST | February 20

Baby Cosette is one month old (corrected) today! She's 8lb 10oz and doing really well. She spends her days sleeping, eating with me, with Ben (bottle), stretching on her back and belly, and listening to books (I'm reading Villette by Charlotte Bronte to her, inspired by her rhyming name). Some have asked about her eyes so if you'd like more of a medical update read on.

We go every other week to the eye doctor to check for return of retinopathy of prematurity. The most likely time for a return is between 45-55 weeks, so she's not yet in that window, but the doctor said she could potentially be showing signs already and she is not, which is good. She has not had much positive growth in her eyes, but has about four months for that to happen. If at around 60 weeks in May/June she has not had much good growth, then she'll need to go to hospital to have the remaining space in her eye lasered so that ROP cannot return, because she cannot keep having this awful experience of an exam every other week for years. She would need to be intubated for this surgery, which is hugely upsetting to imagine. If she has a return of ROP before 60 weeks, then she will need laser surgery immediately. No matter what, at this point she should have adequate vision, just not great peripheral vision, but ROP would threaten the adequate vision. So we are praying for good growth, no bad growth, and patience.

In addition to her eyes, we're hoping for positive results from blood work in two weeks, which could let her cut out or at least decrease the amount of formula she needs each day. We've had a screening for early intervention that will assess what therapies she may need to help her development in these early months. She's also a part of a study at UVa on play therapy for premature babies. She will have twelve home visits from May - August to do the therapy. She'll be tracked for two years. We are grateful to be a part of that. She is a very happy one month/five month-old baby and we are loving spending our days with her.

BABY JOURNAL | February 21

You're one month old corrected. I love you! You're doing great. 8 lb 10 oz.

Friday, February 28

February is almost over. There's a virus called coronavirus that is spreading around the world. It's distressing. Cosette's lung disease puts her at high risk. We can stay in the house, but it's still scary. I did not enjoy my day today because I let the fear take me over. That is not how it should be with her. I will do better tomorrow.

Laura gifted me an appointment with an astrologer who lives in Berlin. I was ten minutes into the talk when someone came into the coffee shop where she was and said she had to leave, that the city was going on lockdown because cases of the virus had been found there. Before that happened, she said Cosette's sudden birth fits my chart. She said Cosette will be an awakening of my femininity and will play this role for a long time. Relationship stuff will be intense until I can merge parts of myself to fully accept myself as a woman. We got cut off then. I want to question what that means and would she warn me against getting pregnant a second time.

I need to calm down about the virus and enjoy the days at home. It's precious time. If we were all going to die for any reason, I would want to enjoy these days. My mind cannot solve it. If we take precautions, we will be okay. I can keep Cosette safe.

BABY JOURNAL | February 29

It's Leap Day. You're five months old! Incredible. You are super sweet and loveable. You are having fussy times at night but overall seem happy.

Thursday, March 5

It is March. It's getting warmer outside. The flu is receding, yet we may be in the house for a lot longer. There's a pandemic out there. It is not in Virginia yet but is in many other states and has affected 100,000 people globally. We will need to stay quarantined. This means Ben may have to move out in order to be with Henry and go to work. It sounds very hard, but there's an overpowering feeling to keep Cosette safe. It would be difficult on our marriage and hard on Ben to be away from Cosette for so long, but if she got sick and died, we would regret not being careful enough and would feel the pain forever. Months split up as a family would be sad, but no more Cosette permanently is unfathomable.

I talked to the astrologer again today. She said things will get lighter in May. I sure hope so. Cosette's birth lines up with my chart as a huge event occurring to wake me up to being more human and loving, to repair breaks in past family lines, as well as my experience of being seen as a little girl. This type of event will not happen for another 28 years. It happened when I was nine, too, going to Ursuline Academy, that initial loneliness of a new school. She said I have a very intense chart and things happen to me in big ways. The start of this transit was when I had my concussion last February. She said this birth experience with Cosette happened in order for me to be a good/right mother, and I will always have a special appreciation for Cosette. She cautioned me to keep my independent Aries side that wants to do things, to not let it go or I will feel dismal, especially during quarantine times ahead. She said Cosette and I will have many adventures as she grows up. She thinks Cosette will be practical, orderly, and good with her hands. And she'll want to stay youthful and will be sensitive to criticism. I should be careful not to squash her energy. She said summer 2021 will be a start to a light time for us. That sounds nice, but I'm also excited for us now. It might be a less fun few more months or weeks inside, but we have been through a lot and can handle it.

Cosette may need eye surgery this week. I will try to meet that with courage, not fear, for her sake. I get really upset at first, feeling like it's all unfair and woe is me, but I am resilient and feel better quickly. I need to make sure Cosette feels that I trust the world, doctors, etc.

Nursing has gotten more difficult and can be hugely depressing. There is another place I need to make sure Cosette does not feel my frustration and disappointment. Sometimes she doesn't latch on or only does for a very brief amount of time. And I cannot get her to take a bottle from me, only from Ben. She'll just cry and cry because she is hungry and not getting what she wants.

BABY JOURNAL | March 7

It's March! We are still inside waiting for flu season to go away. Unfortunately, there's a big virus out there that might keep us inside longer. We'll do it though to keep you safe. I think when May arrives we'll be feeling much lighter. I talked to an astrologer today who told me we will have a lot of adventures together. She said you'll want to stay young for a long time and you will be orderly, practical, responsible, and good with your hands. She said to give you freedom and not criticize too much. She said we'll have a harmonious relationship.

CARING BRIDGE POST | March 7

As many people in the world are feeling unsettled right now, things are no different here with us and Cosette. It is hard to read about coronavirus and how they say it is typically not that serious for those without a preexisting heart or respiratory condition. And what of those who do have that? Cosette's lung disease of prematurity puts her at high risk for complications from a common cold, and so a new, very contagious virus is terrifying. We have stayed in for these six weeks to avoid flu and colds, and I thought we were nearing the end of that time. I am trying my best to not get too swept up in fear, though, for Cosette. I don't want her sensing that from me. We can stay quarantined in the house, and she will be safe.

I tell myself that it won't be like this forever and that Cosette is still so fresh to the world. I am reminded of this when she gives me her first little smiles that look so new and beautiful on her chubby face. She's spending more time awake during the day and has had some fussy evening times like most newborns. We've had some feeding struggles, her and me, with what seems like nipple confusion. She now knows the bottle is easier than breast so fights at the breast sometimes during the day. We may have partially resolved this by changing to a different bottle that mimics the breast more. She would fight taking the other bottle from me too and would only take it from Ben. She'll take this new bottle from me. They say sometimes babies just don't want to bottle feed with their mothers if they're also breastfeeding, which has left me bewildered during times I have been home alone and she won't breastfeed. I am hoping we've turned a corner with that. It is hugely emotional to have Cosette fight me, howling, at the breast.

Another difficult emotional situation that arose was when we found out Cosette would not drink milk that I froze when she was in the hospital. All of the milk I pumped in October she drank during her time there, and I was present giving her milk for much of January, but all of November and December have been waiting for her in the freezer. Some babies don't like the taste of defrosted milk if a woman has high lipase milk, which apparently I do. Cosette won't drink it, and even if disguised with a little vanilla it makes her spit up. Of course I calculated it and know that about 500+ hours of pumping time will be poured down the drain. I needed to do that pumping to have continuous milk, but it is hard because my supply isn't great now so she needs a supplement. I would have preferred for more of that to be this defrosted milk versus formula. Friends who are doctors, or friends who have gone through similar struggles with breastfeeding, tell me that stressing over it is not worth it. It is not worth missing a happy time with Cosette because I'm sad about feeling deficient, or like her backstory has led us to this place that feels unfair (I stopped pumping during the night in October, which is probably why I have less milk now). But it's all just details. The bigger picture is that I have her, and mothering is a lot more than producing milk. And she is getting a large portion of her meals as milk, at least for now. I never knew breastfeeding could be so emotional, challenging, and stressful, though. That wasn't in the baby books I read.

And finally, we find out on Tuesday if Cosette will need laser eye surgery this week. Last Tuesday, the doctor detected some bad membrane growth and prepared us for possible surgery this week if the growth has not regressed. We were sad, of course, but ultimately I trust the doctors, and I want to make sure Cosette feels safe and not like I have a lot of doubt and fear about what she will undergo. It's certainly triggering to imagine returning to the hospital for an overnight visit, but if it needs to happen, I'd prefer this week versus in a few weeks when the hospital may have virus patients. The eye exams she gets every other week are terrible, she screams and screams, so another bright side to surgery is that she would only need a few more of those instead of months more. I am trying very hard to find the positive side of things. It takes a lot of mental work to get to that place and being so isolated without much outside stimulus heightens it all.

My maternity leave ended Friday and I would be returning to work on Monday, but I decided to resign. Now with eye surgery and a looming virus, it really feels like I have no choice. It was certainly a very difficult decision to make a few weeks ago. I miss the kids, my colleagues, and the mental stimulation. Cosette needs me and she's getting me, which is most important right now. Lighter, brighter times are ahead, and for now I am trying to be present each day with her, marveling at her growth and cuteness, and understanding that these small experiences are all part of a bigger life that we get to share together.

CARING BRIDGE POST | March 10

H i everyone, Cosette will be having eye surgery this afternoon. Please think of us. We are hoping for no pain for her, a germ-free hospital visit, a quick recovery, and that everything goes smoothly so we can bring her home tomorrow.

Wednesday, March 11

C osette had eye surgery yesterday. The visit to the doctor on Tuesday morning was brutal. We had such high hopes that she would be okay and not need surgery for a few more months or maybe not at all. I wanted her to get bigger and stronger before needing such an intense procedure. I was also scared about taking her into the hospital with coronavirus looming. The visit started normally with the doctor putting drops in her eyes, and then we waited with her in the dimly lit room for 20 minutes. He returned, she was strapped down on the table, his assistant held Cosette's arms down, and he began the tortuous thing he does. A lot of time went by, what felt like more than usual, with Cosette screaming blood curdling shrieks of misery. I had my hand on her writhing chest, but looked away like I always do. Ben held onto my other hand, hard. I squeezed and squeezed. I didn't cry though. That happens less frequently now. Then suddenly the doctor spoke, which he never does during the actual exam. He always waits until it's over and Cosette is in my arms.

"Looks good, folks," he said cheerily.

I exhaled and squeezed Ben's hand in a pulsing rhythm. I smiled into his shoulder.

"Oh wait," said the doctor. "I spoke too soon." Then silence.

I cursed inaudibly into Ben's shirt. The lights came on, and I grabbed

Cosette off the table as soon as she was released. Her eyes were swollen and her face was red and puffy.

"Baby, baby, baby," I whispered into her ear.

The doctor explained that at first it looked like there was no bad growth, and then he saw one last angle which showed definite growth. "We need to get in there immediately," he said.

"Today?" I asked.

"Today would work for me. The latest I would recommend is tomorrow."

We entered the office knowing this was a possibility. He warned us last time, and he also warned that the next steps would be fast if bad growth was found.

I looked at Ben. "We should do it today," I said.

Ben nodded. "This afternoon? Tell us what we do next."

The doctor left us with his assistant to take care of the details. She gave us paperwork about being admitted to the hospital, where to go, how to check in, etc.

"Are they doing anything different at the hospital because of the virus?" I asked.

She didn't know. She suggested one of us park and the other go in and find out.

Ben drove us home, and I sat in the back next to Cosette. I texted Mom and Cosette's pediatrician to tell them. Mom was upset, of course. The pediatrician said we should wear masks and gloves in the hospital. We didn't have either of those. Mom said maybe they would be available once we entered the hospital.

We packed bags to stay overnight at the hospital. It all felt very strange, to dig out that same bag and I knew exactly what I needed to spend the night. It was all very familiar and sad and terrifying. Cosette was going to be intubated later that day. We worked so hard to get Cosette off her tube; I was scared she would get one again and not be able to have it removed. Like her body would remember it and then forget how to do the work on its own.

We left for the hospital at 1 p.m. We were supposed to check in by 2 p.m. Ben dropped me off in the spot where we had said goodbye to Liza five weeks ago. At the registration desk, I explained that Cosette is premature and at risk for infection. They told me they would text me when it was time to bring her in. I found our car in the parking garage, and we began to wait. We ended up waiting for 1.5 hours in the car. It was beyond miserable. Cosette got upset and she seemed hungry, but she wasn't supposed to consume anything too close to the surgery. I finally gave her some Pedialyte, hating to see her drink the bright orange, sugary liquid. She liked it of course.

Finally, we got the text and took Cosette directly to the pre-op room. It was a tiny room with a large crib. A nurse came in to greet us. She gave me a small, yellow hospital gown to put on Cosette.

"Take off everything but her diaper," she said.

I started to remove Cosette's clothes, and it was around then that I began to feel like crying. But I had promised myself I would hold it together for Cosette. She was not going to see me scared. She had nothing to worry about. I would never make her do something that was dangerous.

She looked adorable in the yellow gown. They told me to put her down in the crib. She rolled around on her back in the gown throwing her legs up in the air. The nurse was loving her. Cosette looked so happy and so smiley. I will never forget how dear and sweet she looked in that tiny, thin gown pulled up to her neck. She had no idea what was going to happen next.

The anesthesiologist came in and talked to us. Then Cosette'e eye doctor came to see us. He was in scrubs and ready to go. Then Cosette was gone. They wheeled her away, and I lost it. I sobbed and sobbed. Ben held me against his chest. I felt deep sorrow come up from the base of my stomach. This was one of the first times I felt like I had to depend on Ben and was relieved he was there to hold me. I needed to be held. I usually felt such resistance but not at that moment. I had been strong for Cosette, but once she was gone I crumbled. Ben was there for me to fall against. I cried until his shirt was wet, then I pushed away.

"I need to pump," I said. "It's been too long. I'm going to find a bathroom and then I'll pump in here."

I walked down the hallway, still crying. Staff looked at me. I didn't care. I pushed open the single-person bathroom with my elbow and washed my hands thoroughly. We were not getting sick.

Back in the pre-op room, Ben said the nurse had come to show us out, but he told them I needed to pump first. I had nowhere to refrigerate the milk, but hopefully it would be okay until Cosette was given her room for the night. They told us the surgery would take about an hour. It was 3:30 p.m. when they took her back. Ben sat next to me in the cramped room. I finished pumping and gathered my things. We made our way to the lobby, but I was afraid of sitting in the crowded space. So we sat outside. It was cold. Over the next hour, I did things on my phone and looked at a book. Ben worked on his laptop. I was supposed to get a text when Cosette was in post-op. It started to get dark outside. It was almost 5 p.m.

We went inside and looked at the electronic board that listed surgery patients and their location. I connected Cosette's ID number with one on the screen. It said Cosette was still in surgery. It was too cold and dark to sit outside any longer. We found two seats away from everyone else in the lobby. Shortly after sitting down, the ophthalmologist found us. He had returned to his normal clothes.

"The surgery went well," he said. "Cosette did great. No issues. Her eyes will be puffy for many days and you need to put drops in three times a day. Those are very important to help her heal. The lasers are a strong burn. They will have the drops in your room tonight, and we'll send you home with them tomorrow. Please call the office if you have any problems. And we'll see you next Tuesday to check on her." The doctor reached out to shake our hands. It felt rude to not do it so we both did. Then we walked to the nearest hand sanitizer station.

It was almost 5:30 p.m. The screen said Cosette was in post-op. I spoke to an administrator at the desk, and she led us to the same door we went in for pre-op. A nurse met us there and took us through the hallways past pre-op, through some doors, and into a different section. Around then I got the text that Cosette was in post-op. And then we saw her. Actually I heard her before I saw her. She was crying hard. My little girl who was so happy in her yellow gown was now beside herself in tears. She was more upset than I ever remember seeing her in the hospital.

The nurses in charge of Cosette looked relieved to see me. "Here's Mom. She will make you feel better." They handed Cosette to me, and I held her close to my chest. Her little fingers desperately gripped my shoulders. Her eyelids were swollen to five times their normal size. She wasn't opening them to look at us. She wailed and wailed. I looked at Ben and started to cry again. Just small tears but the anguish was too intense to keep them back. He put his arms around both of us.

We waited in the post-op area, which wasn't a room but rather a crib with a curtain separating us from the next one. We were there for hours. Cosette nursed some and then fell asleep. I was surprised she was able to nurse because she was so upset, but that must have been more comforting to her than trying the bottle. I put my head back against the headrest and almost fell asleep. It felt good to have her against me sleeping. I probably would have fallen asleep, but a group of nursing students was on the other side of the curtain. They were having a lively conversation about exams and other things. Lots of laughter, joking, teasing. Good for them. If Cosette was a light sleeper I would have said something, but she was solidly asleep.

The nurse came back a few times to check on us and to apologize for the wait. I asked her if it was possible to have a single room and explained Cosette's prematurity and infection risk. The nurse called the peds floor and reported back to me that the few single rooms they had were being kept empty in case a coronavirus patient was admitted. She said she could see the details of the roommate, and we had nothing to worry about in terms of contagion.

At around 9 p.m., the nurse brought a wheelchair so that I could smoothly carry Cosette up to her room. She woke up though and started to cry. She cried in the elevator, down the halls, and all the way into the room. I imagined that whoever was her roommate was very disappointed to hear us enter.

The roommate was a young boy, maybe four. I didn't see him until the next day; he was in bed for the night when we came in. I learned today from being forced to listen to all of the doctors and nurses who spoke to them that he has a rare, genetic intestinal issue. He had surgery a while ago, not at UVa, and something was punctured during the surgery that caused more problems. They are from Virginia Beach and came here for specialists. The boy has been in the hospital for many weeks. The father was on his way out when we arrived, and the mother was spending the night. There was one single flat area that served as a hard couch during the day and could be used as a bed at night. Only one of us was allowed to sleep there, which would have been nice to know ahead of time.

For the next two hours, we tried to get Cosette comfortable. We had brought clothing that wouldn't work with an IV being in her arm. I had forgotten about that. I thought they would take it out when the surgery was over, but I should have known better. They usually leave the PICC line in as long as possible. The nurse brought a short sleeve onesie, and we had her sleep sack from home. Cosette's arm had to stick out of it, though. She did not look comfortable. And she was obviously still affected by the anesthesia. She was not acting like herself and had not yet opened her eyes. I couldn't tell if they were swollen shut from inflammation or she just did not want to open them.

"I need to get food," said Ben. "Do you want anything?"

I had not eaten in so long I wasn't hungry anymore. I was tired and weary and wanted to go home. "Maybe a yogurt? What are we going to do about the one bed?"

"I can stay," said Ben. "If you want to go home."

"Really? I don't think I will sleep at all if I stay here. I can just sit up all night, though."

"That sounds awful. I think I'll be able to sleep here. You go home and take care of Lyle and Teddy."

So that's what I did. At around 11 p.m., I kissed Cosette and did the familiar walk to the parking garage and drove home. I pumped, took a warm shower, and got in bed. I did not fall asleep for a long time. It felt so empty in the house without Ben and Cosette. Being in the bedroom with her vacant crib was awful. She was at the hospital and I was here, again.

At some point, I fell asleep and woke up every hour to check the time. At 4:30 a.m. I finally stayed up. I ate, pumped, and drove to the hospital in the dark. I took the elevator to the seventh floor and pushed the button to get into the peds floor. At the nurse's station, I looked for Cosette's nurse but did not see her. I walked down the hallway and slowly pushed open the door, knowing light would cascade into the space when I did. The first thing I saw when I looked at Cosette was that she had an IV running. She was getting liquids. Shit. Ben was asleep in his clothes on the couch. A blanket was pushed to the end near his feet. I turned around and went back to look for the nurse.

I learned that Cosette woke up at midnight and ate a bottle with Ben, which she immediately threw up. Apparently he tried to feed her multiple times, and she continued to throw up right away. So the nurse contacted the nightshift attending, and she decided to put Cosette on liquids to deter dehydration. I knew that having an IV running meant Cosette was going to stay longer. Maybe not more days but at least more hours. We were not walking out of there with her that morning.

Ben woke up around 7 a.m. and explained how bad the night was. He had vomit on his clothes. I had brought him a new shirt, so he was grateful for that. He left to get breakfast food and coffee. I reminded him to wash his hands often and to not touch the elevator buttons with his bare fingers.

Around 9 a.m. the medical team came in and debated giving Cosette a medicine to help with nausea. Ultimately they decided not to because it could have other effects and generally they didn't want to pump her with medicine. Agreed. It was strange listening to them outside the door before they came in. They were talking about new protocols such as using hand sanitizer every time they went into a new room. And how they were not supposed to wear jewelry or watches anymore.

One woman said, "I sanitize and wash my hands a lot, but I can't imagine doing it between every patient."

"It'll be here by the end of the week, though," said another woman.

The it was coronavirus. We were getting out just in time. I knew it could already be there without them knowing.

Around noon, Cosette was finally able to breastfeed with me and not throw up. Before then, bottle or breast, she ate and vomited. It was hard to watch. She was very upset and cried a lot. I ran in place with her for long sessions throughout the day. That seemed to be the one thing that soothed her. The boy who was her roommate had many doctors visit during the day. The parents listened to so much talking. One doctor tried to explain why they had a tough decision to make, about whether to do more surgery or wait and see what happened on its own. That was a long talk. Then the father reported it all back to the mother who had not been there for it. The boy was very, very, thin and had an IV in his arm, so when he went to use the bathroom he had an IV tower that one parent pushed. It was incredibly sad. All I wanted was to get out of there. I wanted to get back to our little haven at home.

Cosette was discharged at 3 p.m. We went home with orders to put drops in her eyes three times a day for one week. She still had not opened her eyes.

CARING BRIDGE POST | March 11

The last 30 hours have been incredibly difficult, but we're on the road going home now which is what matters most. The doctor was satisfied with the surgery and follow up appointments over the next few weeks will hopefully show it was successful. It was painful to see our girl so distraught post surgery, and I cringe to think of the body experiences being imprinted with something like this, but I also know we couldn't stand by and do nothing and allow her to lose her vision. Thank you for the supportive messages yesterday; I read them all throughout the day.

Friday, March 13

Cosette is slowly making progress. She opened her eyes yesterday, but they are very red and look terrible. She doesn't want anything going in her eyes so inserting the drops is ridiculously difficult and makes me want to throw up. She closes her eye right when it's about to go in, then the drop is lost. It is very important they get in or the inflammation will not go down. It's all just awful. She is tired and seems sad. She has not smiled since before the surgery. I know we had to do this but what if something in her spirit was damaged by this? Was it worth it? I think so because sight is important, but I still wish it didn't need to happen.

The coronavirus, also being referred to as COVID-19, is getting worse around the country. The news warns that people may have it and spread it before they show symptoms. Ben is supposed to get Henry on Sunday. He is still coughing from the virus he had last time he was with us. With that and this virus, we've decided Ben will stay with him at my friend's Air BnB, where Ben's parents stayed at Christmas, for the week. Ben will miss my birthday. Mom will come and stay with me for the week to help with Cosette. It's really hard to put the drops in and hold her still at the same time. It is a two person job. That on top of how challenging it is to feed Cosette means I really need help. Cosette mostly takes bottles from Ben and now Ben won't be here.

BABY JOURNAL | March 14

You had laser eye surgery on Tuesday. You were very brave. I was very sad to put you through that, but I want you to be able to see. We're home now and you're getting better. The virus in the world is getting worse so we have to stay inside. Your dad is leaving tomorrow to be with your brother because we can't all stay together right now. I'm worried he may not be able to come back for a long time. It is a weird time we live in. I hope I can stay present and happy with you. It's hard to not feel distracted.

Tuesday, March 17

I took Cosette back to the eye doctor today. He said her eyes are more red than he would like to see.

Some of her blood vessels have burst which has caused the redness. I have to keep giving her the drops for another week, maybe more, until the inflammation goes down.

Today the governor of Virginia announced measures banning groups of more than ten people from gathering, suggested high-risk populations quarantine, and told people to do what they're calling social distance. Don't see friends and family in person but if it happens then stand apart. This virus is a really big deal.

Saturday, March 21

Today is my birthday. It was nice to spend it with Cosette and Mom. Nothing remarkable but it was fine.

Ben returns tomorrow. I am relieved that he can feed Cosette again. Overnight she breastfeeds with me, but in the evening she won't, and bottle feeding has been terrible. It has been an incredibly hard week. Thank goodness for Mom. I do not know what I would do without her.

BABY JOURNAL | March 24

We made it through a hard week without Dad. Mom Mom helped a lot. Now we're in a quiet week. Things are tense in the world, but I'm trying to stay optimistic and enjoy our time with you. You're still getting over your surgery. You sleep in the bed more with me and I like it a lot. After you nurse in the middle of the night, we both fall asleep sometimes. I half sleep to make sure it's safe, then eventually put you back in your crib.

CARING BRIDGE POST | March 29

Six months ago today, Cosette was born. It has certainly not been an easy six months, but they have been dense with emotion in a way that will be forever memorable, life altering in a good way. Deep sadness and immense joy have followed her arrival into our lives. Today as we enter our tenth week of staying isolated in our home, I am grateful for the consistent happiness I feel each morning when I wake up knowing I will spend the day caring for Cosette. Of course there is fear around her getting sick and how long this will last, and sorrow over the things we are not getting to do out in the world with our baby, and from hearing of the despair being experienced by people around the planet. But in this moment as Cosette sleeps on my chest after a warm bath and meal, I appreciate the safety of our home, the happy birds outside the open window where I can see pink flowering creeping phlox, a cat sunning himself in a basket in the windowsill, and the occasional smile that flutters across my baby's sweet face.

BABY JOURNAL | March 30

You're six months old! We spend all day every day together. The weather has gotten very nice. It's almost April. I think you like wearing short sleeve onesies and no hat for a change. We're all staying inside and keeping safe. We are spending a lot of time in our bedroom this week, especially for naps. It's a chance to read and meditate more versus doing chores and watching television while you sleep. Teddy sleeps on the bed next to us. I love spending my days with you.

Tuesday, April 7

Henry was with us last week because now that quarantine is for everyone, his mom is staying indoors too. I used to be nervous about a rainy Saturday when Henry and Ben would stay in the house all day and now instead it was all week. We made it through. He comes back again on Sunday, Easter. There will be no Easter church service this year. I suggested to Ben that we plan a scavenger hunt and have a cake at the end of it instead of lots of candy. I want us to have nice holidays despite the pandemic.

We took Cosette to the eye doctor today to check on her progress. She still has some burst blood vessels. The doctor asked us to consider taking her for an ultrasound of her eye tomorrow, but then he called when we got home and said he had talked to another specialist and they discouraged it. Not only did we not want to put her through something else, but we also do not want to go into more medical buildings with the virus. Now we don't have to go back to the eye doctor for a month. It is such a nice feeling. It was much more intense to go there today. On top of the usual intensity from her screaming during the exam, we were scared of the virus. Mom sewed us masks to wear. I almost started to cry walking into the waiting room wearing a mask. It surprised me how sad it felt to enter a space in a mask while carrying the baby. This world we have brought her into is full of goodness but is also the home to much pain. There's no telling how long it will all last. Ben and I try not to dwell on it, at least not when talking together, because we have just come out of a very hard time and enjoy being home with Cosette. And she is still our new baby who knows nothing about anything like a virus. So we need to relax and enjoy time with her and understand that as long as we are being safe, we have nothing to worry about. But sometimes Ben and I let ourselves talk about it and wonder if it will still be a problem when school starts at the end of August. That is a very scary idea.

Teddy has been very cute with Cosette. He doesn't let her get close to him, but sometimes he will brush up next to her when she is not paying attention to him. Or he will plant himself at the end of the bed while she is at the top with me. He wants to be close to me like he always has, but Lyle, Henry, and Cosette all make that a little harder. He finds his moments, though, and whenever I get the opportunity to take a nap he's there with me, just him and me like the old days. So much has changed in my life since I met Ben. It was all the same for so long and then click. Once that switch went off, it kept rolling and rolling from dating, to engagement, to marriage, to pregnancy, to my dear Cosette.

BABY JOURNAL | April 8

It's almost Easter. We've been only at the house for about twelve weeks now. We're doing okay. You got a good report from the eye doctor yesterday. That was a relief. You're chewing on your hands and arms a lot, smiling more. We spend a lot of time together every day. The weather is getting very warm.

Friday, April 17

I've started a history club with some of the fifth graders. They're all at home doing school online. We meet three times a week for 45 minutes. I'm doing U.S. history from the start of the colonies to the present. It is a huge span of time, and although I have taught some of this before, that was a very small amount and this much teaching time equals a ton of material. I will do the research necessary; it will be fun to learn some new things while we're home in quarantine. There is a lot going on in our country currently, and I plan to tie that into the lessons. It will be nine weeks of classes, right up to the fifth grade graduation at school. I like seeing the kids over the computer. I can leave Cosette for a short amount of time and return to her right away without leaving the house.

Today before teaching, two friends came to drop off some books for Ben. They're expecting their first child. They told us last month. She's due in October. Because of the quarantine, we have not seen them in person to say congratulations. I went outside to say hi but let them know I was teaching soon. Ben asked about their ultrasound. They answered. Ben asked about what food metaphor the baby is this week according to the apps that do that sort of thing. I used that app because it was amusing and I liked ticking along the weeks. The morning after Cosette was born, I asked Ben to delete it from my phone. I also went into my Life app that tracks my periods and pressed the icon to "end pregnancy." The long green line that cut through nine months until January 20 disappeared.

They politely responded to Ben's questions about pregnancy. Tears came to my throat. I said it was time for me to teach and went inside. I made it past Mom and Cosette in the living room before closing myself in the room where I would be teaching in five minutes. I cried hard and silently, then cried more. I still have a lot of grief in me.

CARING BRIDGE | April 21

Hi everyone. Cosette is now three months corrected, hitting her milestones, and weighs eleven pounds. She enjoys looking and smiling at faces, "talking" to a brightly colored quilt that lives on the couch, as well as talking to her mobile and us, too! Her three month-old clothes are getting a bit tight around the belly and feet, but sleeves always need to be rolled up. As of two weeks ago, she sleeps for a stretch of six hours most nights, which is a joy for me. I'm usually still getting up every three hours to check on her but that will change. She had an eye checkup two weeks ago and the doctor was pleased enough with her progress to have her wait a month for the next appointment. She had her first physical therapy appointment over FaceTime this morning and we got some good tips for increasing her strength and comfort in different positions.

As you have probably assumed, our party for Cosette will not be happening at the end of May. Maybe next summer. Although it's sad to not have you meet her while she's still a small baby, we are glad she is home and safe.

BABY JOURNAL | April 22

You're three months corrected. We're still in the house but the days are very nice. You are talking a lot now, wanting to communicate with us with your voice. It is adorable. You smile big and often. Next you will be laughing and rolling over. You're eleven pounds. Some of your three month clothes are getting tight. I am glad you will get big and healthy, but I love you as a small, cozy baby too.

You only get to see me, your dad, Mom Mom and sometimes Henry. Someday this virus will end and we can take you out. It has been a strange year in the world.

Friday, May 1

Cosette was crowned the May Queen this morning at the school's May Day celebration. It was online, of course, but it was still very sweet. A kind friend said a few words about me and Cosette. She reminisced about how everyone was so excited when they found out I was pregnant because there would be a new baby on campus. But then that baby came very early, too early, and had to stay in the hospital for a long time. But she grew and grew and was finally able to go home with her parents. And now everyone is so happy for her parents and baby Cosette. Like the season of spring, Cosette makes her debut as a new life. Holding her on my lap listening to this short story, I got teary. I wish we could have been on campus, but I felt lifted by this form of gathering too.

Later in the afternoon, I sat on the swing bench in front of the house. I sit there often with Cosette. I like to swing while holding her and tell her stories. Today I told her the story of her birth. I made it more pleasant and cut out many parts. But as I spoke to her, I faced the steps that I crawled up while in labor. When I look down at my feet ascending those steps, I frequently think about what my thoughts were that night. I was in so much pain. I got out the front door on my hands and knees and then took a break a few feet later at the bottom of the stairs. But I made it all the way to the top before I paused again. I crawled the whole way, then lifted myself up on the door frame of the car. I remember all of this during the many occasions I go up the steps, but not every time. I imagine it will happen less and less as the months go by. Similar to how my forehead is tense as I write this, I found myself clenching Cosette as I watched the stairs from the swing. I held Cosette close and whispered a spring song in her ear.

BABY JOURNAL | May 9

Tomorrow is our first Mother's Day. I am excited to share it with you. You're doing very well and seem happy. There are things I'd like to be doing with you that I can't because of the pandemic, but there are few stresses in the house. We have our routine. You are very loved and get a lot of attention.

Sunday, May 10

Today is Mother's Day! I was very excited for this day to arrive. Even though it is only a calendar holiday, it felt special to me. And of course it did, because I very clearly remember my thoughts from last Mother's Day. It is the day I decided I was truly ready to have a baby. And I was already a few days pregnant and didn't know it.

I started the day by wearing my Mama Bear shirt and put Cosette in her Baby Bear shirt. They're part of the set I got for Ben, Henry, and me and Cosette for Christmas. Ben was great about the day. He played with Cosette more so I could take a break outside for an hour. I sat in the sun and read a book. That rarely ever happens these days. We ordered a special takeout barbeque dinner, and Mom came over to celebrate with us. Afterall, it is her day too. Ben humored me and did a photo shoot of Cosette and me. I put a dress on and wore my glasses because Cosette currently loves to look at people who are wearing glasses. Ben took some excellent pictures. It was a lovely day.

Monday, May 18

The baby specialist started a mothers group online. It is for pregnant women, women who have babies six months and younger, and also for practitioners like herself who work with mothers and their babies. The first thing she did was break up the group into dyads to talk for a few minutes. I was wary of that because it meant telling my story, even if just briefly, which is not an easy thing to do. But it turned out that the person I was matched with was a medical practitioner, and she had good sympathy to bestow upon me, as well as some valuable advice. One thing she told me about was a book written by a mother of a baby who was born at 24 weeks. I looked it up and ordered a copy. In doing that, I found a few others also written by mothers of premature babies. One I got on my Kindle and have already started. It was difficult to stop reading once I began. It is very strange to read something so familiar in an autobiographical voice. But it is also extremely intense and is making me think about everything vividly. I find myself comparing my situation to the author's constantly. I've never had such a visceral reading experience. I am not sure if I like the feeling, but I imagine I will finish the book in a few days.

Listening to the lecture today for the mom's group made me feel like Cosette may need help with her trauma. Her difficulty with eating and how it seems almost painful for her to swallow sometimes indicates there is something there. She may have scarring from the intubation tube or a body memory of not wanting it in her throat. I will make an online appointment to assess Cosette. I need to do whatever I can to help her.

Summer camps are not happening. There are so few options of places to go outside of the house. At parks Henry can't safely use the playground equipment. They say the virus can be passed on surfaces. A lot of people out there have it worse than me, I know that. It's still hard, though, especially when trying to get Cosette to nap and the house is loud.

BABY JOURNAL | May 23

We have moved through May quickly. It's getting warmer out. You and I have been taking long walks because that's the best way for you to nap. The pandemic is still happening. Most people have been inside for eight weeks. It's longer for us. It is hard but we're making it. You are smiling a lot and love watching us eat and do all the things we do. We have been spending more time in your room playing with your gym and taking naps on the couch.

Saturday, May 30

Today was supposed to be Cosette's big debut party. And tomorrow her baptism. Obviously neither is happening. As today went by as a normal day, I had the realization that a large celebration might not have been that great anyway. It was a dismal thought but also reassuring because it means life is not somehow worse right now. Cosette's first year at home is not deficient due to the pandemic. Each day is just a day. They float on, party or no party. Introducing Cosette to a lot of people would have been fun but also extremely tiring. She may have gotten grouchy or overstimulated by all of the activity. She also may have loved it. But the reality is the day we had, which was pleasant and happy.

Wednesday, June 3

The book I read by the mother of the premature baby inspired me to look up support groups for NICU parents. I found a site called Hand to Hold. At the top of the homepage, it lists tabs to select and one is Bereaved Parents. That almost made me shut the whole thing down. I could not stand to think about being that parent regarding Cosette. But I quickly clicked on NICU Families and learned that I could request a mentor, a mother who formerly had a child in the NICU. I decided to sign up.

Tonight I talked to a woman from Alabama. Her son is seven now. He was born at 24 weeks and weighed less than Cosette. He spent almost the amount of time in the NICU as Cosette did, about a week less. I was nervous and excited to talk to her. I was eager to tell my story but still wary of hearing someone else's. And that inclination was correct. It was nice to talk but at times hard to listen. The thing that was most difficult to hear was that she kept her son protected and away from groups and chances to get sick until he was four. She let him go to pre-school then and he got RSV, but she said it wasn't that bad because he was old enough to handle it. She has a stepson who was a teenager when she had her baby and she said that was challenging too, but agreed having a five year-old at home sounded much harder regarding bringing in germs. She said other mothers thought she was crazy for staying home so much, but she felt like that's what she needed to do and has no regrets. I suppose it would have been easier to hear someone say that they were lax about such things and their child did not get sick. That was not the message, though. The message was you've gone through hell to have your child survive, you cannot stop now. And the can't was not just a direction but also empathizing. Like I understand you physically cannot stop working to protect your daughter. In that way, the call was good. She validated things in a way no one else has for me.

BABY JOURNAL | June 4

I t's definitely summer now. You wear lots of rompers. Hopefully the summer won't be too hot so we can still go on long walks. You're 12 lbs 6.5 oz now. Such a big girl! You love holding onto your feet.

Tuesday, June 9

I had an appointment over the computer today for Cosette. It was not easy to do with the screens, but we managed. When she talked to Cosette about her time in the hospital, Cosette whimpered and seemed to understand what was being said. The specialist encouraged me to speak to Cosette about it and tell her it was bad, but it's over and it will not happen again. It was emotional but felt good to do. She said Cosette was very present and attentive, which was nice to hear. She sees a lot of babies.

Wednesday, June 10

I think often about having another baby. I'm embarrassed to talk about it because I expect most people would frown and shake their head, then decide I must be joking. Cosette is only eight months old, there is a pandemic happening, and I don't know the level of risk for having another premature birth. I don't want another baby just to have it work out correctly. I am not trying to redo it and mend the wounds. No, I think it is because Cosette is so amazing and I love her so much that I want to have a second. I acknowledge how hard it would be to have two babies, but at the same time, it feels like they could grow up together and go through their young years side by side. I also want Cosette to have lots of undivided attention. And I worry about being exhausted when pregnant and not being present for her. She deserves one hundred percent of my energy. We have talked about trying for another child in the summer of 2021. The astrologer even told me not to complicate my life before the summer of 2021. When I said, "You mean not to have another child before then? And she said, "Yes, oh my goodness, definitely not before then."

Maybe this idea is being pushed along by hormones. I don't think about it so often that I am not being grateful for Cosette, but it has crossed my mind a lot.

Tonight, sitting outside on the porch admiring the beautiful vine of purple flowers, the world looked so gorgeous and was calling to be consumed by me and everyone I love. Even though there is so much difficulty right now, those precious moments still happen and I want to create another life who can also enjoy them. At this point, the question isn't baby or not but when.

Friday, June 12

I went to graduation at school yesterday. I delivered a speech that felt meaningful. It was sad to see friends and students and not get close. I was nervous to be somewhere public even though it was outside, but once there it was impossible to imagine a virus reaching me behind my mask so spaced out from everyone else. I calmed down and felt safe. Many of the kids mentioned how hard it was to have three different teachers because of me leaving. That was not pleasant to hear, but they have every right to express their hardship. Of course, I wish it had all gone differently too. They also said very kind things and I will take those with me. The next day a parent texted me and said my speech was the highlight of the night for her. I appreciated hearing that. I have now written four graduation speeches, each one quite different and all very personal and significant to me.

Sunday, June 14

We are halfway through two weeks of the four of us being in the house together. It is hard. Very, very hard. It is two weeks because Henry's mother can go out and see people during these two weeks, and then she keeps Henry in for two weeks when she has him so he can come back safely to us. I look forward to the day that Henry and Cosette can play as siblings. Right now she's not very exciting to him and he's going through his own struggles of being an active kid separated from friends and a normal routine.

Breastfeeding is not going well again; I think I'm not making enough to satisfy Cosette. She has less interest in eating with me because it's harder work and less food. I am not ready to give up though, so I'm pumping five or six times a day. Finding the time to do that while mostly taking care of her alone is extremely challenging. Breastfeeding has been an emotional thing for me from the start, as I think it is for a majority of women, so when a layer of frustration is added because I can't pump because Ben is preoccupied, it wipes away any cool I may have had.

Wednesday, June 17

Today an empathic friend of mine and I talked about Cosette having a sibling. She said she thought it would be wonderful and something Cosette deserves. She imagined me having another girl, which is what I want, and the two girls would be similar in many ways and have a deep bond. She had an image of this little girl waiting out there to be born to me. This girl saw how I took care of Cosette in the hospital, and although she will be healthy to term, she honors that journey. I am so fortunate to live in a time when babies born at 23 weeks can survive. That has only started to happen in the last few decades since surfactant was invented. Before then, the lungs collapsed and could not work. Having this talk makes me feel like I do not need to think about another baby as much now. I will let it rest and try not to feel badly that this baby is out there waiting. Cosette needs more time with just me while I'm rested and absorbed in only her.

BABY JOURNAL | June 17

I am in your room with you. You don't sleep here yet but that's coming soon. You're playing with a puffy book toy. You're trying to eat the pages. You love your toys. This is the longest you've stayed on your back in a few days. You love flipping onto your belly. You're wearing yellow and purple striped pants and pink socks. Last night we took your arms out of your sleep sack for the first time and you happily slept on your belly all night.

Wednesday, June 24

I took Cosette to see the baby specialist in person today. We met outside and she and I both wore masks. It was very pleasant; I didn't feel worried once we were there with her. It felt safe. She worked on Cosette, doing her baby massage. She said Cosette looked really good. Hearing this is helpful to me. I trust her expertise so much. She worked on Cosette's neck and head, which she said might loosen her up for eating more easily. She also mentioned that it might just take time for Cosette to trust everything going down her throat. That was also good for me to hear. Cosette is fine, but she might need more healing time. I can give that to her. I needed to know I was not missing something, some help I could be giving to her but wasn't.

The mothers' group is ending, or rather it is taking on a new form that will not involve me. I learned a lot from it in the number of sessions I attended. The last one was Monday, and I was paired with a practitioner who told me that quarantine at home with her parents is probably the best possible thing for a long-stay NICU baby. That was very comforting to hear. The group talked about how important it is for mothers to feel connected to each other and supported. Mom definitely supports me but otherwise, with no groups or friends around, I have no one else. I'm really feeling that this summer as Ben attends to Henry and I spend hours alone with Cosette, either interacting with her or trying to get her to nap. If we could just go to a park or a class, that would fill and change the mood of the whole day.

All of that being said, in the afternoon today, Cosette and I sat on the swing and appreciated the warm, summer breeze. The days, although repetitive, are enjoyable. As I sat there, I thought *This is as good as it gets.* Cosette seems happy just being with me, and so that can be enough for me too. She needs me and I love being with her. Everything else is extra.

Friday, June 26

The baby yoga studio is closing permanently. An email went out this morning. They couldn't see a path forward through the pandemic. Everyone is realizing it is going to last for a very long time. With the population they serve, pregnant women and babies, it will be even longer before they could hold classes safely. It is incredibly sad to know that such a unique, lovely place is closing because of this virus. I wanted so badly to go back there with Cosette for the Sweet Pea class. I anticipated going there with a second pregnancy, too. There was some real healing waiting to happen by returning to that studio. And now, nothing.

In February, I made a list of things I want to do with Cosette as a baby once she can go out. It includes: Mom & baby swim lessons, Mom & baby yoga class, and parent/child class at the Waldorf school. Swimming and Waldorf require Cosette to be a little older than she is now, but by the time she can go out, she will be much older than the minimum. I deleted the yoga class from the list today.

BABY JOURNAL | June 5

You're getting so close to crawling. You spend so much time on your belly and complain less about it. You're in your crib now wearing a blue and yellow flower dress and looking at your fairy mobile. Your aunt, uncle, and cousins drove for two days to see us, especially you. We all had a cookout for the 4th. It's an abnormal summer, but I'm enjoying it.

Tuesday, July 7

I have decided to start a writing group with any of the fourth and fifth graders who want to do it. Just an hour once a week. We start next Tuesday. I do not miss the prep of the history classes, but I do miss the interaction and the chance to talk about something entirely different. I really do love teaching. I love all of the places I ended up along the way of explaining something, connections made, realizations discovered. The spontaneity of teaching has always been attractive to me, like improvisational acting. It makes sense why I'm craving that now during a time of such deep routine.

Thursday, July 16

I took Cosette to the pool at Mom's neighborhood today. Cosette was not too sure about the water, it was a little chilly, but I will try again another time. She took a two hour nap after being there, the length she should be sleeping. That made me feel like maybe she is not getting enough stimulation in her days. But I also know less stimulation is good for her after the start she had. The pool is a good place to take Henry too. When we're all there outside in the water things feel more normal.

BABY JOURNAL | July 20

You're six months corrected today. You're doing so great. You met more of your family this month. That was special. You're almost ready to crawl! You are always on the move, you love your toys and watching people, especially when they eat.

Tuesday, July 28

Teddy has been acting odd, and I'm worried about him. He is sleeping in strange places and for long periods of time. He slept on the bed the whole night last night. I am taking him to the vet tomorrow because it seems like he's having trouble walking. Maybe he hurt one of his other legs. I know it is a lot to expect him to be okay on three legs. He just moves so easily and fast, it's hard to remember sometimes how much impact is being put on the other legs. I hope he's okay and they can give him some cat Advil. Of course my fear is that the cancer is back somewhere in his body. And that he is very sick and I will not be able to save him a second time.

Thursday, July 30

The vet said Teddy has arthritis because of using his three legs so much. It makes a lot of sense. His heart and lungs sounded fine. That means no cancer most likely. He gave him an anti-inflammatory medicine to take. I am very relieved. I had a strong intuition that something really bad was wrong with him, but I must have been scared and imprinted from last summer. Hopefully the medicine will work quickly and he will be back to his old self. He did not come to the bed this morning, didn't ask for breakfast or dinner, although he ate them eventually.

Sunday, August 2

I had to take Teddy back to the vet on Friday. The medicine was not helping and he seemed worse. They did blood work and all was fine. The doctor listed off Teddy's symptoms: circling around as he walks, seeming unsteady, walking on his hind feet like a rabbit rather than on toe pads, not focusing or blinking. Putting it all together in a list sounded very bad. Hearing his blood work was good is a positive, though. It's not cancer because his white blood count would be up. The doctor thinks Teddy had a stroke, which is totally unrelated to his tumor or amputation. I could take him to a neurologist in Richmond or try prednisone. We're trying prednisone. If there was a bleed, then this could decrease the swelling and make him feel better. The doctor did not sound confident that this would definitely work. But he also did not bring up quality of life or ending Teddy's life. I am upset, but it seems like there is a big chance he could recover and be okay.

Tuesday, August 4

Teddy died today. I had to end his life. The prednisone made him very thirsty and hungry, but he couldn't eat without me putting food mixed with water, like soup, on my fingers and having him lick. When I put dry food in front of him, he scattered it and seemed to not see it at all, only smell it. I thought he was drinking a lot, but the doctor said that he was dehydrated. The biggest problem became constipation. His brain forgot how to tell his body to have a bowel movement. He had not had one since Friday when he was at the vet so that's why I made the appointment on Monday to take him on Tuesday. The doctor said he could keep him overnight and give him an IV and enema, but it would just happen again. Then he brought up quality of life, that he didn't see it there anymore. Before going to the vet today, I sat with Teddy, crying and telling him our memories together. I knew he was dying before the doctor told me, just like I knew it last week when I started noticing differences. I wasn't overreacting, I was sensing the truth. Maybe I could feel him telling me to let him go.

The doctor spoke to me on the phone in the car because of COVID. Ben was with me this time, this third time, because we knew it was bad. I thought we wouldn't be allowed in and I would not get to hold him in his last moments, but the doctor said they make exceptions. We went in, and I held him while he received the sedation. I stroked his back and told him how much I love him and how great a cat he is and how he was safe and I was there with him. I cried and cried. My mask filled with snot. I blew my nose over and over.

Saying goodbye to Teddy is one of the hardest things I have experienced. Going home without him. Leaving him on the table with his paws shaved to reveal a vein for the overdose injection of ketamine. Those images will live with me forever. It's like the image of Cosette in the transport isolette with her tiny hat, looking uncooked and too fragile. Those images will always burn in my brain. Why does life have to be so cruel? I know that if we didn't love so hard, then it wouldn't hurt, but still, the pain is deep and aches and aches. I keep crying. All my thoughts are of him. He should be everywhere in the house and he is nowhere. It feels like a breakup with a love of ten years, yet in a breakup there's often some anger, some realization that it was not meant to be, that there are others out there who might be a better fit. I do not feel that way about Teddy. There was nothing bad about him, and yes, there are other cats in the world, but none of them will have lived in one apartment and two houses with me. That's only him. I held my hands on his warm fur once he passed, then raised them up and grabbed at the air, trying to hold his soul. I placed my hands on my heart. I want him with me always. My dear, dear cat. My best friend.

Wednesday, August 19

Cosette's sleeping habits are very challenging. I am afraid we did this to her by not letting her learn to self soothe. We held her constantly, then bounced her to sleep at night to go in her crib. We bounce her in the middle of the night after she eats too. It's just not sustainable. I saw a post on Facebook where someone had asked for sleep advice and a whole list of moms raved about a local Charlottesville sleep coach. It is expensive to hire her, but I'm considering it. Holding or walking Cosette for two naps a day plus long sessions during the night will drive me insane if I have to do that alone in October when Ben is gone to take care of Henry. It's the plan we figured out to make sure Cosette does not get exposed to COVID. Every other month starting in October our family will be split.

Monday, August 24

I went to see a doctor today about the riskiness of me having another baby. I had to wait for an hour and a half from the start of my appointment until he came in to talk to me for ten minutes. He didn't have any information from Martha Jefferson hospital about Cosette's birth. He asked me if I had pain during labor or did the baby just slip out. Pain. He said that's preterm labor and I have a 30% chance of it happening again. There was no attempt at explaining why it happened. No one is going to do that for me. There are too many unknowns and questions about what came first, infection or labor. He was there to tell me what he could offer for the future. It's only one thing -- an injection of progesterone once a week for twenty weeks during the pregnancy. From week 16 to 36.

It's supposed to keep the uterine environment calm.

I imagined my interior, my uterus, as a dark cave of unrest, a place where bad things suddenly decide to happen. It was calm, then it wasn't. An alarm went off, something broke down in the system, a tiny perforation appeared, because it just did. Cosette and I did not ask for it or give permission. And then little invisible flecks of poison entered and pushed her out.

The drug is designed specifically for women who have had a preterm baby. It is not given to anyone else. Someone cannot take it preventatively if they think they may have a preterm baby for their first. It is only for someone like me. The average woman who has a preterm baby is from lack of availability of nutritious food, or someone who smokes, drinks or does drugs during pregnancy. Or it is someone who does not have any of these risk factors and is simply unlucky.

A study was done recently that said these progesterone shots do not work, so the FDA may revoke approval. It could be off the market before I want to have another baby. The doctor said the main reason women stop taking it once they've started is because it hurts a lot.

"We alternate butt cheeks each week," he said as he pointed to his own rear end, using his index finger to demonstrate a shot. "Think about it like a flu shot on steroids. The hormone goes in an oil. It's thick and sticks in the muscle."

Listening to him, it sounded like I should definitely get the injections because it is my only chance at help. I could not spend four months in the NICU with Cosette at home as a two year-old. And we were lucky with her, we know that. Another baby born early could have major difficulties that could threaten all of our livelihoods. But when I got home, I read about the drug and all the doctors who say it's despicable that it was given for so long without being effective. Now I'm less sure. He did say I have a 70% chance of everything going smoothly without assistance. I do not want to inject something into my growing fetus if it is not necessary and could potentially cause issues.

We are waiting until the virus subsides and Ben has a full-time job lined up, so next summer. Maybe it will be off the market by then, and I won't have to decide for or against it. Even though there is a risk, I don't feel a pull toward the question: do we have another child at all? I cannot imagine not having Cosette or saying no to her. How could I do that to a child who is not yet born? I imagine women who have five or more children fall into that rut, like how could I not have one more? My age will determine that a second child will be the only other. There are many final things about being human. Things we do not get to question or fight.

It has been very hard at home this month. We are halfway through our four weeks as a group of four. Ruth told me to scream into pillows to let out pent up emotions. I should be doing that. I tried to restart meditating after Cosette falls asleep, right there in the room with her. I do it some nights.

In September, Ben will start working during the day. I will be okay with Cosette, just the two of us all day. That's how it was supposed to be starting last April. I get upset with Ben when he's here but unavailable to help. If he's not here but instead working, I will not feel angry at him. I am so ready to be less volatile.

BABY JOURNAL | August 30

You're seven months/eleven months old. Your birthday month is a few days away. Summer is almost over. Then it'll be you and me all day together while Dad is at work. The weather will get cooler and our walks will be easier. You're crawling all over! You are a very happy baby.

Saturday, September 5

I signed up with the sleep coach. We had a long phone call this morning. We start two weeks of sleep training on Monday. I'm excited and scared.

Sunday, September 13

We had a small memorial service for Teddy this morning. I cried hard. There is still a lot of sadness in me.

Sleep training is going really well. Cosette is napping in her crib, which is incredible. My free time has opened up so suddenly. I'm exercising during her first nap and preparing dinners during the second. I feel like an efficient homemaker. I plan to do some writing during the day, too. This all feels very satisfying following the summer I had. It was great with Cosette but stifling in other ways. Mom comes over during the day for a couple of hours. She plays with Cosette and gives me someone to talk to who can respond.

Ben and I are doing well together. He seems fulfilled by working and being around lots of people again. And I am happy to have quiet times in the house again. We don't talk about what is coming in October.

BABY JOURNAL | September 13

We got you a sleep trainer. It's somewhat working but is still hard. We're trying to help you!

BABY JOURNAL | September 27

It is two days until your birthday. My baby is going to be one! You're eight months old, too, but you were born a year ago. It was a difficult day and months that followed, but we have you now. I will write you an entry for your birthday on Tuesday.

You have been sleeping much better and in your crib. It gives me time to exercise, cook, and write. Dad is working hard. I am very lucky that I get to stay home with you.

BABY JOURNAL | September 29

Here we are! It is your birthday. You're sleeping right now. Dad will be home early today. We'll open presents, eat applesauce, and blow out a candle. You were very excited to wear your special dress and have your picture taken. Mom Mom and Pop will be over, too. I got you new clothes and some books. Mom Mom made you a crossstitch of your birth announcement. She got you books, silks, pajamas, and a snowsuit. Daddy got you a little St. Michael doll, and a pumpkin full of Halloween friends, and little slippers. Nana got you your birthday crown and a xylophone, a brush, and clothes. Your aunts got you a rain jacket and your first pair of shoes for when you start walking and a drum. Henry got you a dinosaur toy. Everyone is so happy that it's your birthday. We'll celebrate a little in January on your due date, but today is the day you will celebrate your birthday over your whole life.

On our walk this morning I told you your birth story and also about Michaelmas. I hope to do that every year. When you go to the Waldorf school, your birthday will be a festival day, which will be very fun. You are a very special baby and your birthday being a special day makes sense. When you were born, people all reached out to support us and hear about you. You brought people together. Friends and family who were distant got closer. I'm glad your birth year is 2019 because 2020 will be remembered as a hard year. You are a very happy baby and I hope you are happy for a long time. I am so honored to be your mother. It was a hard start but watching all of your movies from the beginning of your life last night brought big smiles to my face. It was a difficult and intense time and my love is stronger and greater for it. I love you, dear one. I am so glad you are here with us.

Wednesday, September 30

Cosette turned one yesterday. It has been twelve months since she was born in the parking lot of the emergency room. I wondered how I would feel, if I would get sad or feel frozen, but I felt none of that. I just felt happy to celebrate my girl.

It was a workday for Ben, but Mom came over mid-morning to help me take some photos of Cosette in her birthday dress and generally be around in a celebratory mood. She went home in the afternoon but came back soon after with Dad so that we could all have an early dinner together. Ben was able to leave work early in order to make it home before Cosette went to bed. I made applesauce in the slow cooker. Cosette loved it. She scooped it up by the handful and shoved it into her mouth. She also enjoyed opening her gifts.

I have decided to stop pumping milk. I get hardly anything out, it just does not seem worth it. Cosette breastfeeds once overnight and that's it. So I have been pumping in the middle of the day and before bed. And then I cut down to just once a day and was getting less than an ounce. I made it to her birthday, one whole year of pumping. Hopefully she will still nurse once a night or in the morning for a little longer. I will miss the experience with her, but I also understand my body is done with this stage.

Ben leaves on Sunday for four weeks, maybe a little more. I have not been thinking about it very much because I was excited about Cosette's birthday.

CARING BRIDGE ENTRY | October 1

As Cosette turns one, I want to say thank you again to everyone who supported us during this time last year. The change of season definitely reminds me of the many beautiful days when I was headed inside to be with Cosette in the dimly lit NICU. I feel so grateful to now be taking walks with her every morning in the crisp, fresh air. And then we have the whole day ahead of us to spend together.

Ben is working full-time at UVa hospital as a chaplain. It's a lot of work and many hours, but he seems to be enjoying it. He has been back to visit nurses and doctors in the NICU. Apparently they still talk about Cosette and bring her up in meetings as an example of a purely positive outcome. There is a television screen in the lobby of the NICU that has photos of babies when they entered the NICU alongside a later photo when they're home and healthy. I probably had the rotation of photos memorized by the time we left. Cosette is going to be on that board now!

Cosette has met all of her eight month milestones. She crawls everywhere, is trying to stand, sits steadily, and babbles delightfully. Presently she is learning to clap and wave. Her favorite foods are apple, pumpkin, sweet potato, and carrots. For her birthday, I made her applesauce from apples we picked at a local orchard on a rainy day. She couldn't have cake, but there will be other birthdays for that. It was a sweet, small celebration.

A party together feels far off in the future, but it will happen someday. Much love to all.

Friday, October 9

B en left in the afternoon while Cosette and I were on a walk to soften the goodbye. When we returned from our walk and his car was gone from the driveway, it felt so final and empty. I said out loud to Cosette, "Dad's gone. He's going to be away for a very long time." It was as if I needed to hear it out loud to believe it.

The first week has been okay. We're in a routine, and I find the alone time at night to be pleasant. And now I know I can take care of Cosette on my own and enjoy it quite a lot. Of course I miss Ben but my resilience endurance level has increased so much over the past year.

BABY JOURNAL | October 12

W e've had one week on our own, just you and me, and we're doing well. We have our routine. You're sleeping great. Your dad has visited outside three times. He misses you a lot. You've been happy to see him, but I think it's also confusing for you. You have me, and Mom Mom comes over almost every day for a few hours. You're healthy and happy and safe.

Sunday, October 18

I have been thinking a lot over this past week about wanting to have a second child soon. The thoughts that were so present in June are back. Maybe it's from all of the alone time in the house, like I want to fill the house. Or maybe it's because Cosette has fully stopped breastfeeding. There are all sorts of reasons why it could be wise to start trying soon, like in December, but after much thinking (and list making), I have decided it is better to wait. I do want Cosette to have a full-time sibling. A little sister to play with would be so lovely. I can see the three of us together having a wonderful time. And then five of us when Henry is here. I'm sure there would be fighting and jealousy and problems too, but also so much love.

BABY JOURNAL | October 22

It's been a beautiful fall. Just terrific weather. We have a nice routine. We're at the end of the third week without Dad. He's coming today to see us outside. I made a Thanksgiving card with pictures of you to send to family and friends. It's hard to pick which photos to put on it because there are so many adorable ones.

Friday, October 23

I took Cosette to school today. There was a small reunion of last year's fifth grade class, the class that went virtual for their last months. It was nice to see kids and parents and David, but we were only able to stay for less than an hour because of Cosette's dinner time. I imagine visiting the school will feel differently once the pandemic is over, but some of the faculty who I looked forward to seeing and introducing to Cosette no longer work there. The pandemic has changed so much everywhere. It was good to talk to David, though, and it made me miss him. He is such a dynamic person and someone who I wish was still in my daily life.

Saturday, October 31

Cosette and I spent Halloween day listening to Halloween music and playing. We went to Mom and Dad's in the afternoon, and she wore her ladybug costume. I carried her around in my arms while we looked at decorations in their neighborhood. Then we went upstairs to their apartment where she crawled around in her costume looking very cute. She is such a fast crawler now. When we got home, I walked her up our street, but it was too early to see anyone out trick-or-treating. A few people had baskets and tables set up at the curb with the intention to give out candy in a socially distanced way.

Before Cosette went to bed, I held her on one hip and we danced to the Monster Mash for the last time this season. I must have played her that song fifty times this month. It was a happy moment and I was able to take a video of us. I rewatched it so many times tonight. Cosette and I look so happy in it.

I missed Ben today, but we did okay. It was a fine day and tomorrow will be a new one. When we first made the plan for Ben to be away, he was going to be gone for four weeks. We thought maybe he could get tested yesterday and come home today. That all changed, a lot. He will not be home for three more weeks. Four down, three to go. It is a familiar feeling to counting down the weeks in the NICU, those awful realizations when I knew we were only one fourth or one half the way to forty weeks. This is nothing like that in terms of desperation and sadness. It still hurts, but nothing compares to that.

Monday, November 9

After Halloween, the election was the next big thing to think about, the next distraction to help me move positively through these weeks of single parenting. But it has gotten really hard over the past week. Cosette did not adjust to daylight savings time and has been waking up once or twice in the middle of the night every night. Sometimes it takes me a long time to fall back to sleep after feeding her or I don't go back to sleep at all.

I took Cosette to the eye doctor today. It has been six months since she was there. The doctor told us last time that it would not be the excruciating setup where she was strapped down. I was expecting it to be simple and easy. It was not. Instead of strapping her down, I held her on my lap and he performed all of the tests he needed to do. I had to keep her arms down by her sides and squeeze her to try to keep her still. It was awful. She screamed a brutal scream and the whole thing lasted for many, many minutes. I was drenched in sweat by the end.

Cosette's vision is fine for now, but she is near-sighted in her right eye. She will most likely need glasses at some point when she is a young kid. Considering everything her eyes have gone through, this was mostly expected and fairly easy to accept. She does not return to see the ophthalmologist for an entire year.

Friday, November 20

B en came home last night. It was very nice to have him walk inside and put down his things and hug me. It felt good to hug him. I wondered what it would be like, if it would feel awkward at first, but it didn't. There has been so much in the seven weeks he was away.

He returned last night after Cosette was asleep. When he walked into Cosette's room this morning, at first she seemed scared and cautious, but she adjusted quickly. He's her dad and she knows it even if he has not held her in seven weeks. I think it has been to her detriment to not have him here in terms of her verbal progress and overall stimulation from various people, so it was a relief to see she didn't seem emotionally disturbed by his absence. We will keep moving forward.

BABY JOURNAL | November 24

I t's two days until Thanksgiving and a month until Christmas. You are definitely what I'm thankful for this year. I'm so glad you're here with me. Dad is back with us, which is great. We've missed him. He's a very good dad. We will be getting the house ready for Christmas soon. I've had fun buying you Christmas presents. Your first Christmas!

Sunday, November 29

C osette was baptized today. It was just our pastor, me, Ben, Mom, and Cosette. It was small and lovely. We all dressed up which felt nice to do. Ben wore his suit pants and jacket from our wedding, and I wore my burgundy shoes from the wedding. We would rather have had family and friends present, but it still felt important and sacred. Cosette's aunts are her godparents and they joined us virtually. A few friends also joined in that way, which was sweet of them. They have not met Cosette in person, but they love her enough already to tune in at noon on a Sunday to watch her baptism.

Cosette did great with the whole thing. She wore my old baptismal gown and looked adorable. She was fascinated by the water in the font. She was very agreeable when he splashed the water over her hair and applied oil to her forehead. She seemed to like it all. My face clenched in tears during the moment of baptism. No tears fell, but they could have, perhaps if I had not been wearing a mask. Or maybe it happened because I was masked and I felt protected from the view of others.

When we got home, I fed Cosette and put her down for a nap. Ben left to pick up groceries. When I came downstairs, Mom was sitting on the couch.

"You should open this before I go." Mom gestured toward the small gift bag on the kitchen table.

She had put it there when I was feeding Cosette lunch before we left for the church. There hadn't been time then to open it. I had almost forgotten about it.

I opened the card first which was a christening card for Cosette. It had a money gift inside. "Thank you," I said. "I'll put it in her college fund." I said this half joking, but it is probably something we should start thinking about.

A small box remained in the bag. I lifted the lid and saw a folded piece of paper. I picked it up, revealing a blue rosary beneath it. This had been my grandmother's rosary. I remember seeing it in her bedroom. Mom's mother, who I called Mom Mom, just like Cosette calls Mom now. My grandmother's name was Adeline, the reason for Cosette's middle name.

I read the note and began to cry as I finished. *Mom wrote Dear Cosette Adeline, This rosary once belonged to your great-grandmother, Adeline Elizabeth Keeney McGrory. She loved your mother very much and would be so glad to know how much happiness you have brought to her life. You share her name so I thought on your christening day you should have a keepsake of hers. Love, Mom Mom*

"Thank you," I said, looking at Mom through tears. Her eyes were glassy, but she wasn't crying. This was a moment of strong feeling for me, for me more than anyone else. It was my moment of being a mother, feeling like a mother, loving my daughter so fiercely, and being moved to tears when it was pointed out.

"It's true," she said. "She would be so happy to see you with her."

I nodded. "I know," I said. "I know."

After Cosette woke from her nap, she and I went for a walk. With her strapped around my front, we headed down our familiar street, doing our routine walk for the second time that day. The temperature was pleasantly warm. Birds were singing joyfully. The air smelled of no season, like nature was temporarily locked in an in-between place. I know more about those in-between places now. The transition between death and life, life and more life.

As we walked, I thought about Mom's note and about how Mom Mom gave birth to Mom who gave birth to me who gave birth to Cosette. And one day Cosette may have her own child. Is this the point of life? To give each other the gift of having children? It makes sense on an animal level, that a continuation of the life cycle depends on enjoying it, treasuring it, and feeling so deeply. I am okay with that, if this is the reason for living, I accept. If everything that has happened to me so far, the good and the bad, has led me to this moment of being Cosette's mother, then great. Thank you world and nature and all of the pieces that aligned. Each new day means more smiles, more squeezes, and more Cosette. My sweet, victorious Cosette.

EPILOGUE

In early 2021, Ben and I started trying for a second child. After months of ovulation predictor kits, basal body thermometers, a painful saline sonogram that showed no issues, acupuncture, herbs, chiropractor appointments, treating hyperthyroidism, and praying, we sought help from a fertility center. After two unsuccessful intrauterine inseminations in 2022, I had mostly given up. I went back to Dr. H and she encouraged me to get a test called a hysterosalpingography to clear my fallopian tubes. I had avoided this test because it was similar to the saline sonogram, which had caused me abnormal pain for weeks after the procedure. I had the HSG test. It showed that my fallopian tubes are entirely blocked off. There is no explanation for this, because obviously Cosette's egg made it through in 2019. Another layer of mystery was added to the story. I am no longer able to have a baby naturally and the IUIs never had a chance of working. In 2023 we decided to commit to one round of in vitro fertilization. It did not end in success. Cosette will be the one child to whom I give birth, and in my life I will only ever be pregnant for 23 weeks, and we are all okay.

At age three, Cosette is a healthy, happy, vibrant child. She is smaller than her peers and is in the one percentile for her age regarding weight and height. She completed physical therapy and speech therapy up until she turned three. She did well in both and had loving, wonderful therapists. She started wearing glasses in 2021. She immediately agreed to wear them and they've never caused a problem for her. It is hard to have such a unique feature as a child, though, especially something that strikes others as cute. *Readers, please take this advice: don't comment on toddlers' glasses in casual passing! They hear it every time they go out in public and it's confusing to them why people they don't know want to talk about this thing that seems very normal to them.*

Cosette and Henry are good friends now and she plays with him in that special sibling way that is different from any other person. Cosette will start a part-time preschool program in the fall of 2023 at the Waldorf school where I am working again part-time. We'll drive to and from school together. Our bond we made in her first weeks and months of life has continued to strengthen. She is agreeable, hilarious, dramatic, imaginative, and brings so much joy to everyone who knows her.

In the past year, a few of my friends had babies in the NICU for short term stays. I saw them blindly enter a situation that is so foreign and so different from how most people expect their births to go. This made me decide to publish Cosette's story. I hope it can inform those who don't know anything about prematurity and serve as a story about being human and of love. For those more closely connected to complicated births, I hope this story can direct you to a place of understanding, self-compassion, and acceptance. Life can feel massively unfair and tremendously benevolent. It is hard, it will pass, there is so much good ahead, and the resilience built during this time will serve your family forever.

www.ingramcontent.com/pod-product-compliance
Lightning Source LLC
Chambersburg PA
CBHW022007080426
42733CB00007B/507